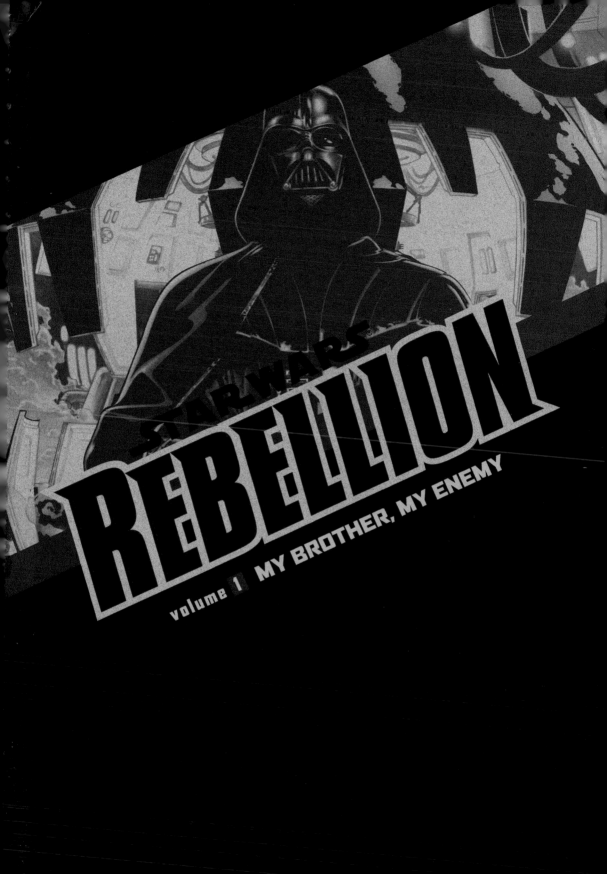

STAR WARS

REBELLION

volume 1 MY BROTHER, MY ENEMY

THE REBELLION (From the Battle of Yavin to five years after) Open resistance begins to spread across the galaxy in protest of the Empire's tyranny. Rebel groups unite, and the Galactic Civil War begins. This era begins with the Rebel victory that secured the Death Star plans, and ends a year after the death of the Emperor high over the forest moon of Endor. This is the era in which the events in *A New Hope*, *The Empire Strikes Back*, and *Return of the Jedi* take place. **The events in this story take place approximately nine months after the Battle of Yavin.**

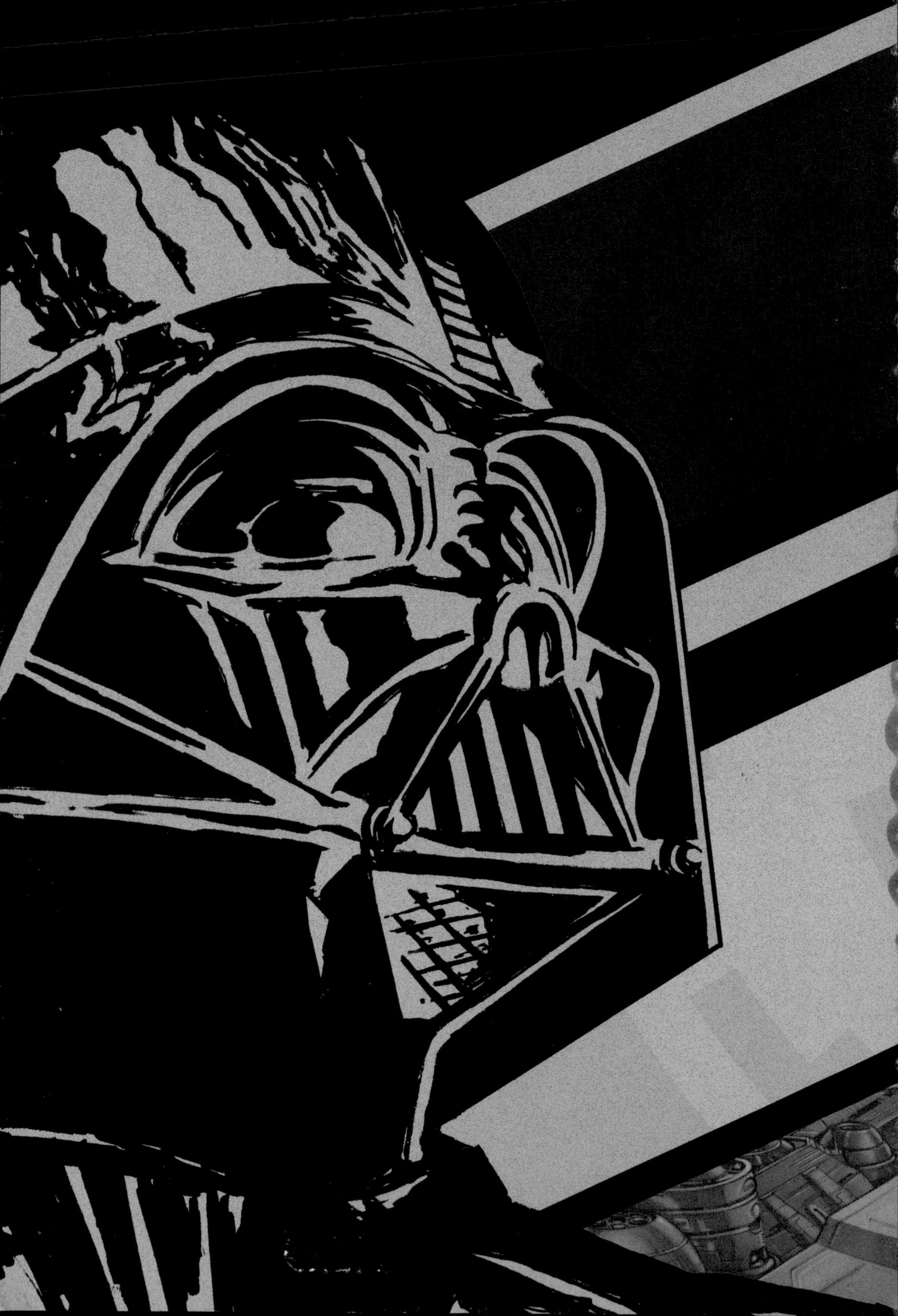

STAR WARS®

REBELLION

volume 1

MY BROTHER, MY ENEMY

script ROB WILLIAMS

"crossroads" script THOMAS ANDREWS

art BRANDON BADEAUX and MICHEL LACOMBE

colors WIL GLASS

lettering MICHAEL HEISLER

front cover art BRANDON BADEAUX and BRAD ANDERSON

back cover art BRANDON BADEAUX and WIL GLASS

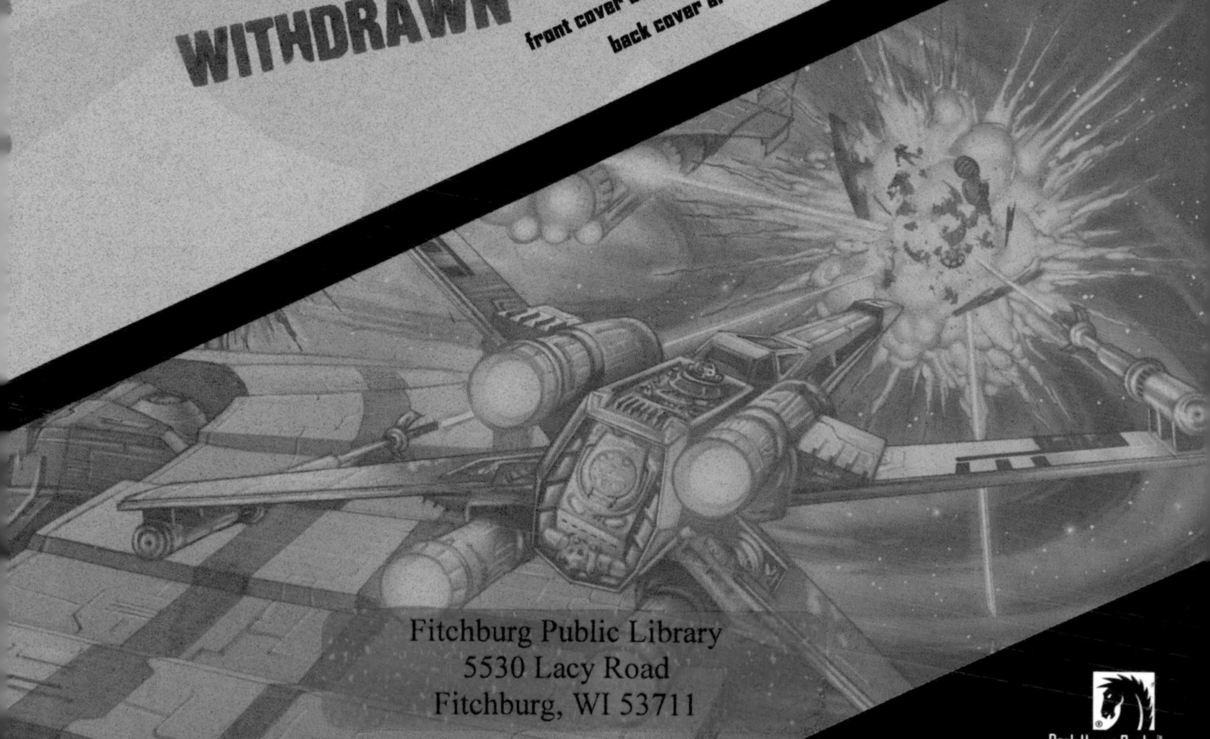

Dark Horse Books™

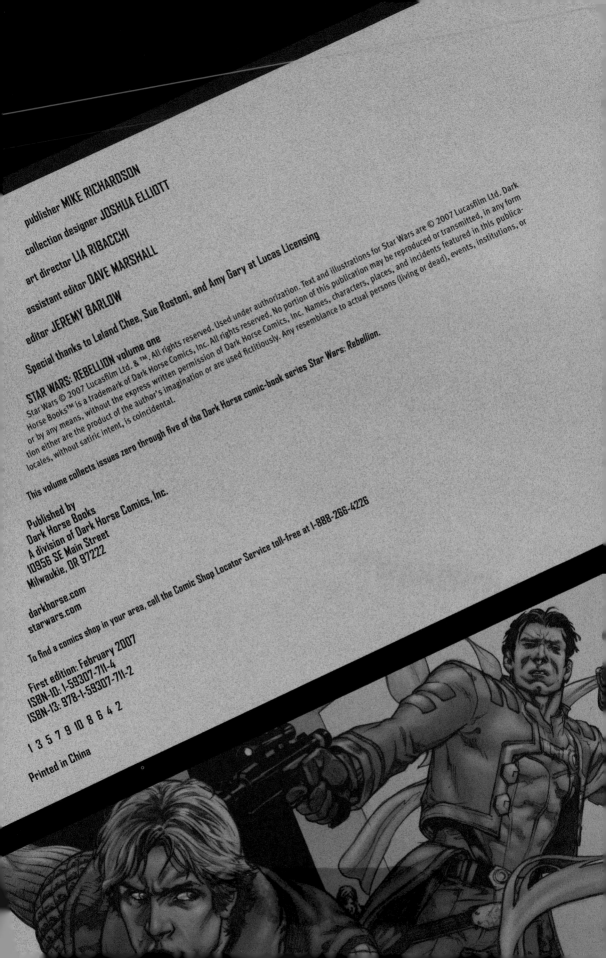

publisher MIKE RICHARDSON

collection designer JOSHUA ELLIOTT

art director LIA RIBACCHI

assistant editor DAVE MARSHALL

editor JEREMY BARLOW

Special thanks to Leland Chee, Sue Rostoni, and Amy Gary at Lucas Licensing

STAR WARS: REBELLION volume one

This volume collects issues zero through five of the Dark Horse comic-book series Star Wars: Rebellion.

Published by
Dark Horse Books
A division of Dark Horse Comics, Inc.
10956 SE Main Street
Milwaukie, OR 97222

darkhorse.com
starwars.com

To find a comics shop in your area, call the Comic Shop Locator Service toll-free at 1-888-266-4226

First edition: February 2007
ISBN-10: 1-59307-711-4
ISBN-13: 978-1-59307-711-2

1 3 5 7 9 10 8 6 4 2

Printed in China

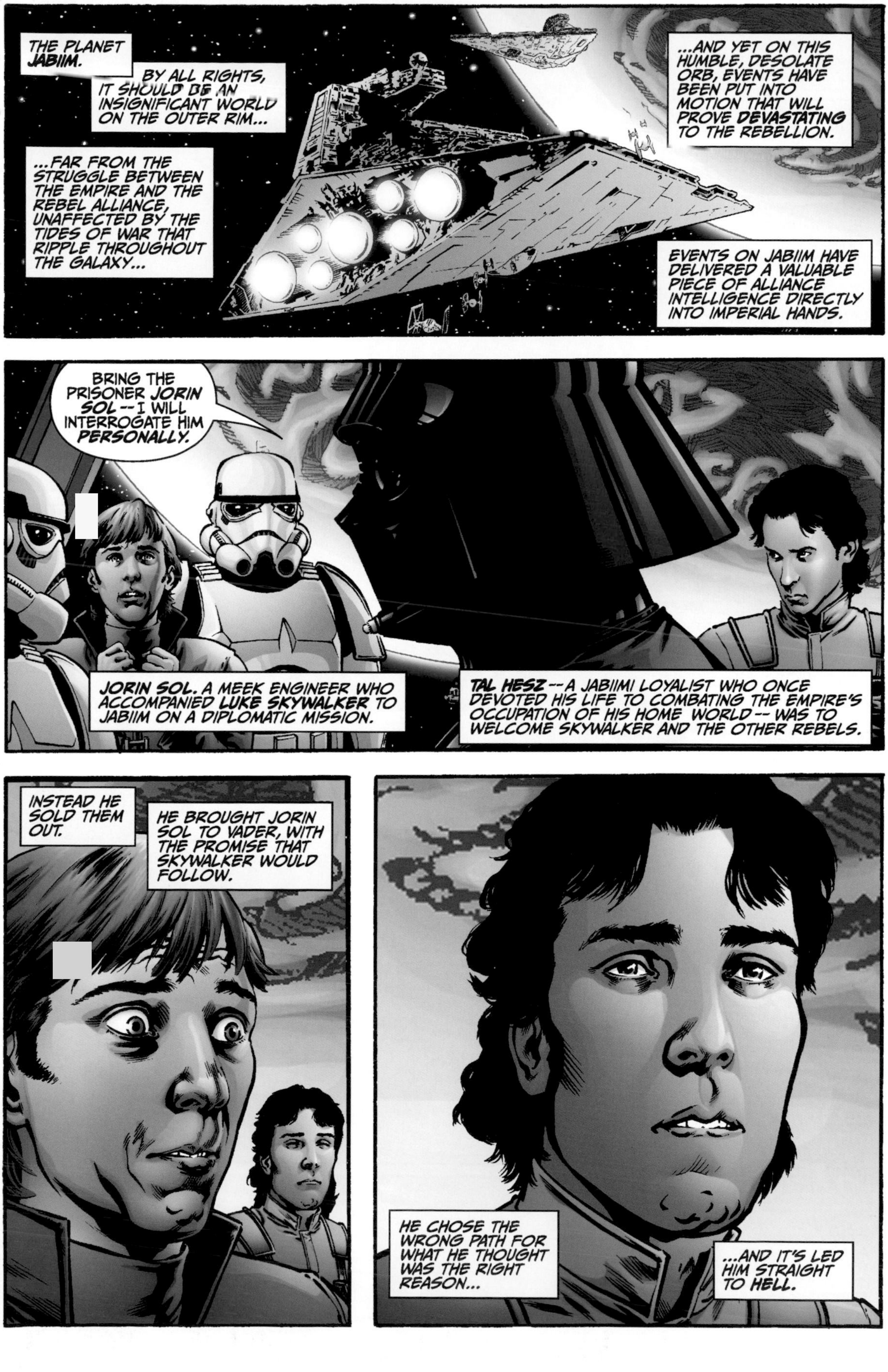
THE PLANET JABIIM.
BY ALL RIGHTS, IT SHOULD BE AN INSIGNIFICANT WORLD ON THE OUTER RIM...
...FAR FROM THE STRUGGLE BETWEEN THE EMPIRE AND THE REBEL ALLIANCE, UNAFFECTED BY THE TIDES OF WAR THAT RIPPLE THROUGHOUT THE GALAXY...
...AND YET ON THIS HUMBLE, DESOLATE ORB, EVENTS HAVE BEEN PUT INTO MOTION THAT WILL PROVE DEVASTATING TO THE REBELLION.
EVENTS ON JABIIM HAVE DELIVERED A VALUABLE PIECE OF ALLIANCE INTELLIGENCE DIRECTLY INTO IMPERIAL HANDS.
BRING THE PRISONER JORIN SOL -- I WILL INTERROGATE HIM PERSONALLY.
JORIN SOL. A MEEK ENGINEER WHO ACCOMPANIED LUKE SKYWALKER TO JABIIM ON A DIPLOMATIC MISSION.
TAL HESZ -- A JABIIMI LOYALIST WHO ONCE DEVOTED HIS LIFE TO COMBATING THE EMPIRE'S OCCUPATION OF HIS HOME WORLD -- WAS TO WELCOME SKYWALKER AND THE OTHER REBELS.
INSTEAD HE SOLD THEM OUT.
HE BROUGHT JORIN SOL TO VADER, WITH THE PROMISE THAT SKYWALKER WOULD FOLLOW.
HE CHOSE THE WRONG PATH FOR WHAT HE THOUGHT WAS THE RIGHT REASON...
...AND IT'S LED HIM STRAIGHT TO HELL.

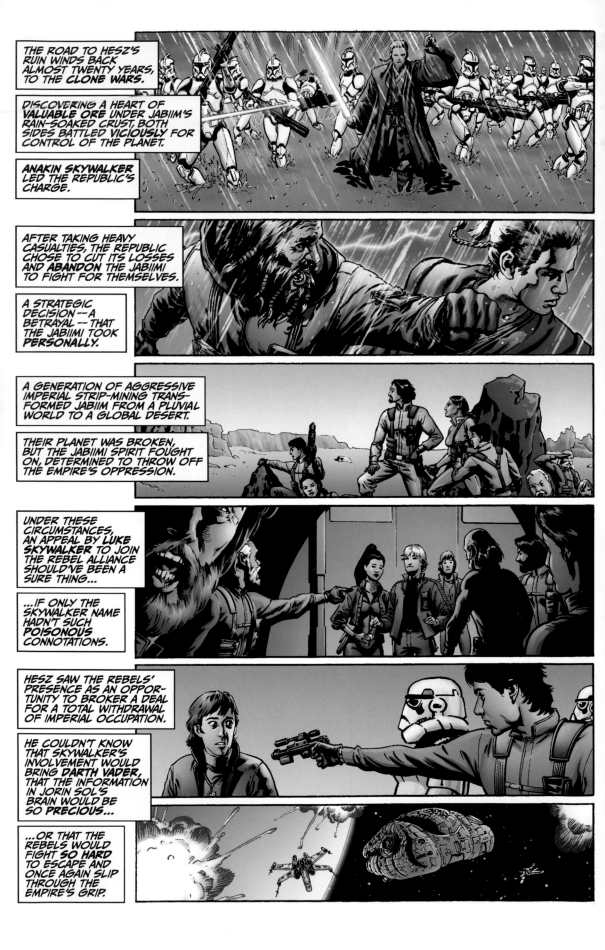

THE ROAD TO HESZ'S RUIN WINDS BACK ALMOST TWENTY YEARS, TO THE *CLONE WARS.*

DISCOVERING A HEART OF *VALUABLE ORE* UNDER JABIIM'S RAIN-SOAKED CRUST, BOTH SIDES BATTLED VICIOUSLY FOR CONTROL OF THE PLANET.

ANAKIN SKYWALKER LED THE REPUBLIC'S CHARGE.

AFTER TAKING HEAVY CASUALTIES, THE REPUBLIC CHOSE TO CUT ITS LOSSES AND *ABANDON* THE JABIIMI TO FIGHT FOR THEMSELVES.

A STRATEGIC DECISION--A *BETRAYAL*--THAT THE JABIIMI TOOK *PERSONALLY.*

A GENERATION OF AGGRESSIVE IMPERIAL STRIP-MINING TRANS-FORMED JABIIM FROM A PLUVIAL WORLD TO A GLOBAL DESERT.

THEIR PLANET WAS BROKEN, BUT THE JABIIMI SPIRIT FOUGHT ON, DETERMINED TO THROW OFF THE EMPIRE'S OPPRESSION.

UNDER THESE CIRCUMSTANCES, AN APPEAL BY *LUKE SKYWALKER* TO JOIN THE REBEL ALLIANCE SHOULD'VE BEEN A SURE THING...

...IF ONLY THE SKYWALKER NAME HADN'T SUCH POISONOUS CONNOTATIONS.

HESZ SAW THE REBELS' PRESENCE AS AN OPPOR-TUNITY TO BROKER A DEAL FOR A TOTAL WITHDRAWAL OF IMPERIAL OCCUPATION.

HE COULDN'T KNOW THAT SKYWALKER'S INVOLVEMENT WOULD BRING *DARTH VADER,* THAT THE INFORMATION IN JORIN SOL'S BRAIN WOULD BE SO PRECIOUS...

...OR THAT THE REBELS WOULD FIGHT *SO HARD* TO ESCAPE AND ONCE AGAIN SLIP THROUGH THE EMPIRE'S GRIP.

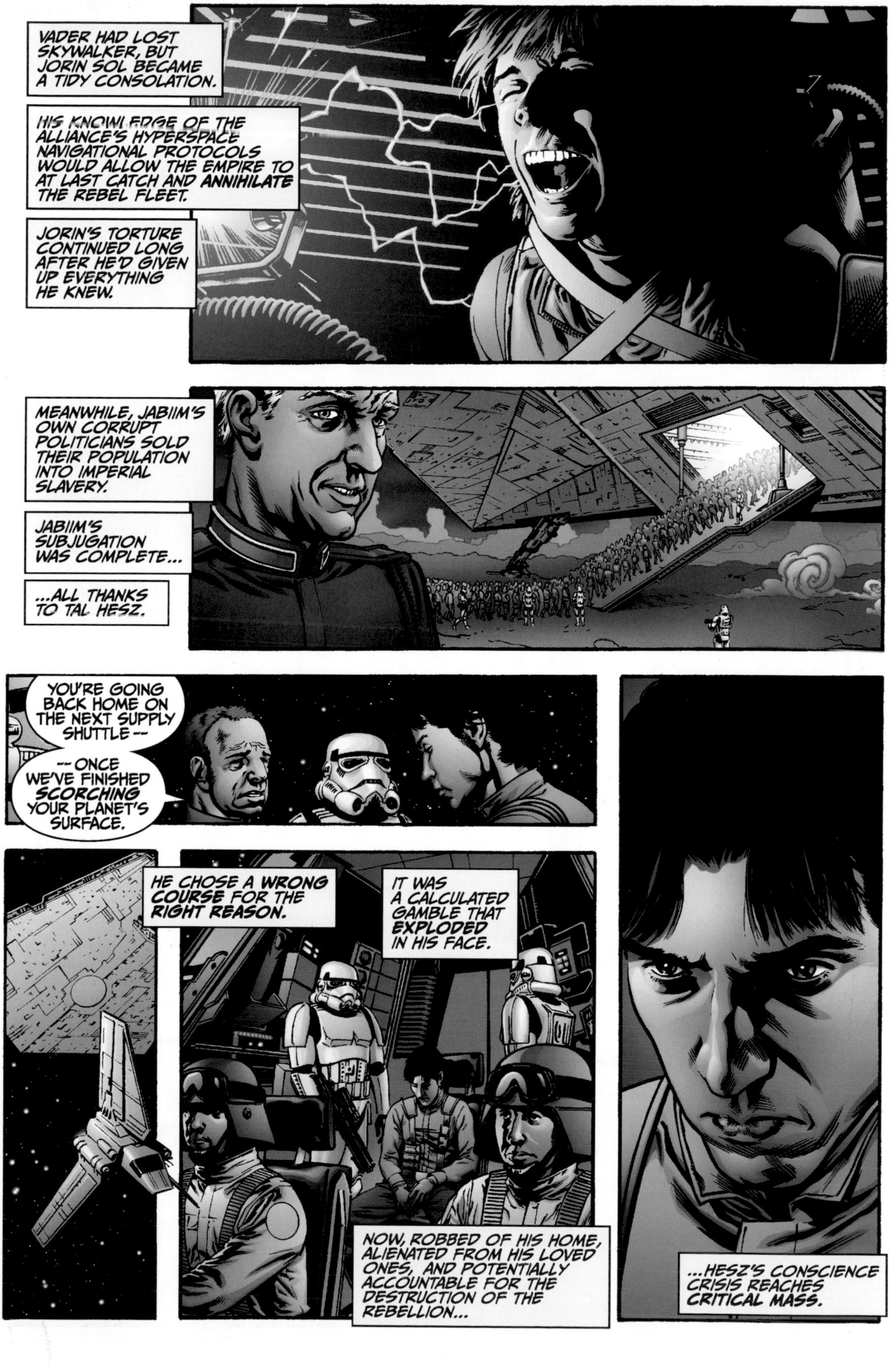
VADER HAD LOST SKYWALKER, BUT JORIN SOL BECAME A TIDY CONSOLATION.
HIS KNOWLEDGE OF THE ALLIANCE'S HYPERSPACE NAVIGATIONAL PROTOCOLS WOULD ALLOW THE EMPIRE TO AT LAST CATCH AND ANNIHILATE THE REBEL FLEET.
JORIN'S TORTURE CONTINUED LONG AFTER HE'D GIVEN UP EVERYTHING HE KNEW.
MEANWHILE, JABIIM'S OWN CORRUPT POLITICIANS SOLD THEIR POPULATION INTO IMPERIAL SLAVERY.
JABIIM'S SUBJUGATION WAS COMPLETE...
...ALL THANKS TO TAL HESZ.
YOU'RE GOING BACK HOME ON THE NEXT SUPPLY SHUTTLE --
-- ONCE WE'VE FINISHED SCORCHING YOUR PLANET'S SURFACE.
HE CHOSE A WRONG COURSE FOR THE RIGHT REASON.
IT WAS A CALCULATED GAMBLE THAT EXPLODED IN HIS FACE.
NOW, ROBBED OF HIS HOME, ALIENATED FROM HIS LOVED ONES, AND POTENTIALLY ACCOUNTABLE FOR THE DESTRUCTION OF THE REBELLION...
...HESZ'S CONSCIENCE CRISIS REACHES CRITICAL MASS.

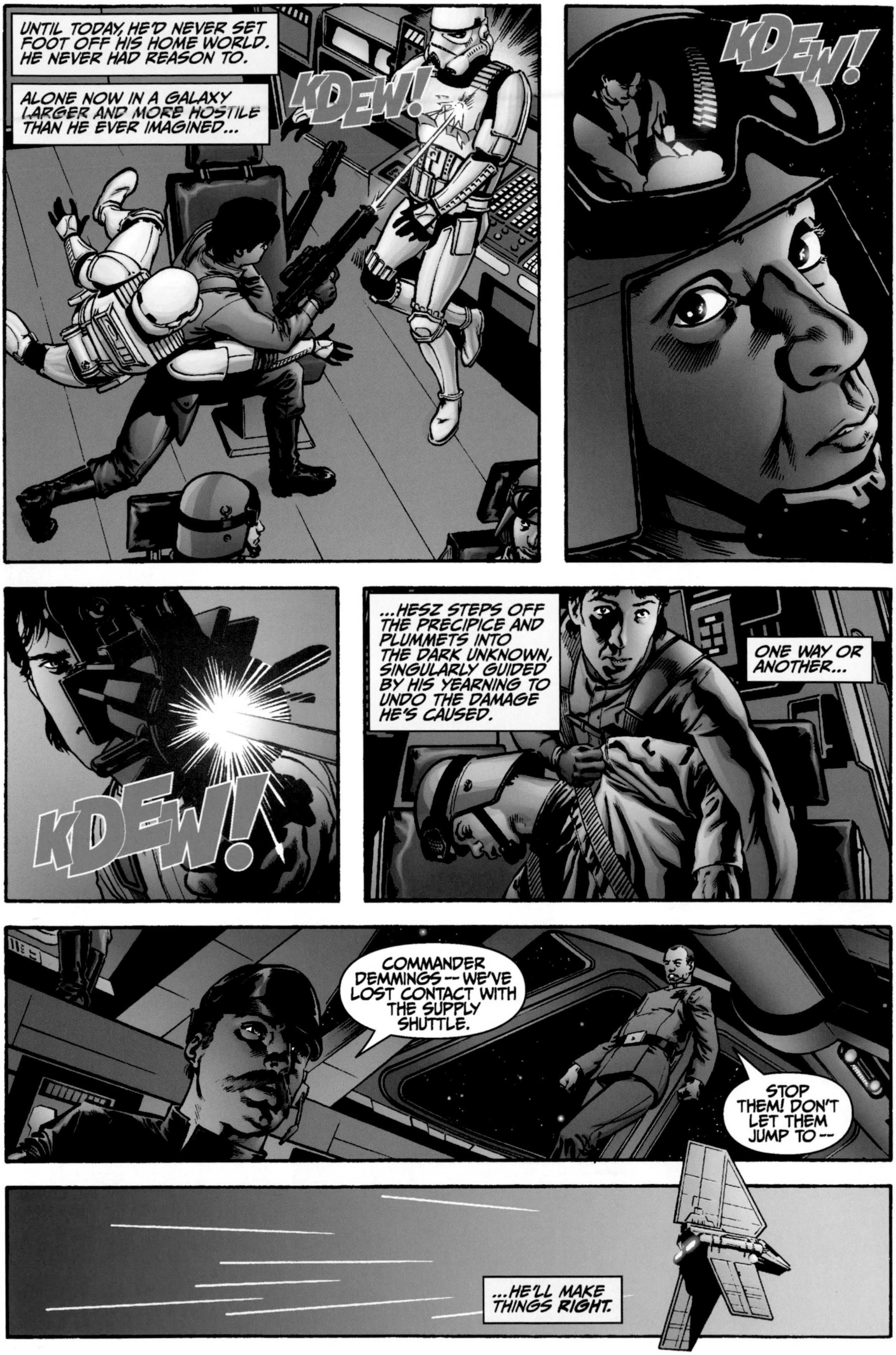

UNTIL TODAY, HE'D NEVER SET FOOT OFF HIS HOME WORLD. HE NEVER HAD REASON TO.
ALONE NOW IN A GALAXY LARGER AND MORE HOSTILE THAN HE EVER IMAGINED...
KDEW!
KDEW!
KDEW!
...HESZ STEPS OFF THE PRECIPICE AND PLUMMETS INTO THE DARK UNKNOWN, SINGULARLY GUIDED BY HIS YEARNING TO UNDO THE DAMAGE HE'S CAUSED.
ONE WAY OR ANOTHER...
COMMANDER DEMMINGS -- WE'VE LOST CONTACT WITH THE SUPPLY SHUTTLE.
STOP THEM! DON'T LET THEM JUMP TO --
...HE'LL MAKE THINGS RIGHT.

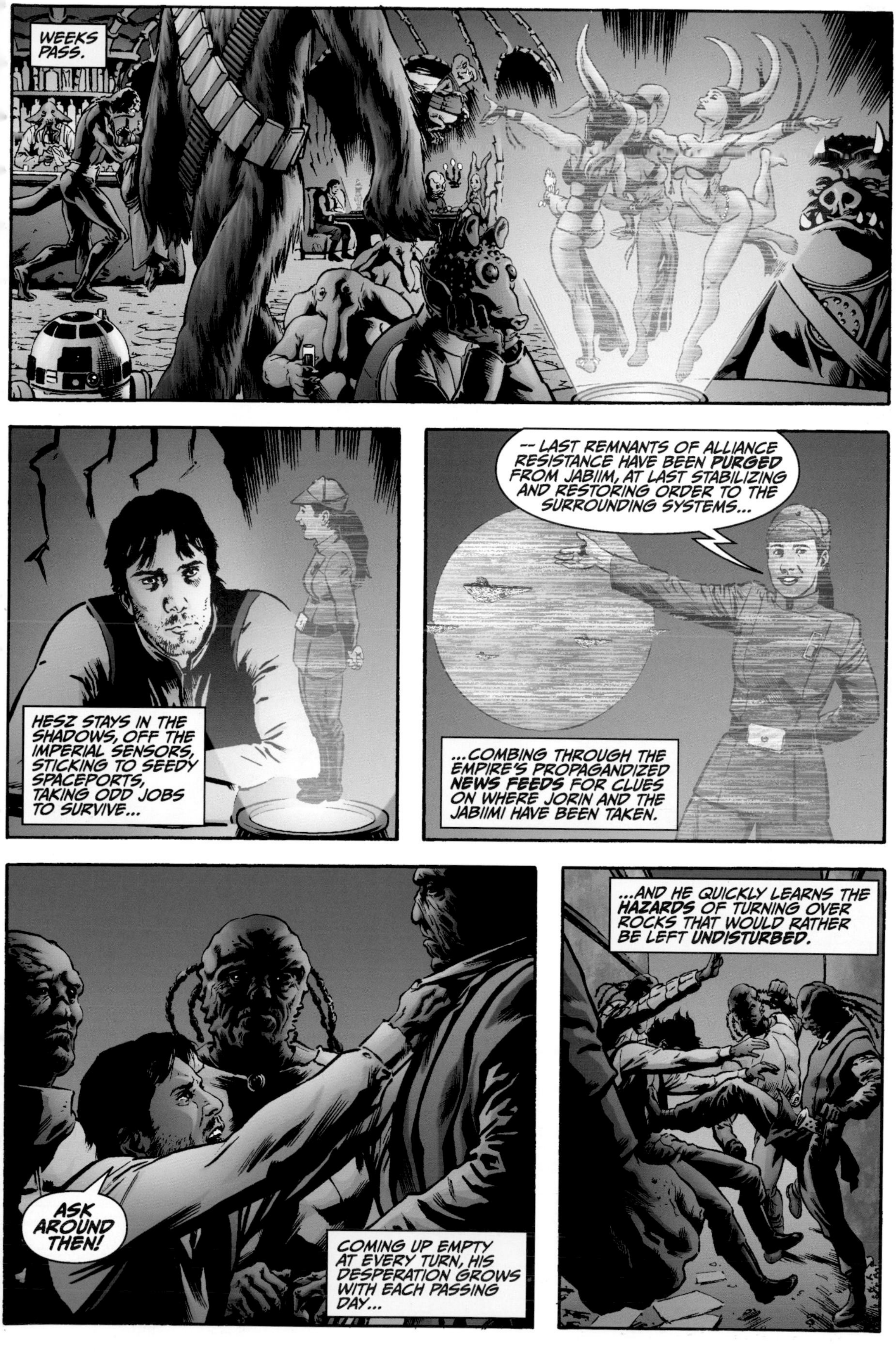
WEEKS PASS.
HESZ STAYS IN THE SHADOWS, OFF THE IMPERIAL SENSORS, STICKING TO SEEDY SPACEPORTS, TAKING ODD JOBS TO SURVIVE...
-- LAST REMNANTS OF ALLIANCE RESISTANCE HAVE BEEN PURGED FROM JABIIM, AT LAST STABILIZING AND RESTORING ORDER TO THE SURROUNDING SYSTEMS...
...COMBING THROUGH THE EMPIRE'S PROPAGANDIZED NEWS FEEDS FOR CLUES ON WHERE JORIN AND THE JABIIMI HAVE BEEN TAKEN.
ASK AROUND THEN!
COMING UP EMPTY AT EVERY TURN, HIS DESPERATION GROWS WITH EACH PASSING DAY...
...AND HE QUICKLY LEARNS THE HAZARDS OF TURNING OVER ROCKS THAT WOULD RATHER BE LEFT UNDISTURBED.

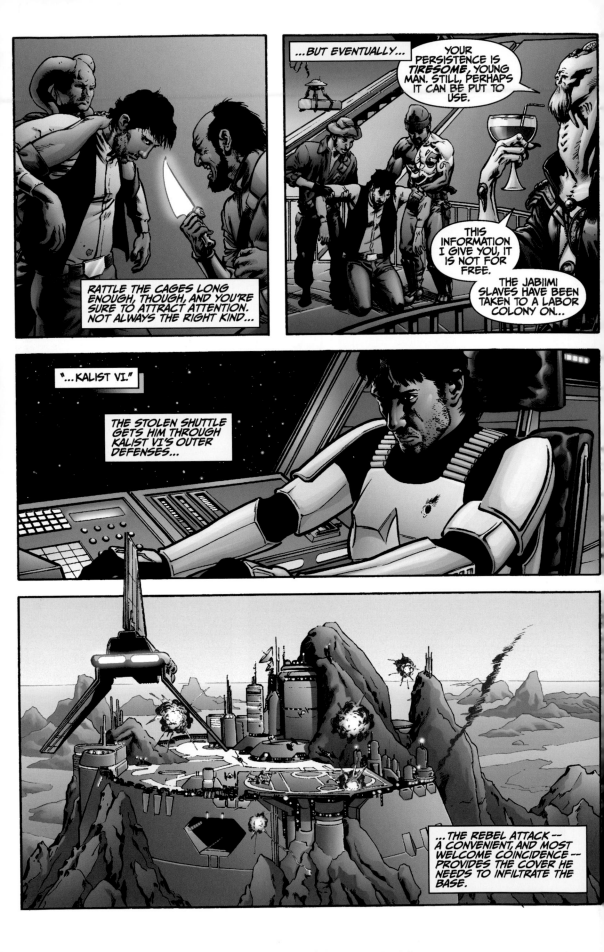

...BUT EVENTUALLY...

YOUR PERSISTENCE IS *TIRESOME*, YOUNG MAN. STILL, PERHAPS IT CAN BE PUT TO USE.

THIS INFORMATION I GIVE YOU, IT IS NOT FOR FREE.

THE JABIIMI SLAVES HAVE BEEN TAKEN TO A LABOR COLONY ON...

RATTLE THE CAGES LONG ENOUGH, THOUGH, AND YOU'RE SURE TO ATTRACT ATTENTION. NOT ALWAYS THE RIGHT KIND...

"...KALIST VI."

THE STOLEN SHUTTLE GETS HIM THROUGH KALIST VI'S OUTER DEFENSES...

...THE REBEL ATTACK -- A CONVENIENT, AND MOST WELCOME COINCIDENCE -- PROVIDES THE COVER HE NEEDS TO INFILTRATE THE BASE.

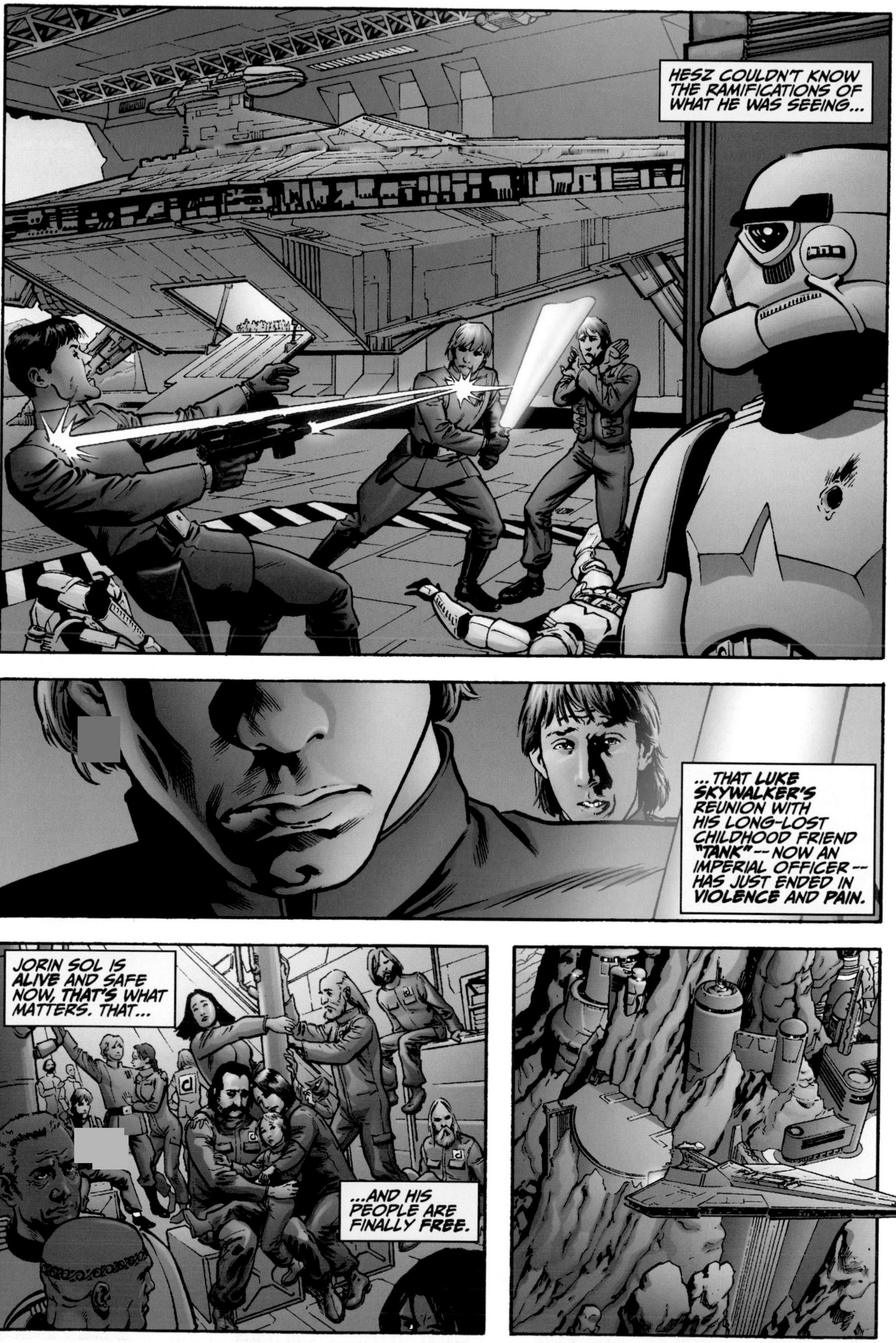
HESZ COULDN'T KNOW THE RAMIFICATIONS OF WHAT HE WAS SEEING...
...THAT LUKE SKYWALKER'S REUNION WITH HIS LONG-LOST CHILDHOOD FRIEND "TANK" -- NOW AN IMPERIAL OFFICER -- HAS JUST ENDED IN VIOLENCE AND PAIN.
JORIN SOL IS ALIVE AND SAFE NOW, THAT'S WHAT MATTERS. THAT...
...AND HIS PEOPLE ARE FINALLY FREE.

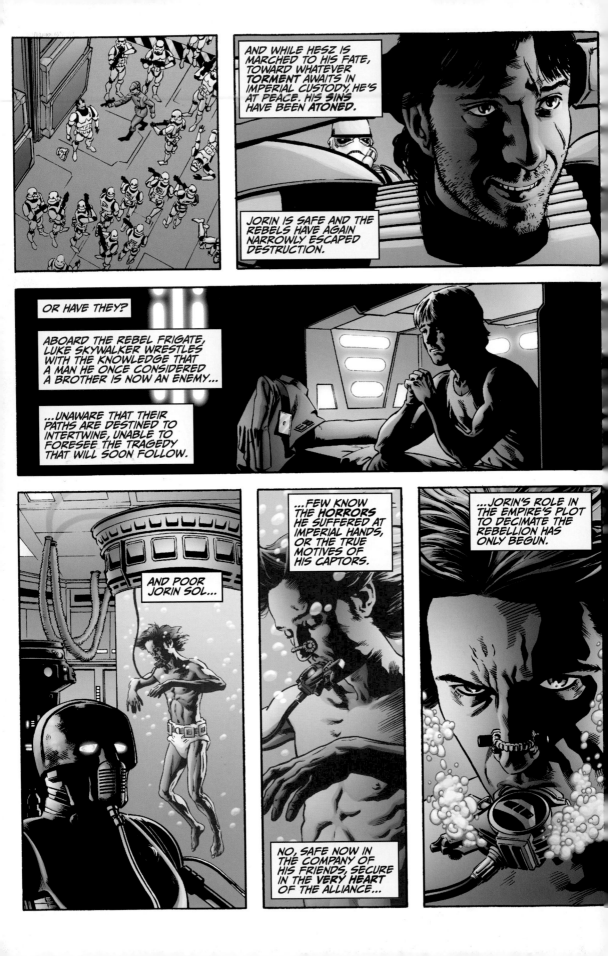

AND WHILE HESZ IS MARCHED TO HIS FATE, TOWARD WHATEVER TORMENT AWAITS IN IMPERIAL CUSTODY, HE'S AT PEACE. HIS SINS HAVE BEEN ATONED.

JORIN IS SAFE AND THE REBELS HAVE AGAIN NARROWLY ESCAPED DESTRUCTION.

OR HAVE THEY?

ABOARD THE REBEL FRIGATE, LUKE SKYWALKER WRESTLES WITH THE KNOWLEDGE THAT A MAN HE ONCE CONSIDERED A BROTHER IS NOW AN ENEMY...

...UNAWARE THAT THEIR PATHS ARE DESTINED TO INTERTWINE, UNABLE TO FORESEE THE TRAGEDY THAT WILL SOON FOLLOW.

AND POOR JORIN SOL...

...FEW KNOW THE HORRORS HE SUFFERED AT IMPERIAL HANDS, OR THE TRUE MOTIVES OF HIS CAPTORS.

NO, SAFE NOW IN THE COMPANY OF HIS FRIENDS, SECURE IN THE VERY HEART OF THE ALLIANCE...

...JORIN'S ROLE IN THE EMPIRE'S PLOT TO DECIMATE THE REBELLION HAS ONLY BEGUN.

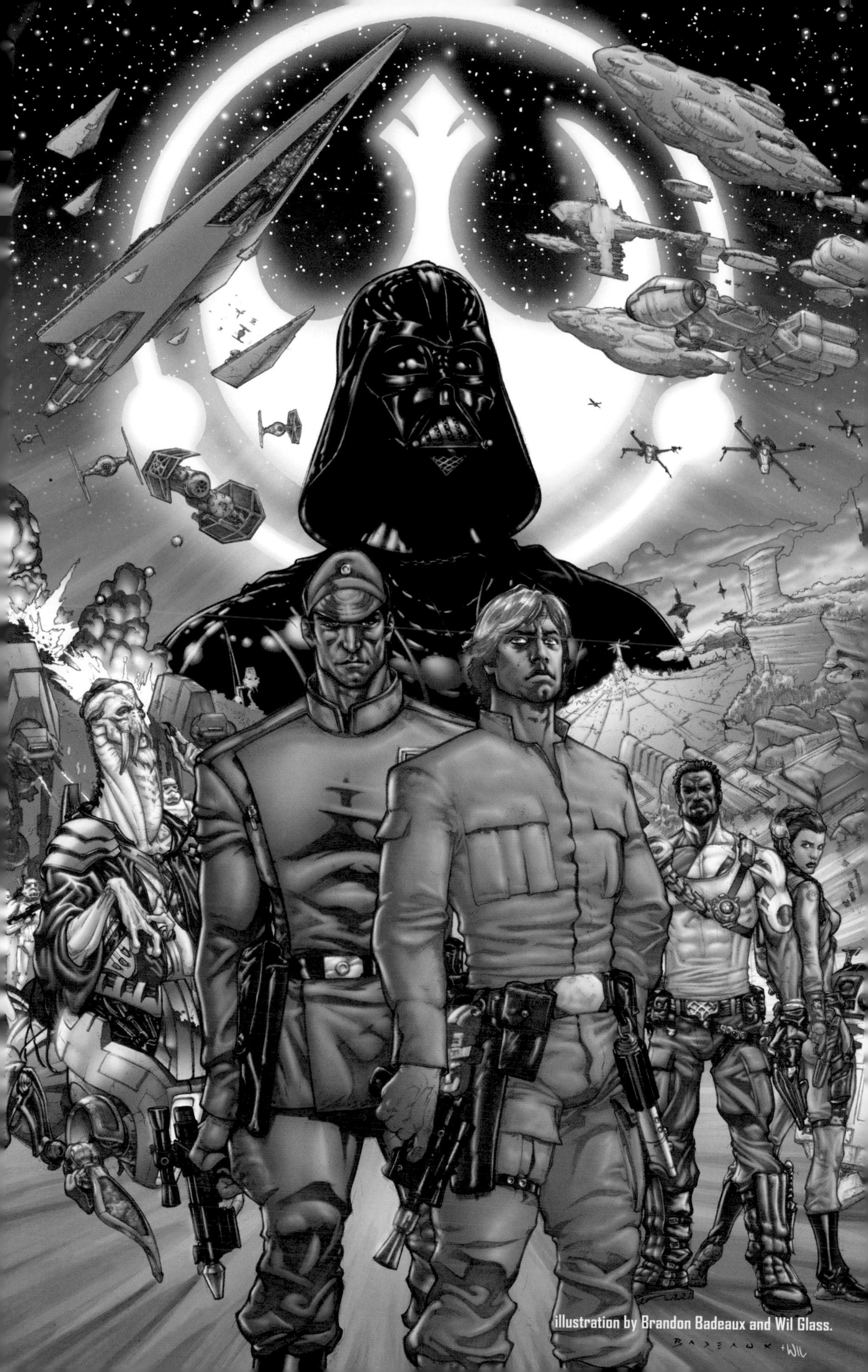

illustration by Brandon Badeaux and Wil Glass.

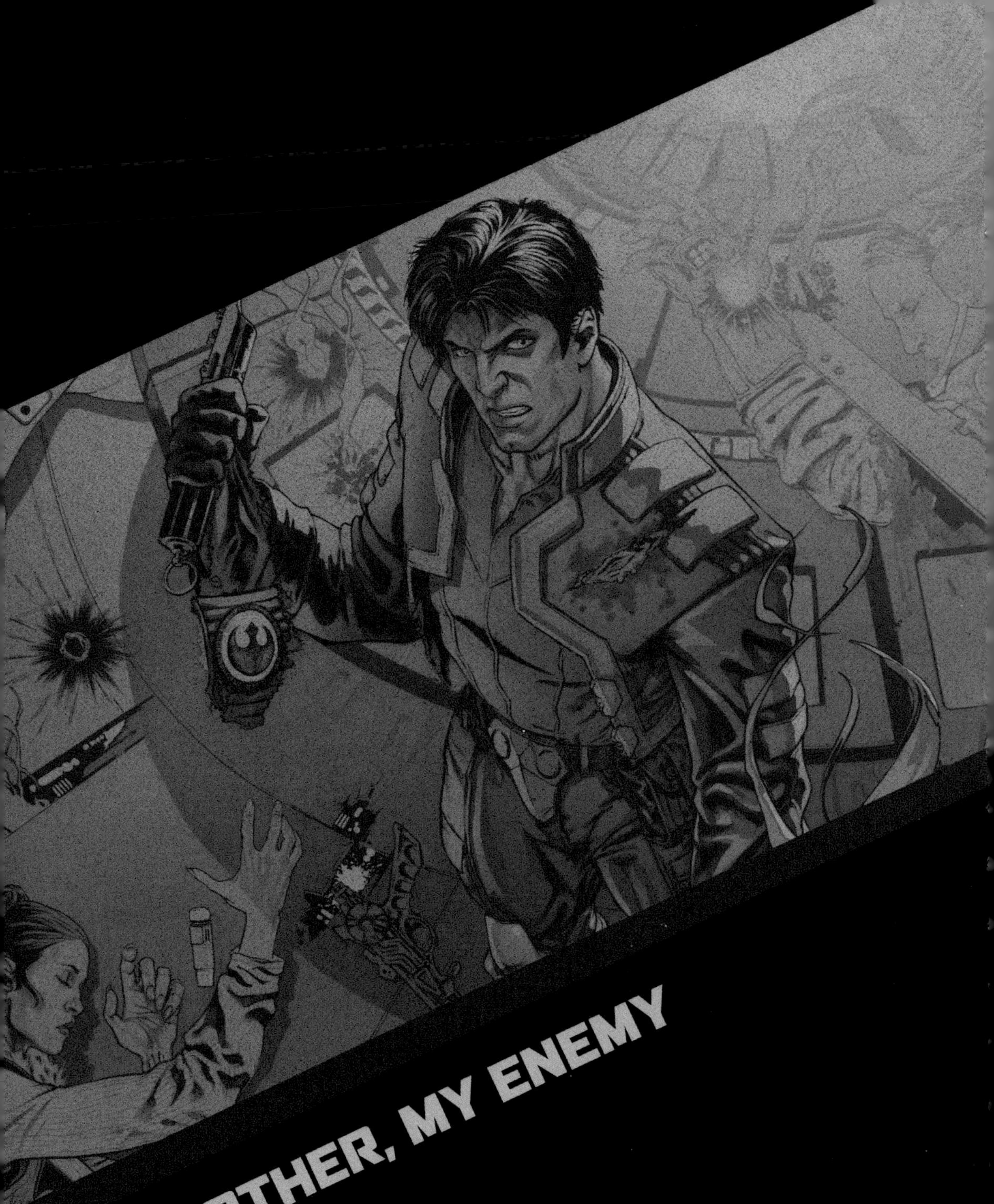

MY BROTHER, MY ENEMY

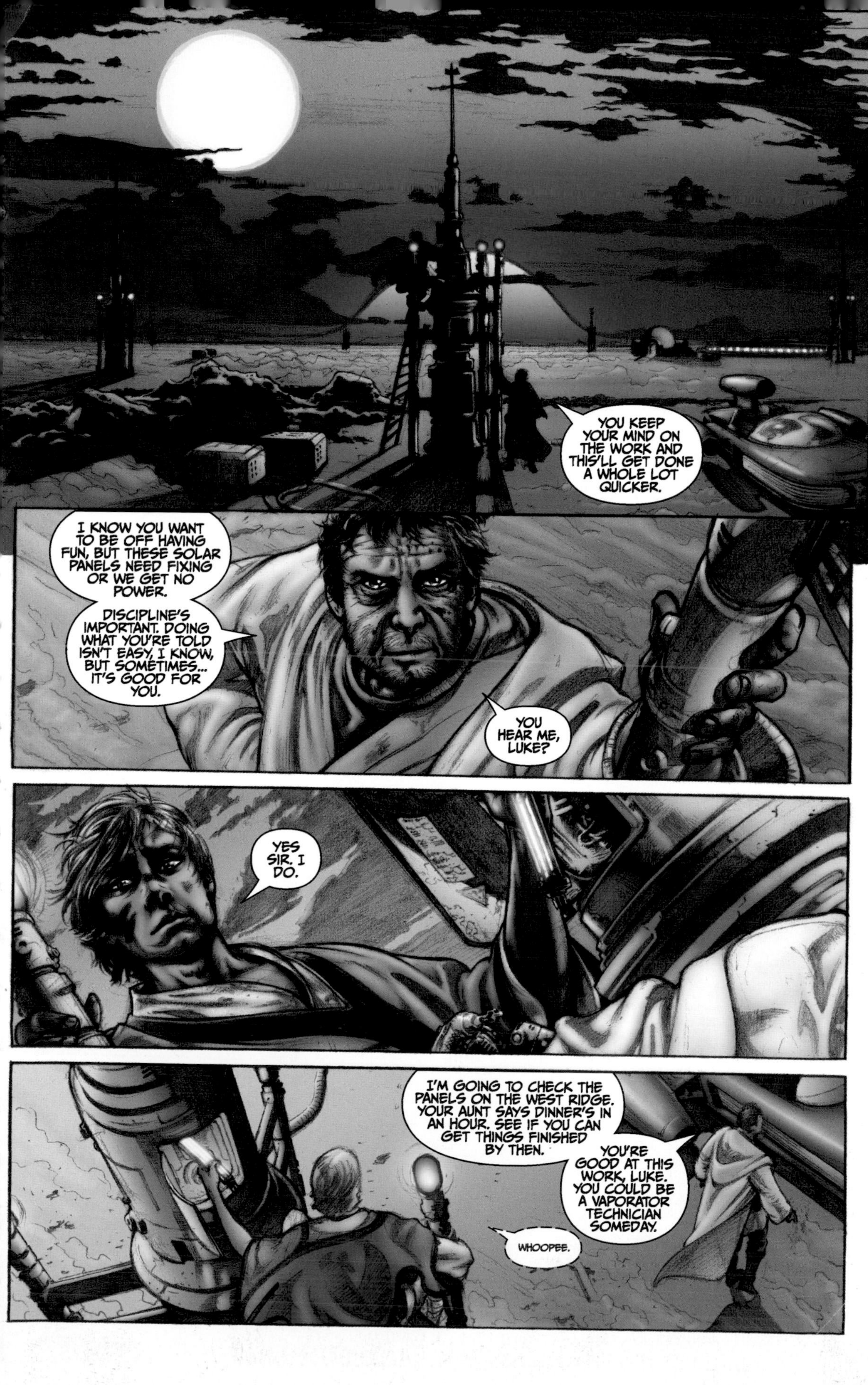
YOU KEEP YOUR MIND ON THE WORK AND THIS'LL GET DONE A WHOLE LOT QUICKER.
I KNOW YOU WANT TO BE OFF HAVING FUN, BUT THESE SOLAR PANELS NEED FIXING OR WE GET NO POWER.
DISCIPLINE'S IMPORTANT. DOING WHAT YOU'RE TOLD ISN'T EASY, I KNOW, BUT SOMETIMES... IT'S GOOD FOR YOU.
YOU HEAR ME, LUKE?
YES SIR. I DO.
I'M GOING TO CHECK THE PANELS ON THE WEST RIDGE. YOUR AUNT SAYS DINNER'S IN AN HOUR. SEE IF YOU CAN GET THINGS FINISHED BY THEN.
YOU'RE GOOD AT THIS WORK, LUKE. YOU COULD BE A VAPORATOR TECHNICIAN SOMEDAY.
WHOOPEE.

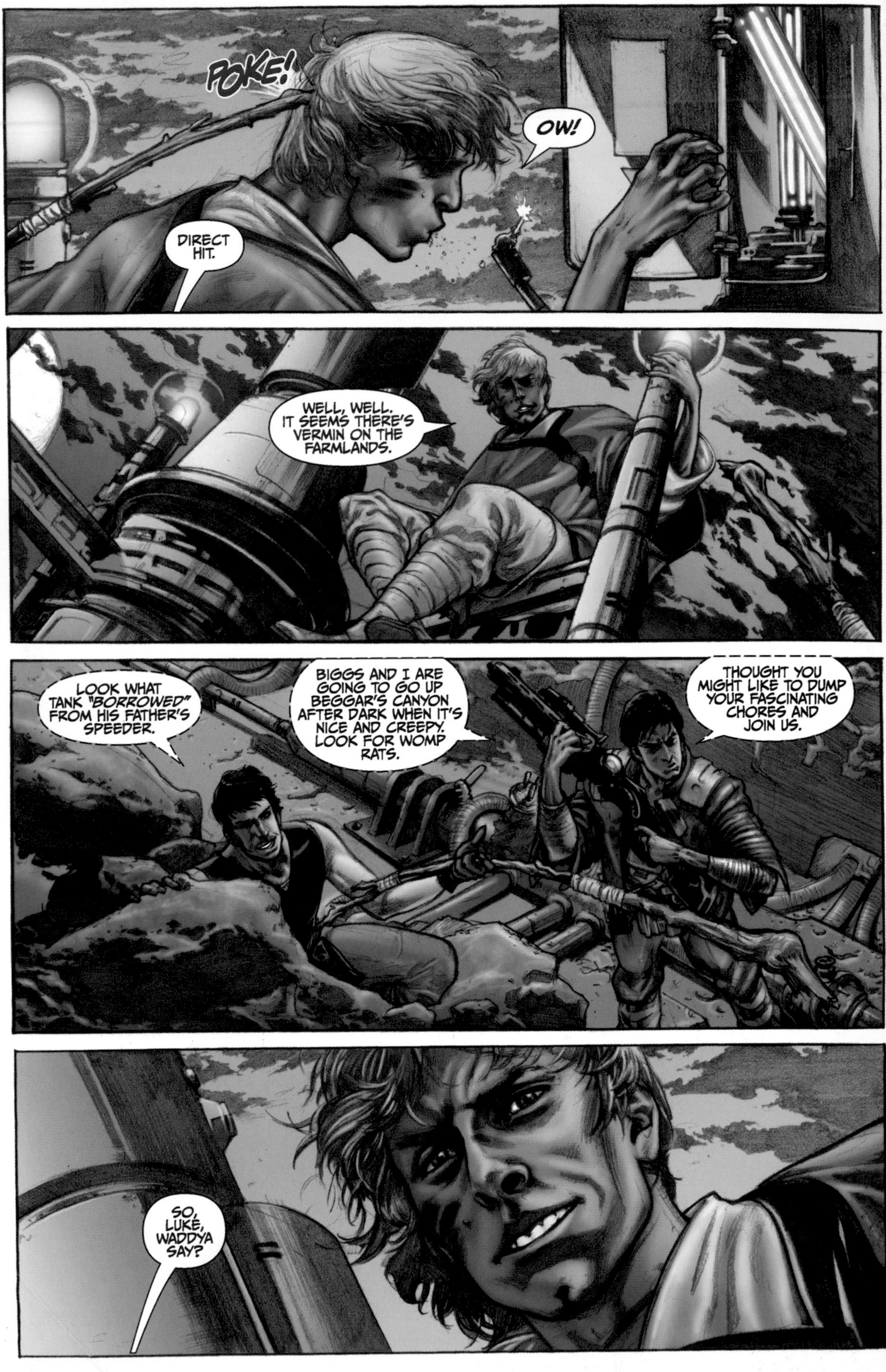
POKE!
OW!
DIRECT HIT.
WELL, WELL. IT SEEMS THERE'S VERMIN ON THE FARMLANDS.
LOOK WHAT TANK "BORROWED" FROM HIS FATHER'S SPEEDER.
BIGGS AND I ARE GOING TO GO UP BEGGAR'S CANYON AFTER DARK WHEN IT'S NICE AND CREEPY. LOOK FOR WOMP RATS.
THOUGHT YOU MIGHT LIKE TO DUMP YOUR FASCINATING CHORES AND JOIN US.
SO, LUKE, WADDYA SAY?

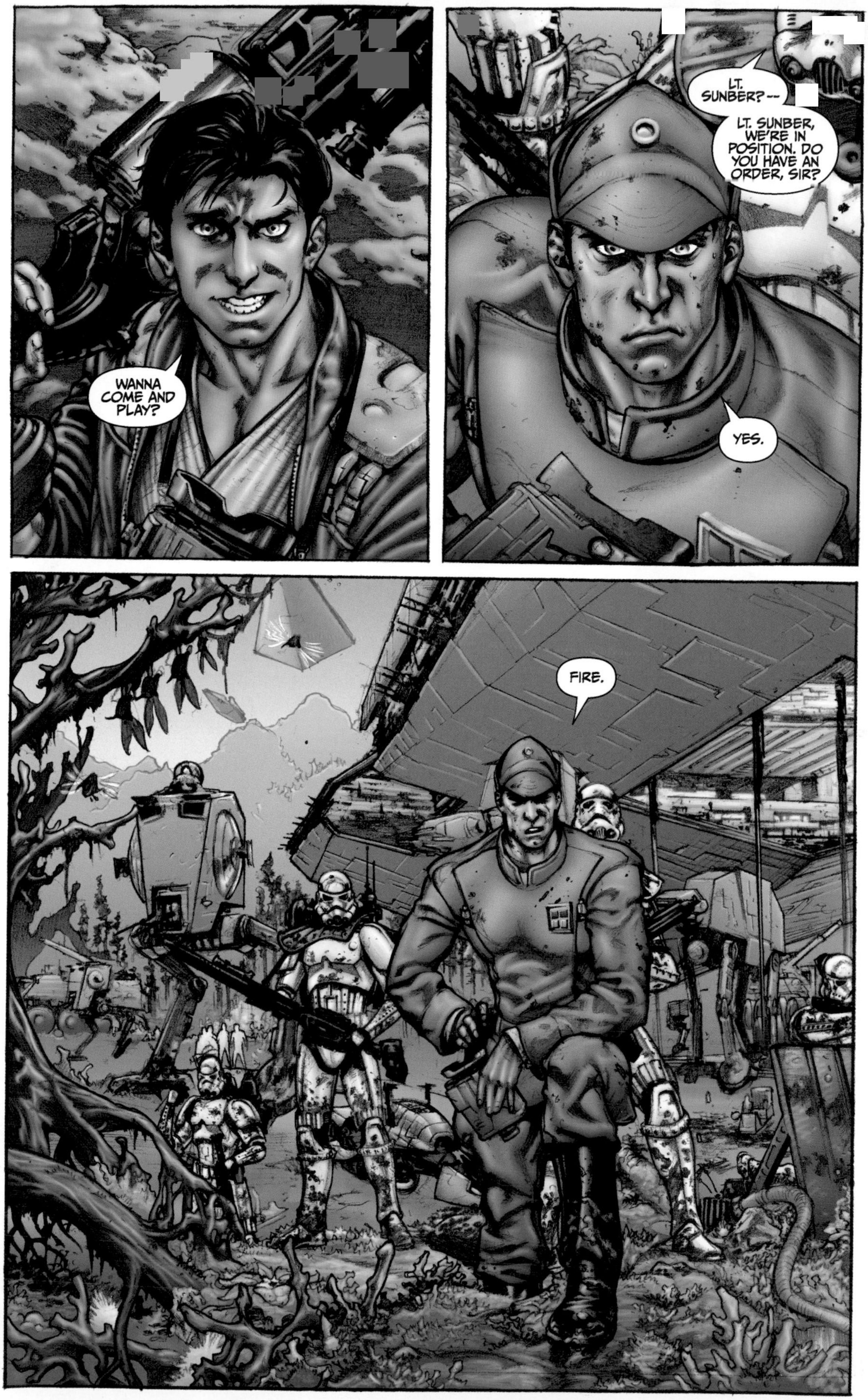
WANNA COME AND PLAY?
LT. SUNBER?--
LT. SUNBER, WE'RE IN POSITION. DO YOU HAVE AN ORDER, SIR?
YES.
FIRE.

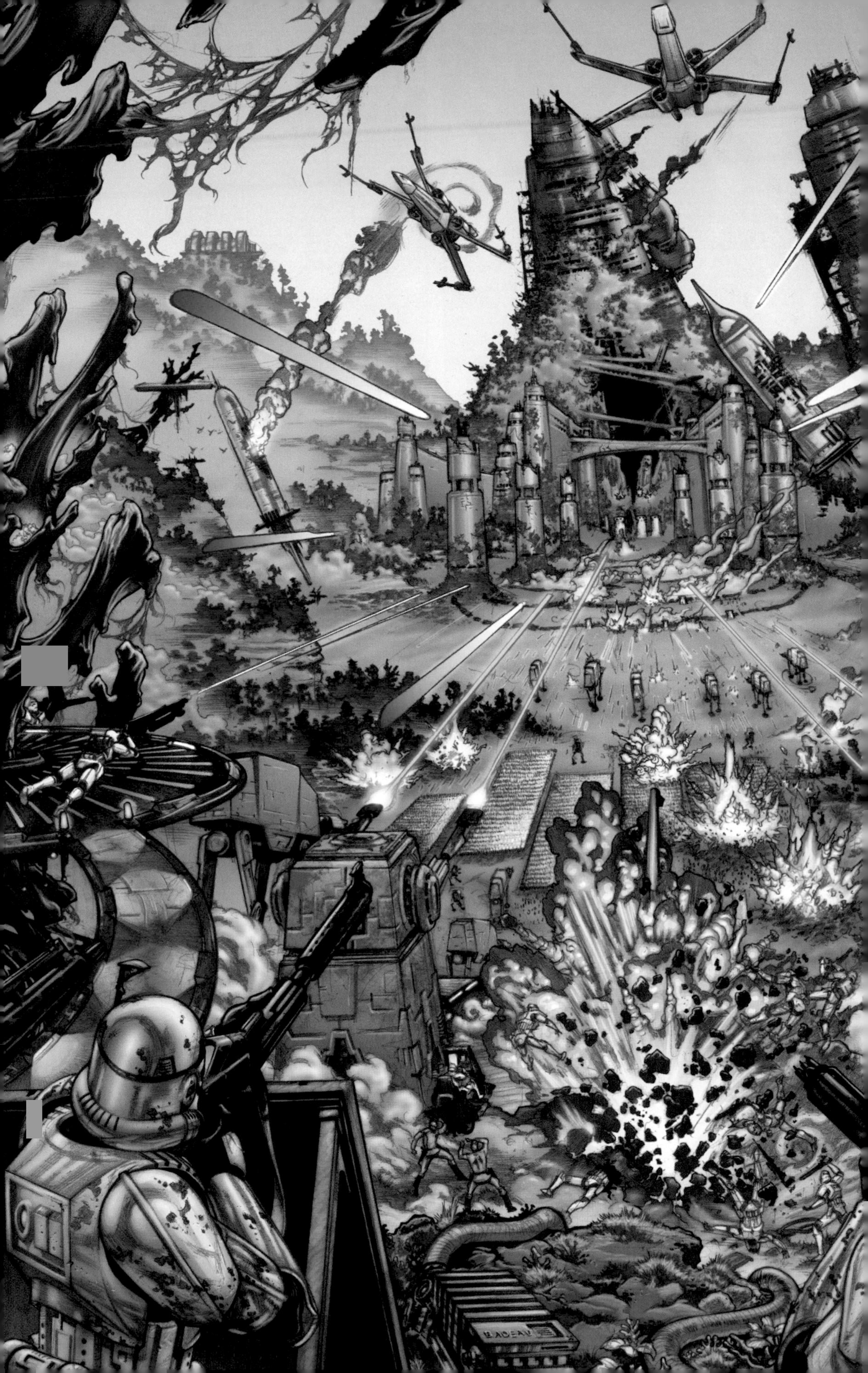

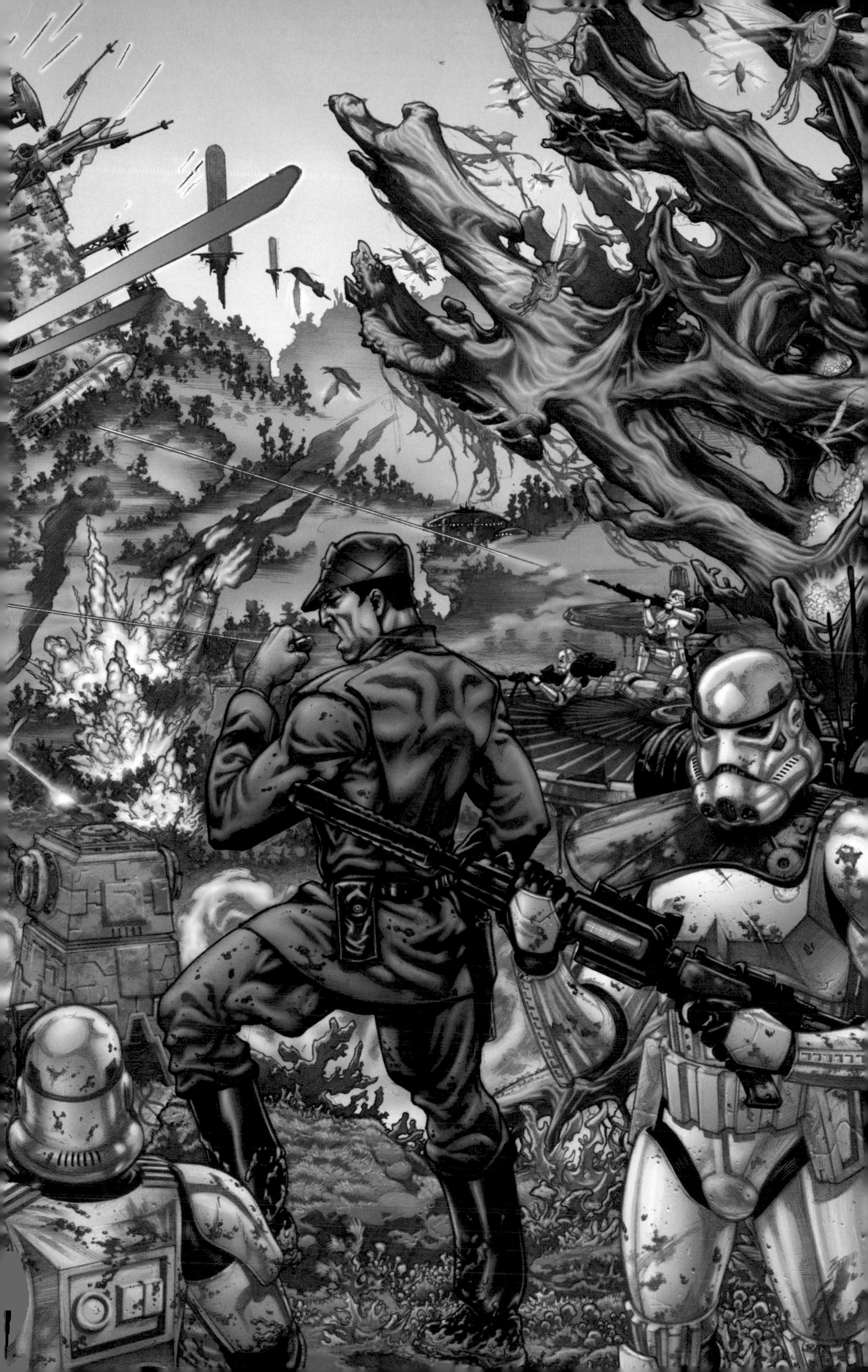

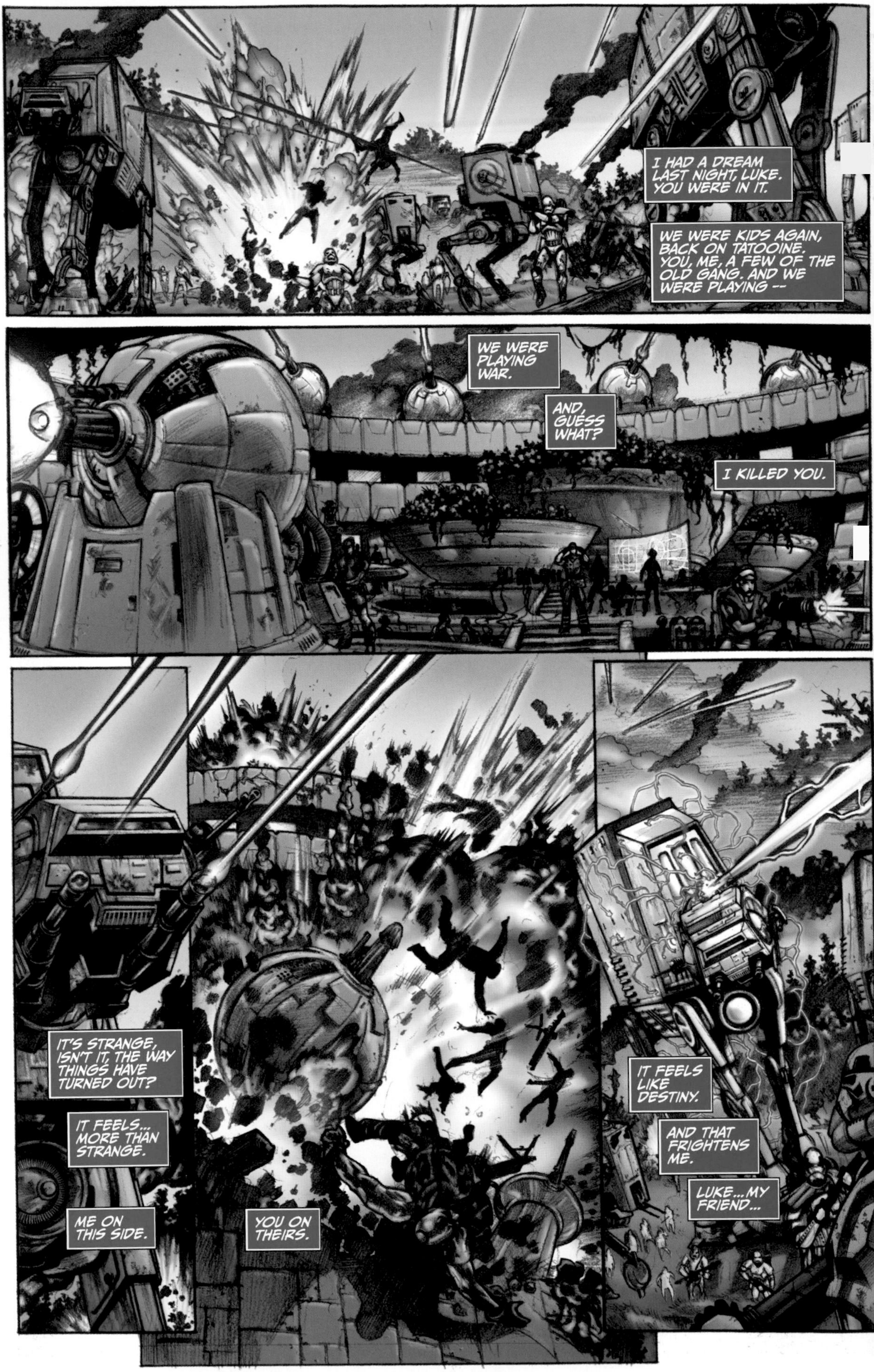
I HAD A DREAM LAST NIGHT, LUKE. YOU WERE IN IT.
WE WERE KIDS AGAIN, BACK ON TATOOINE. YOU, ME, A FEW OF THE OLD GANG. AND WE WERE PLAYING --
WE WERE PLAYING WAR.
AND, GUESS WHAT?
I KILLED YOU.
IT'S STRANGE, ISN'T IT, THE WAY THINGS HAVE TURNED OUT?
IT FEELS... MORE THAN STRANGE.
ME ON THIS SIDE.
YOU ON THEIRS.
IT FEELS LIKE DESTINY.
AND THAT FRIGHTENS ME.
LUKE... MY FRIEND...

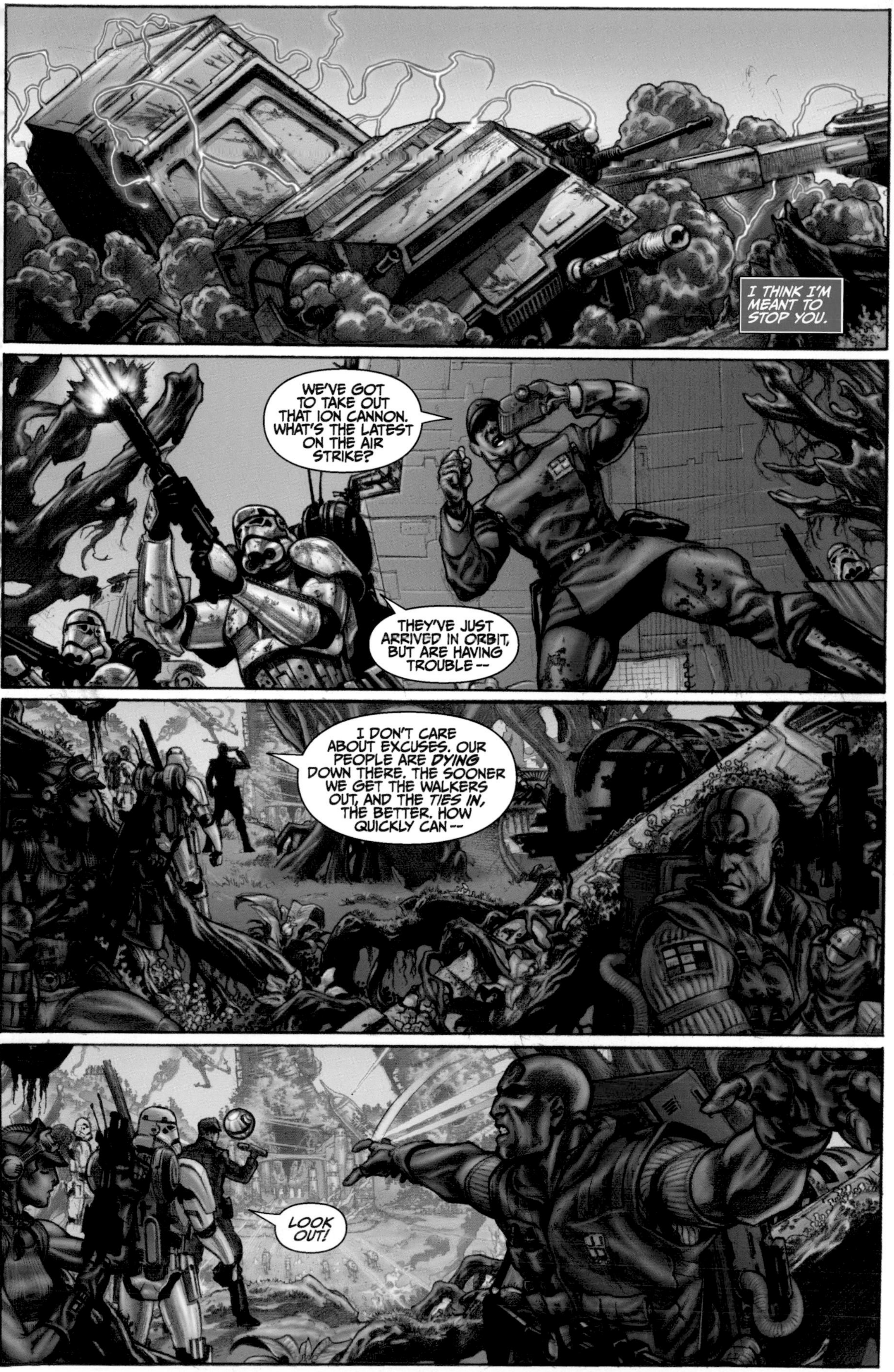
I THINK I'M MEANT TO STOP YOU.
WE'VE GOT TO TAKE OUT THAT ION CANNON. WHAT'S THE LATEST ON THE AIR STRIKE?
THEY'VE JUST ARRIVED IN ORBIT, BUT ARE HAVING TROUBLE --
I DON'T CARE ABOUT EXCUSES. OUR PEOPLE ARE *DYING* DOWN THERE. THE SOONER WE GET THE WALKERS OUT, AND THE *TIES IN*, THE BETTER. HOW QUICKLY CAN --
LOOK OUT!

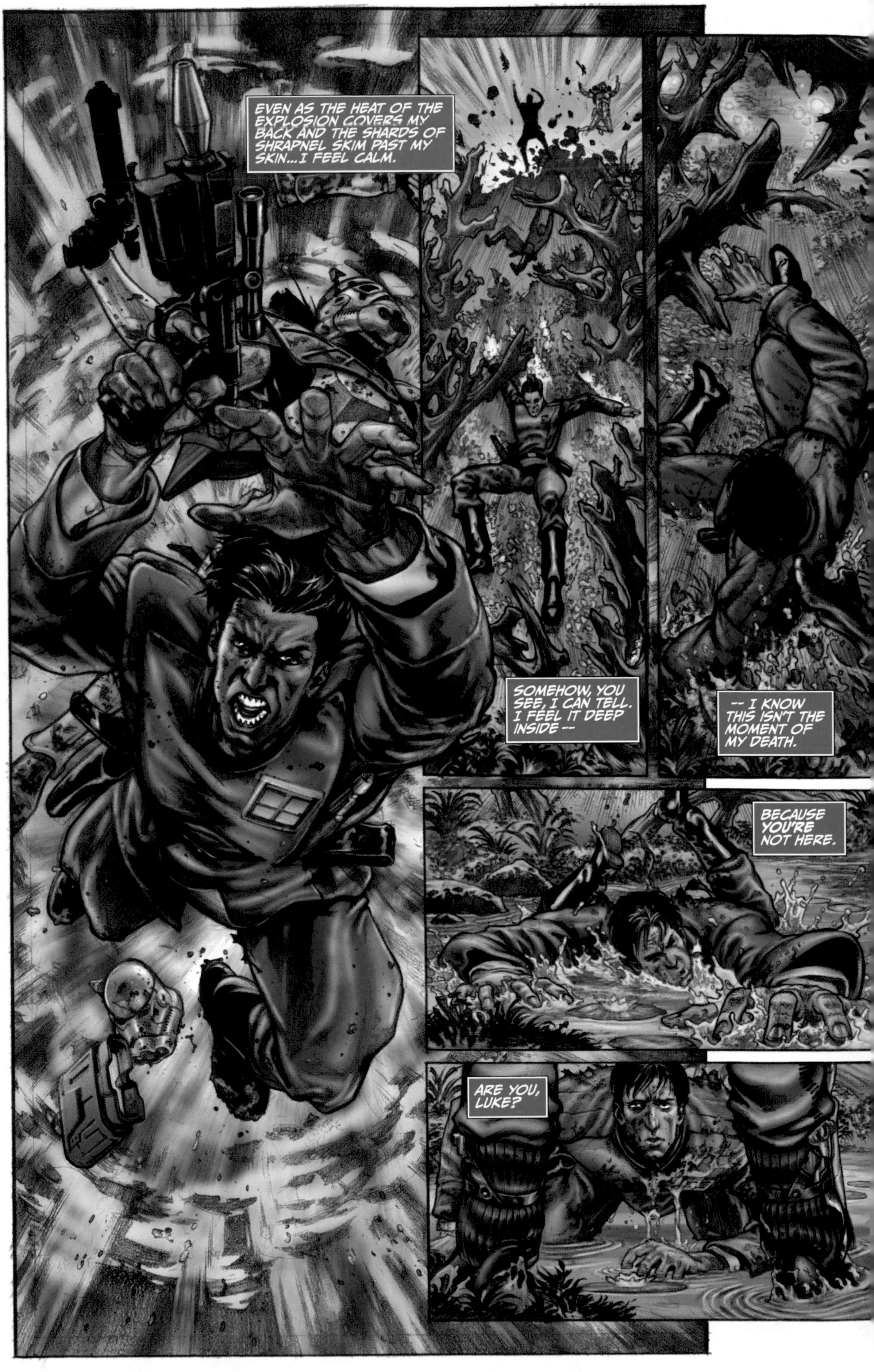
EVEN AS THE HEAT OF THE EXPLOSION COVERS MY BACK AND THE SHARDS OF SHRAPNEL SKIM PAST MY SKIN...I FEEL CALM.
SOMEHOW, YOU SEE, I CAN TELL. I FEEL IT DEEP INSIDE --
-- I KNOW THIS ISN'T THE MOMENT OF MY DEATH.
BECAUSE YOU'RE NOT HERE.
ARE YOU, LUKE?

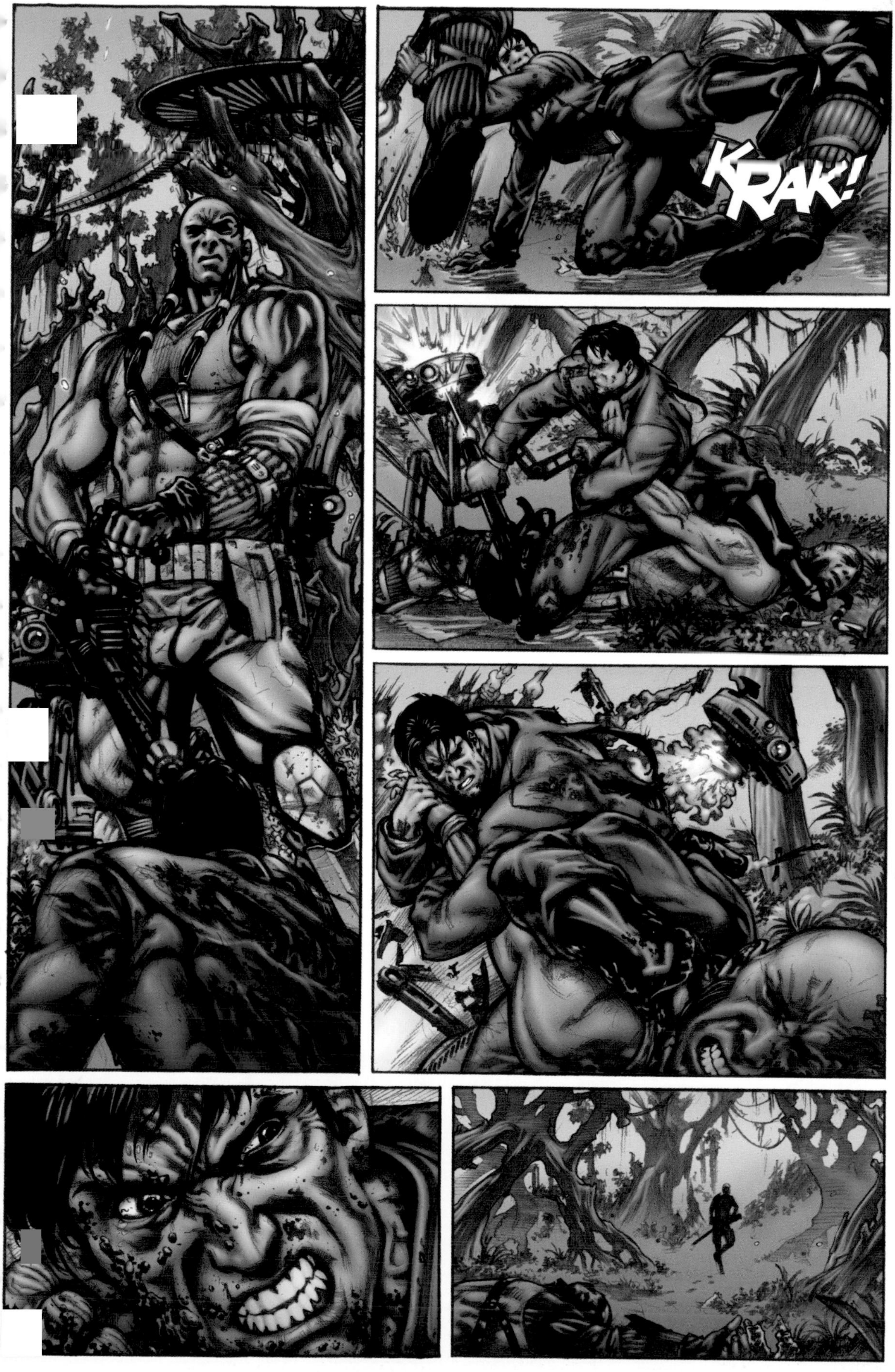
KRAK!

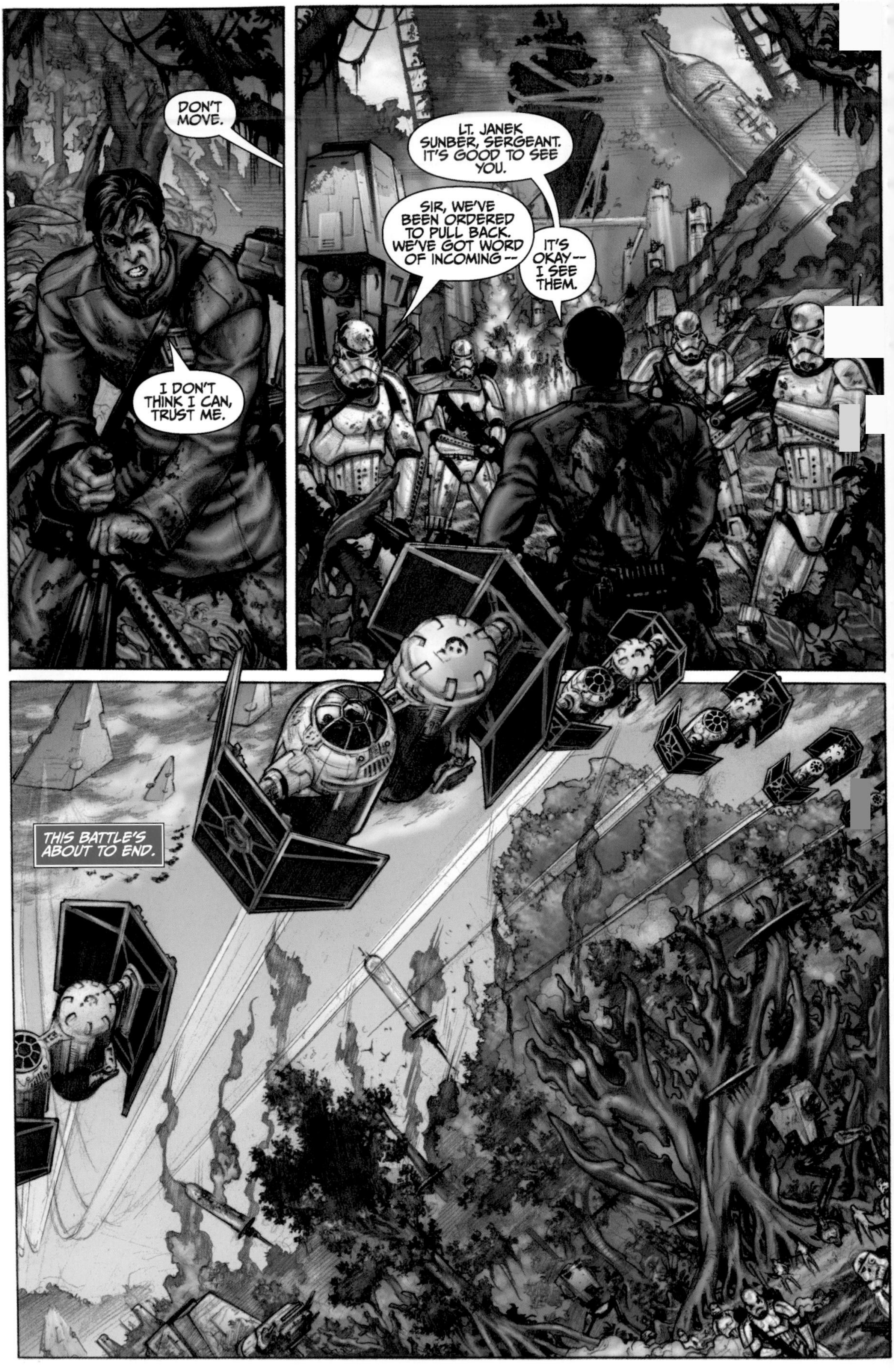
DON'T MOVE.
I DON'T THINK I CAN, TRUST ME.
LT. JANEK SUNBER, SERGEANT. IT'S GOOD TO SEE YOU.
SIR, WE'VE BEEN ORDERED TO PULL BACK. WE'VE GOT WORD OF INCOMING --
IT'S OKAY -- I SEE THEM.
THIS BATTLE'S ABOUT TO END.

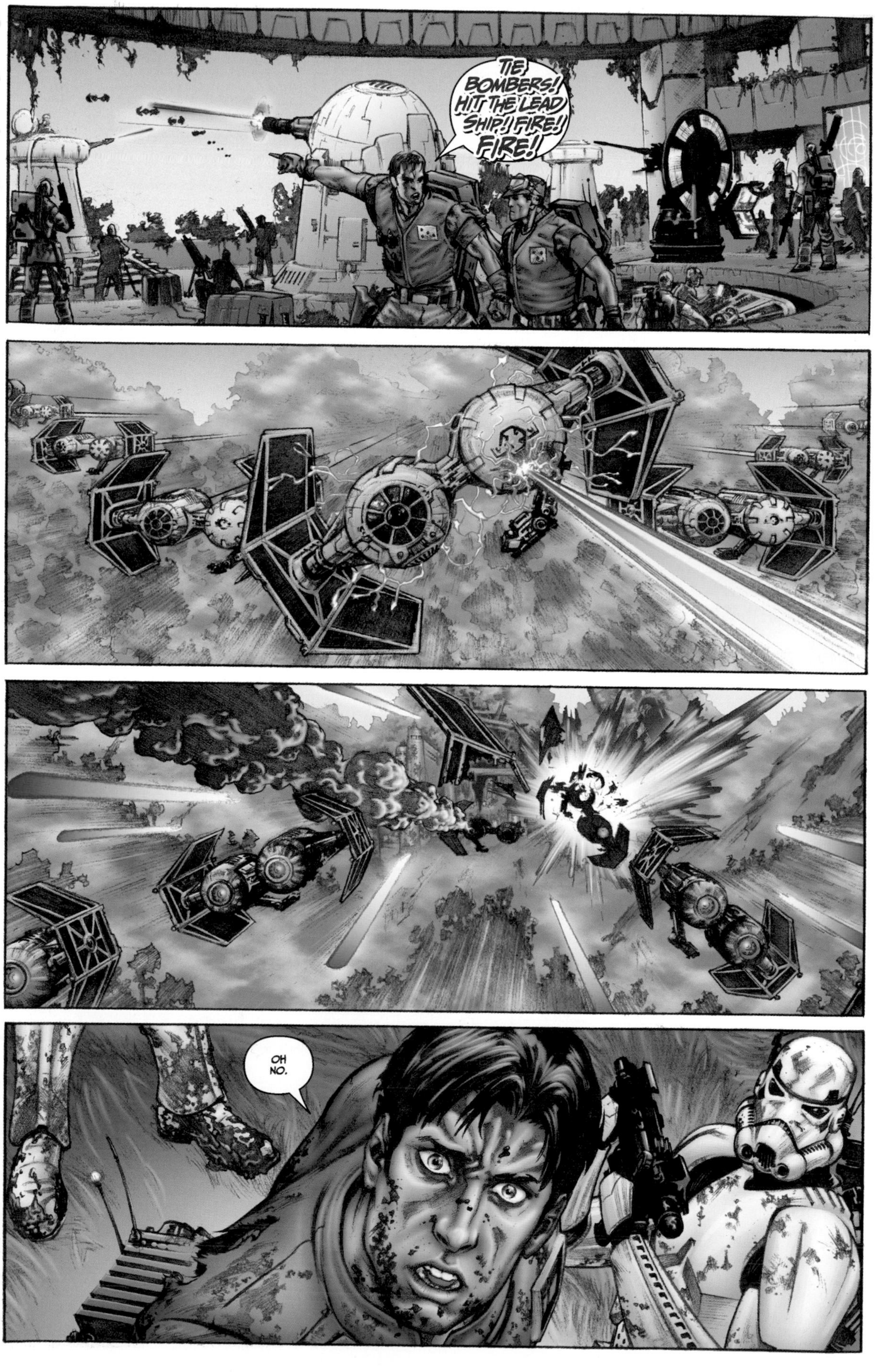
TIE BOMBERS! HIT THE LEAD SHIP! FIRE! FIRE!
OH NO.

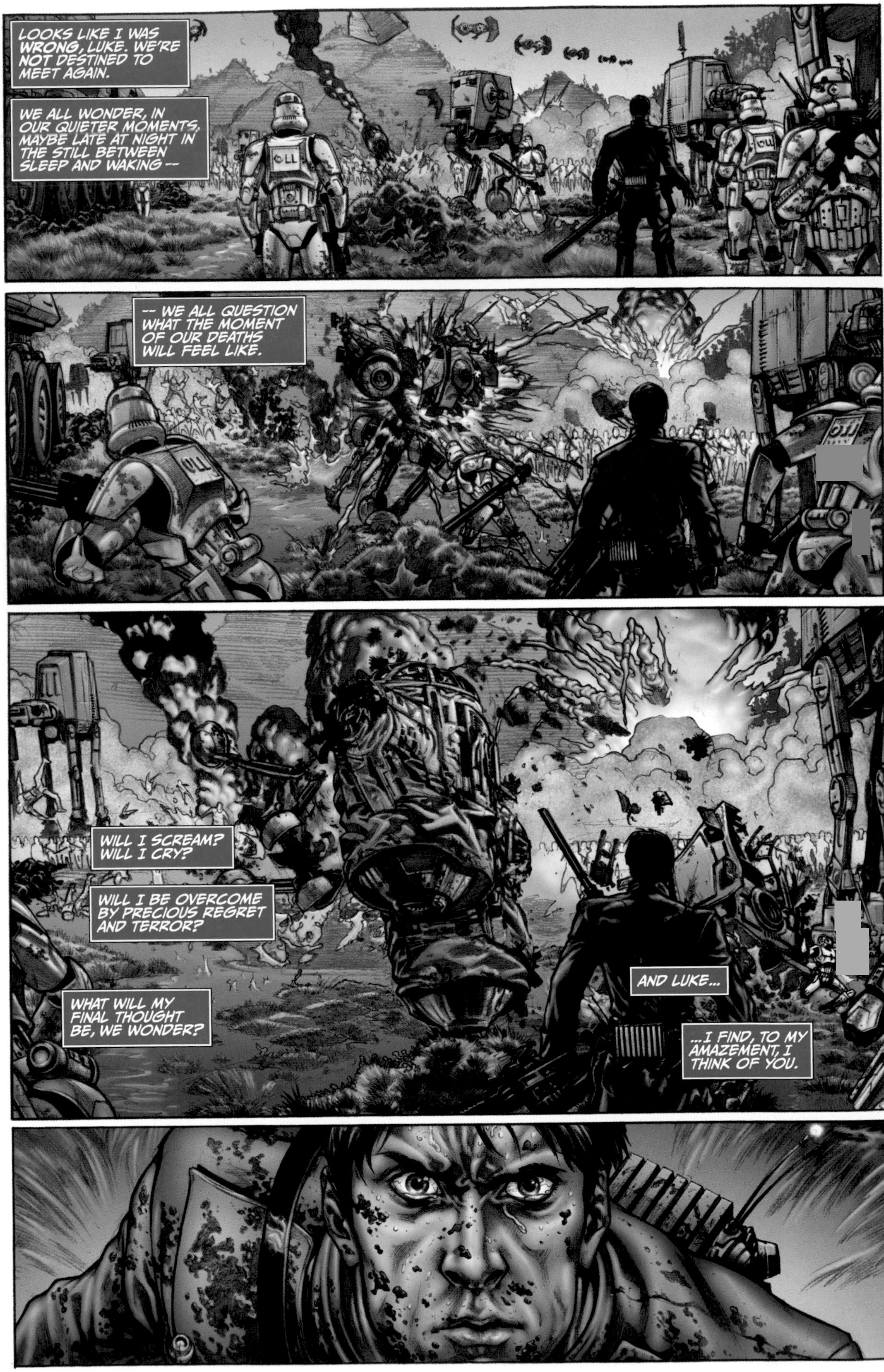
LOOKS LIKE I WAS WRONG, LUKE. WE'RE NOT DESTINED TO MEET AGAIN.
WE ALL WONDER, IN OUR QUIETER MOMENTS, MAYBE LATE AT NIGHT IN THE STILL BETWEEN SLEEP AND WAKING --
-- WE ALL QUESTION WHAT THE MOMENT OF OUR DEATHS WILL FEEL LIKE.
WILL I SCREAM? WILL I CRY?
WILL I BE OVERCOME BY PRECIOUS REGRET AND TERROR?
WHAT WILL MY FINAL THOUGHT BE, WE WONDER?
AND LUKE...
...I FIND, TO MY AMAZEMENT, I THINK OF YOU.

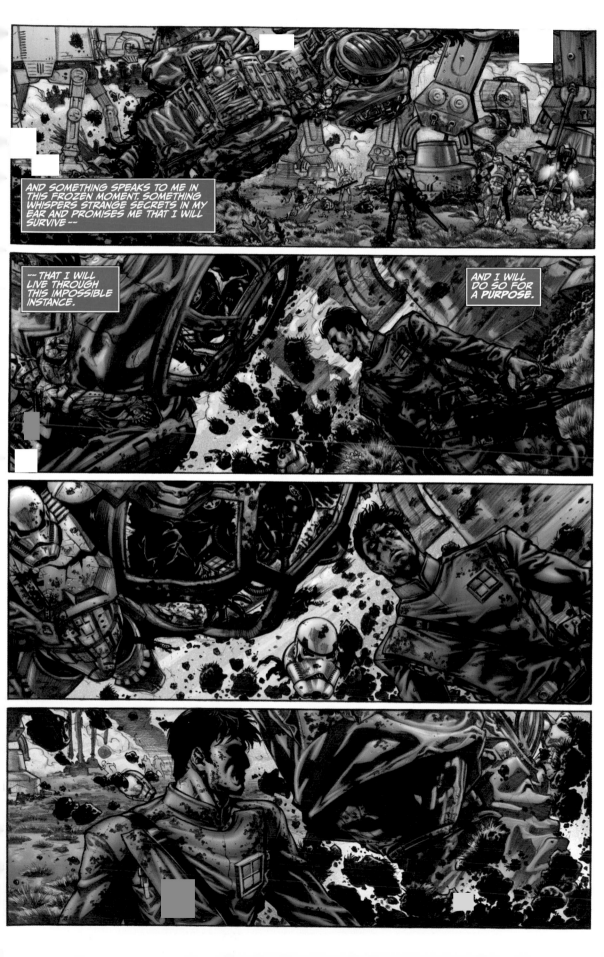

AND SOMETHING SPEAKS TO ME IN THIS FROZEN MOMENT. SOMETHING WHISPERS STRANGE SECRETS IN MY EAR AND PROMISES ME THAT I WILL SURVIVE --

-- THAT I WILL LIVE THROUGH THIS IMPOSSIBLE INSTANCE.

AND I WILL DO SO FOR A PURPOSE.

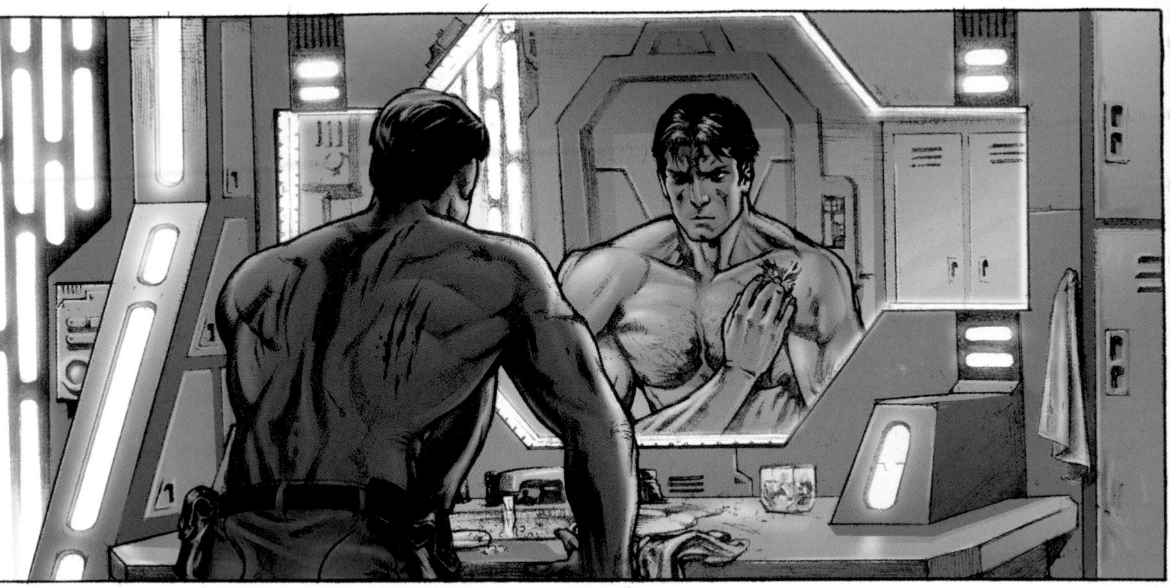

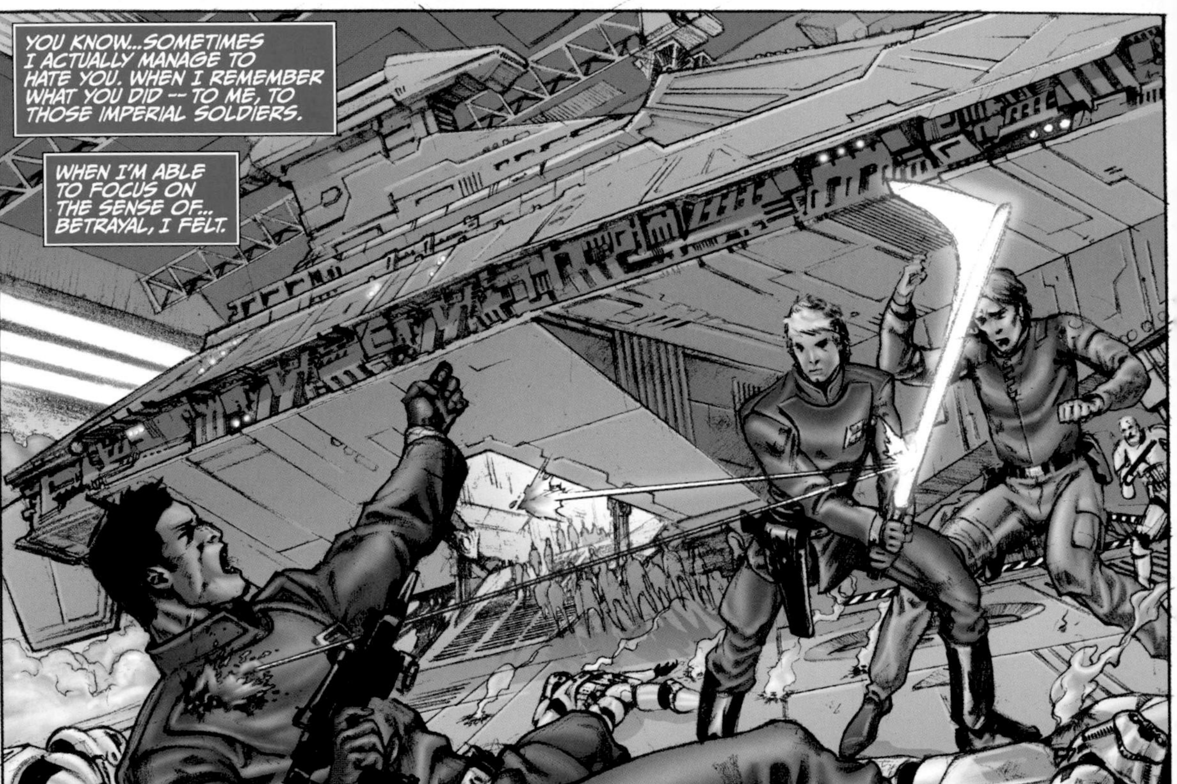
YOU KNOW...SOMETIMES I ACTUALLY MANAGE TO HATE YOU. WHEN I REMEMBER WHAT YOU DID -- TO ME, TO THOSE IMPERIAL SOLDIERS.
WHEN I'M ABLE TO FOCUS ON THE SENSE OF... BETRAYAL, I FELT.

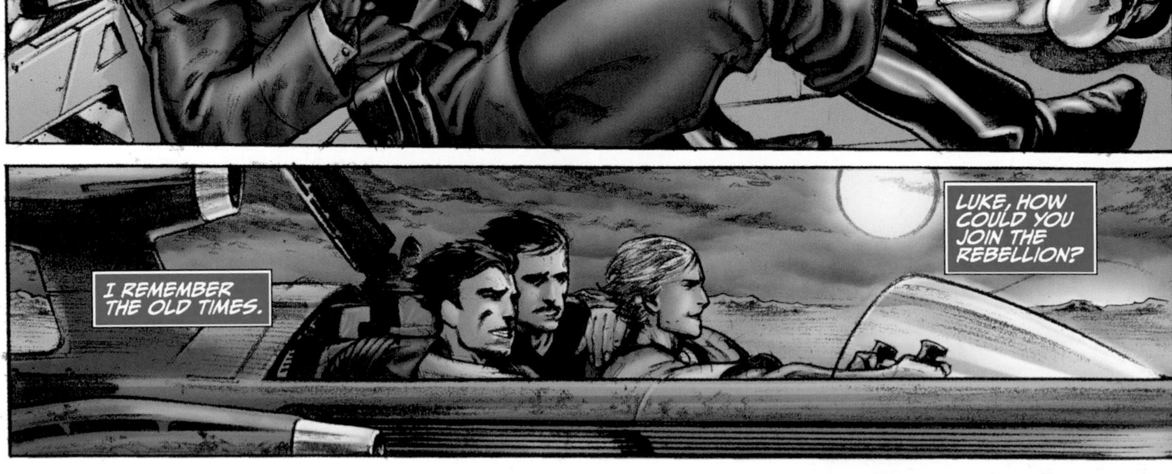
I REMEMBER THE OLD TIMES.
LUKE, HOW COULD YOU JOIN THE REBELLION?

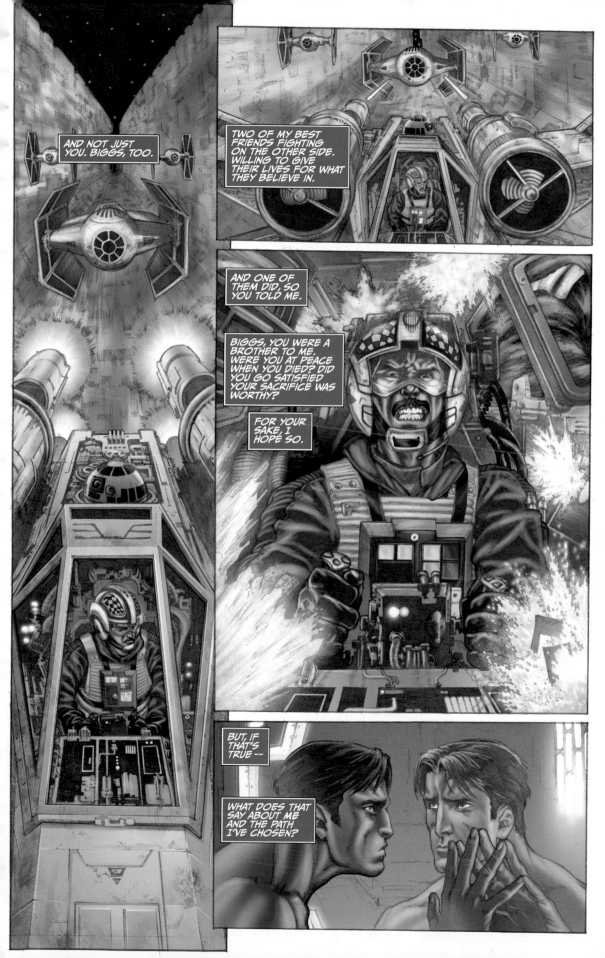

AND NOT JUST YOU. BIGGS, TOO.

TWO OF MY BEST FRIENDS FIGHTING ON THE OTHER SIDE. WILLING TO GIVE THEIR LIVES FOR WHAT THEY BELIEVE IN.

AND ONE OF THEM DID, SO YOU TOLD ME.

BIGGS, YOU WERE A BROTHER TO ME. WERE YOU AT PEACE WHEN YOU DIED? DID YOU GO SATISFIED YOUR SACRIFICE WAS WORTHY?

FOR YOUR SAKE, I HOPE SO.

BUT, IF THAT'S TRUE --

WHAT DOES THAT SAY ABOUT ME AND THE PATH I'VE CHOSEN?

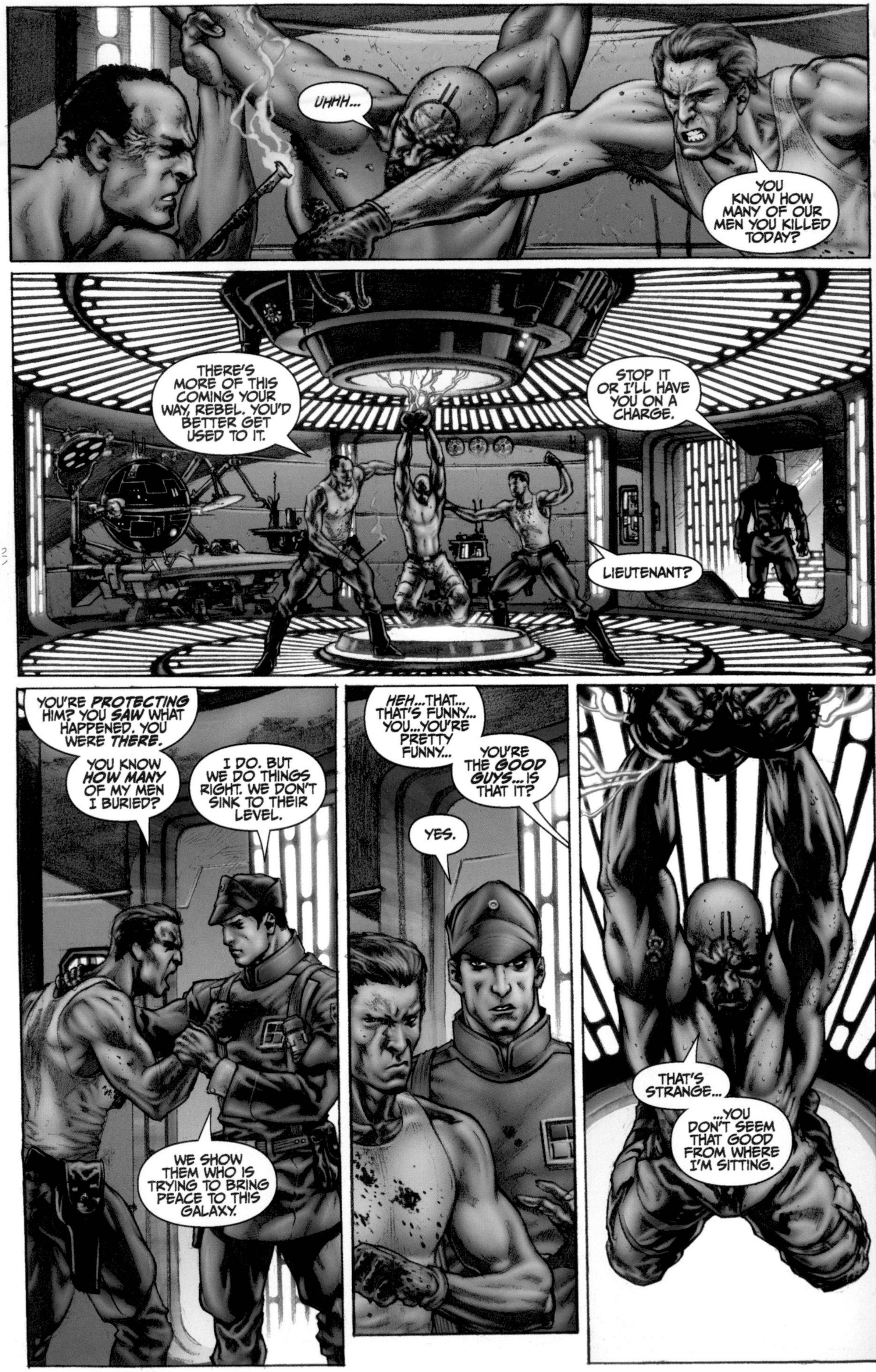
UHHH...
YOU KNOW HOW MANY OF OUR MEN YOU KILLED TODAY?
THERE'S MORE OF THIS COMING YOUR WAY, REBEL. YOU'D BETTER GET USED TO IT.
STOP IT OR I'LL HAVE YOU ON A CHARGE.
LIEUTENANT?
YOU'RE *PROTECTING* HIM? YOU *SAW* WHAT HAPPENED. YOU WERE *THERE*.
YOU KNOW *HOW MANY* OF MY MEN I BURIED?
I DO. BUT WE DO THINGS RIGHT. WE DON'T SINK TO THEIR LEVEL.
WE SHOW THEM WHO IS TRYING TO BRING PEACE TO THIS GALAXY.
HEH...THAT... THAT'S FUNNY... YOU...YOU'RE PRETTY FUNNY...
YOU'RE THE *GOOD GUYS*...IS THAT IT?
YES.
THAT'S STRANGE...
...YOU DON'T SEEM THAT GOOD FROM WHERE I'M SITTING.

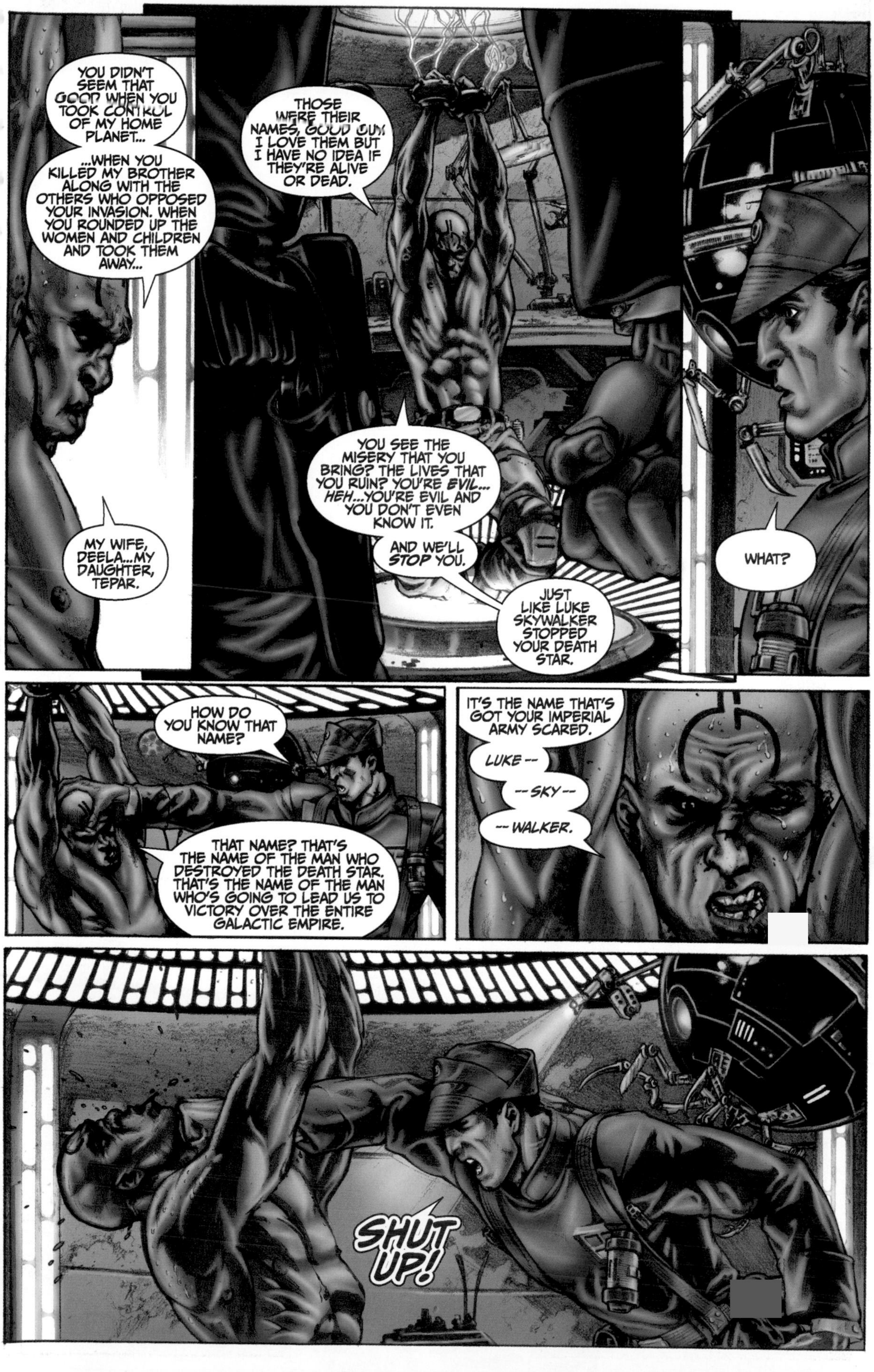
YOU DIDN'T SEEM THAT GOOD WHEN YOU TOOK CONTROL OF MY HOME PLANET...
...WHEN YOU KILLED MY BROTHER ALONG WITH THE OTHERS WHO OPPOSED YOUR INVASION. WHEN YOU ROUNDED UP THE WOMEN AND CHILDREN AND TOOK THEM AWAY...
MY WIFE, DEELA...MY DAUGHTER, TEPAR.
THOSE WERE THEIR NAMES, GOOD GUY. I LOVE THEM BUT I HAVE NO IDEA IF THEY'RE ALIVE OR DEAD.
YOU SEE THE MISERY THAT YOU BRING? THE LIVES THAT YOU RUIN? YOU'RE *EVIL*... *HEH*...YOU'RE EVIL AND YOU DON'T EVEN KNOW IT.
AND WE'LL *STOP* YOU.
JUST LIKE LUKE SKYWALKER STOPPED YOUR DEATH STAR.
WHAT?
HOW DO YOU KNOW THAT NAME?
THAT NAME? THAT'S THE NAME OF THE MAN WHO DESTROYED THE DEATH STAR. THAT'S THE NAME OF THE MAN WHO'S GOING TO LEAD US TO VICTORY OVER THE ENTIRE GALACTIC EMPIRE.
IT'S THE NAME THAT'S GOT YOUR IMPERIAL ARMY SCARED.
LUKE --
-- SKY --
-- WALKER.
SHUT UP!

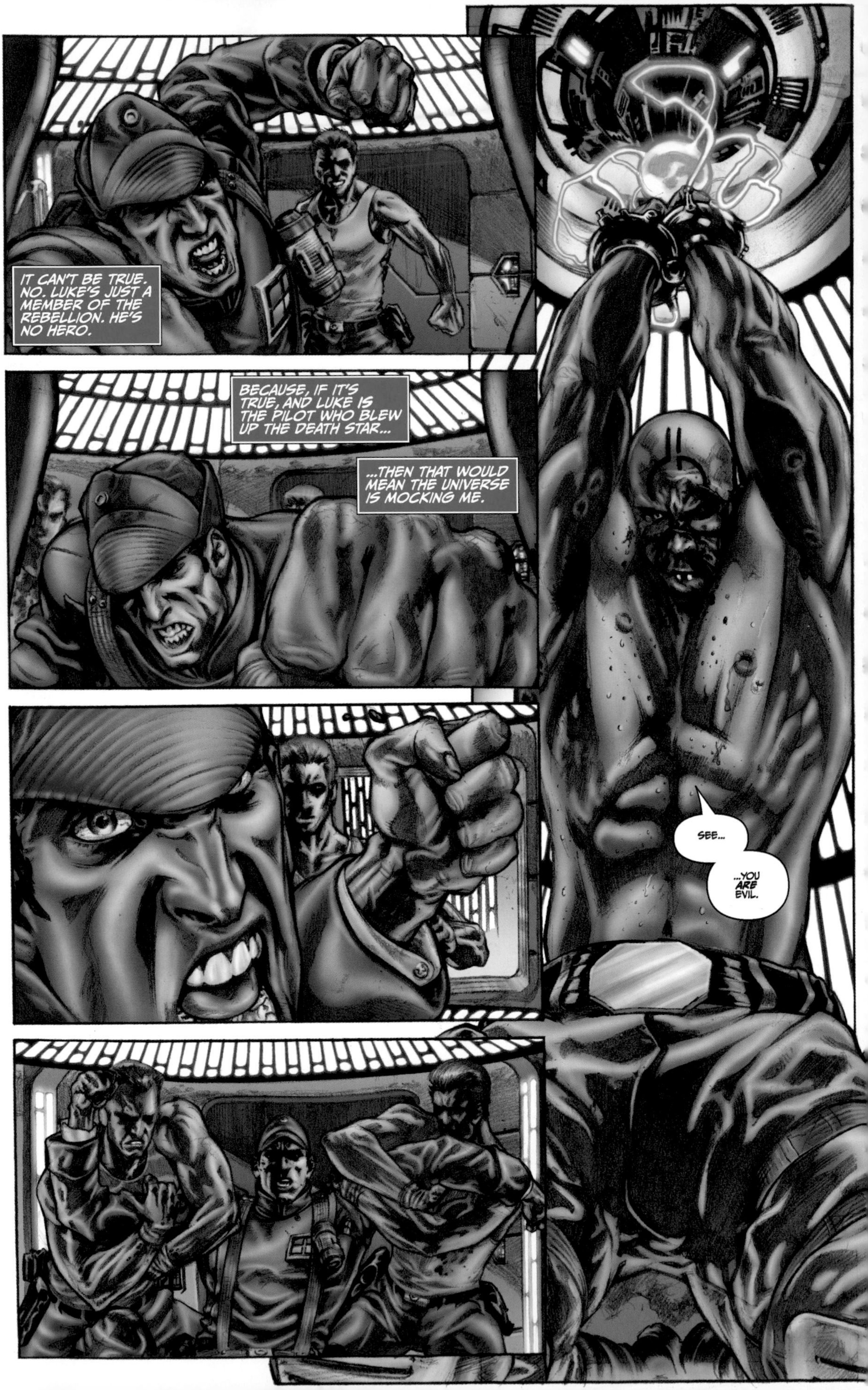
IT CAN'T BE TRUE. NO. LUKE'S JUST A MEMBER OF THE REBELLION. HE'S NO HERO.
BECAUSE, IF IT'S TRUE, AND LUKE IS THE PILOT WHO BLEW UP THE DEATH STAR...
...THEN THAT WOULD MEAN THE UNIVERSE IS MOCKING ME.
SEE...
...YOU ARE EVIL.

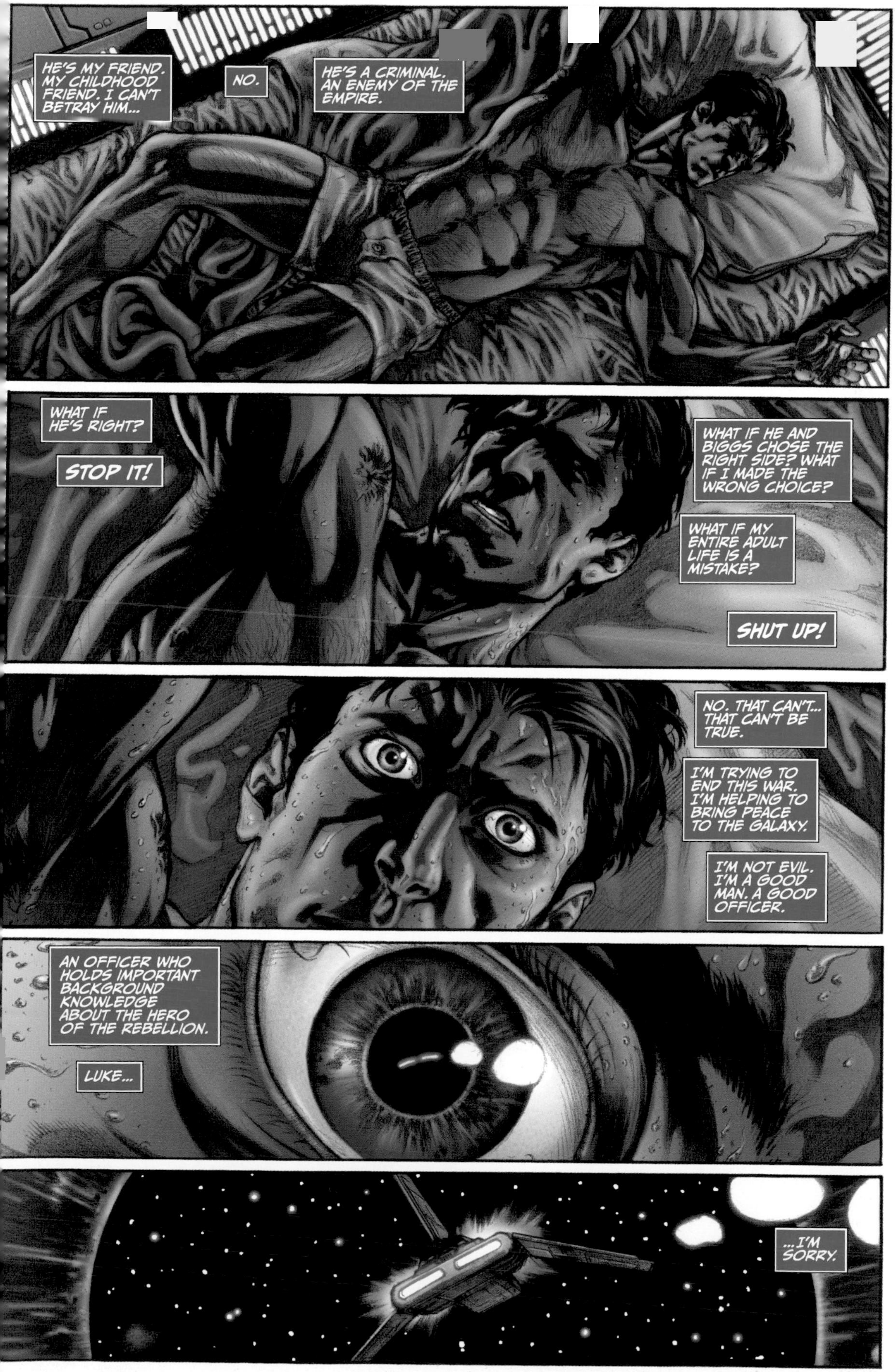
HE'S MY FRIEND. MY CHILDHOOD FRIEND. I CAN'T BETRAY HIM...
NO.
HE'S A CRIMINAL. AN ENEMY OF THE EMPIRE.
WHAT IF HE'S RIGHT?
STOP IT!
WHAT IF HE AND BIGGS CHOSE THE RIGHT SIDE? WHAT IF I MADE THE WRONG CHOICE?
WHAT IF MY ENTIRE ADULT LIFE IS A MISTAKE?
SHUT UP!
NO. THAT CAN'T... THAT CAN'T BE TRUE.
I'M TRYING TO END THIS WAR. I'M HELPING TO BRING PEACE TO THE GALAXY.
I'M NOT EVIL. I'M A GOOD MAN. A GOOD OFFICER.
AN OFFICER WHO HOLDS IMPORTANT BACKGROUND KNOWLEDGE ABOUT THE HERO OF THE REBELLION.
LUKE...
...I'M SORRY.

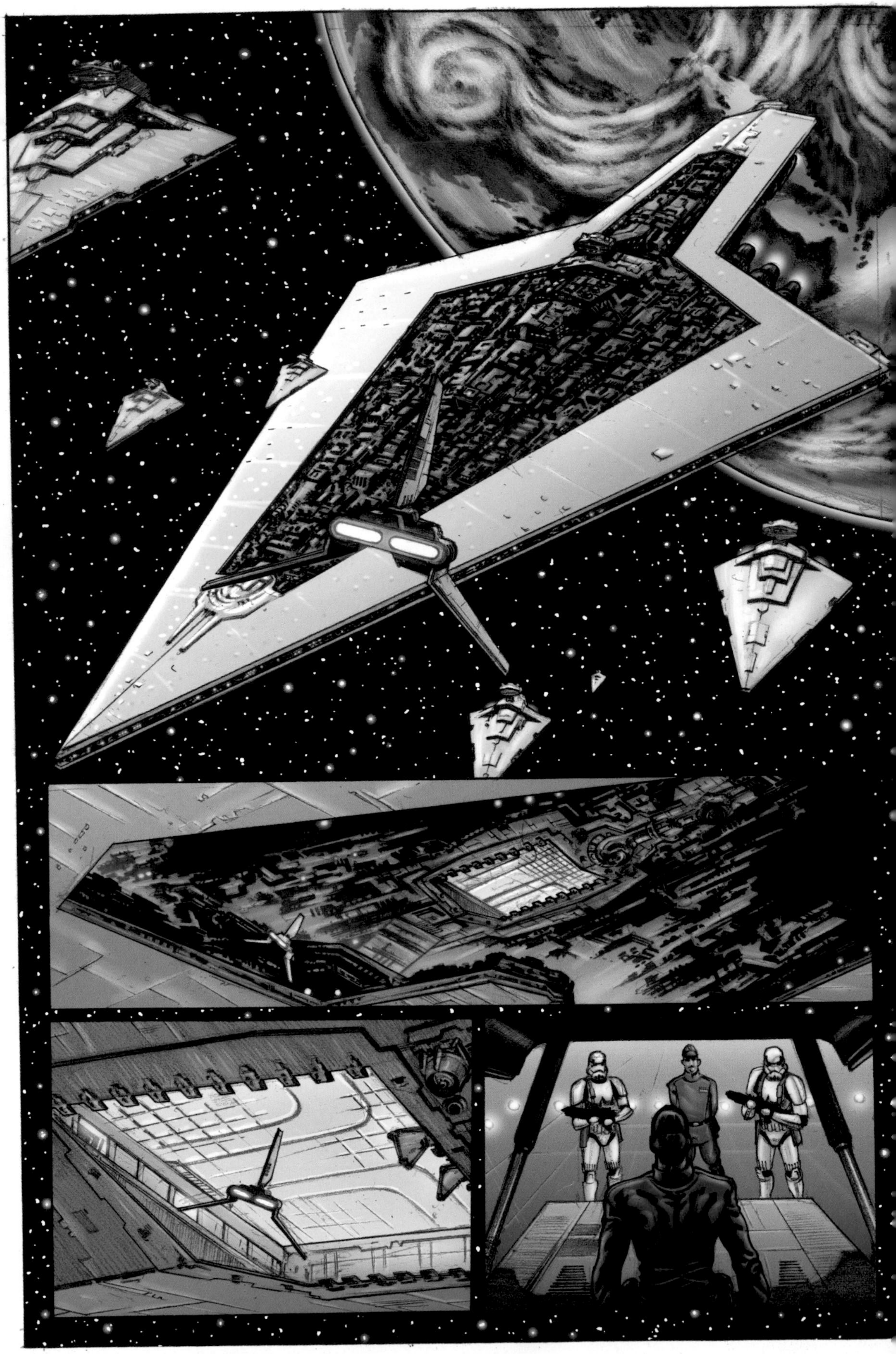

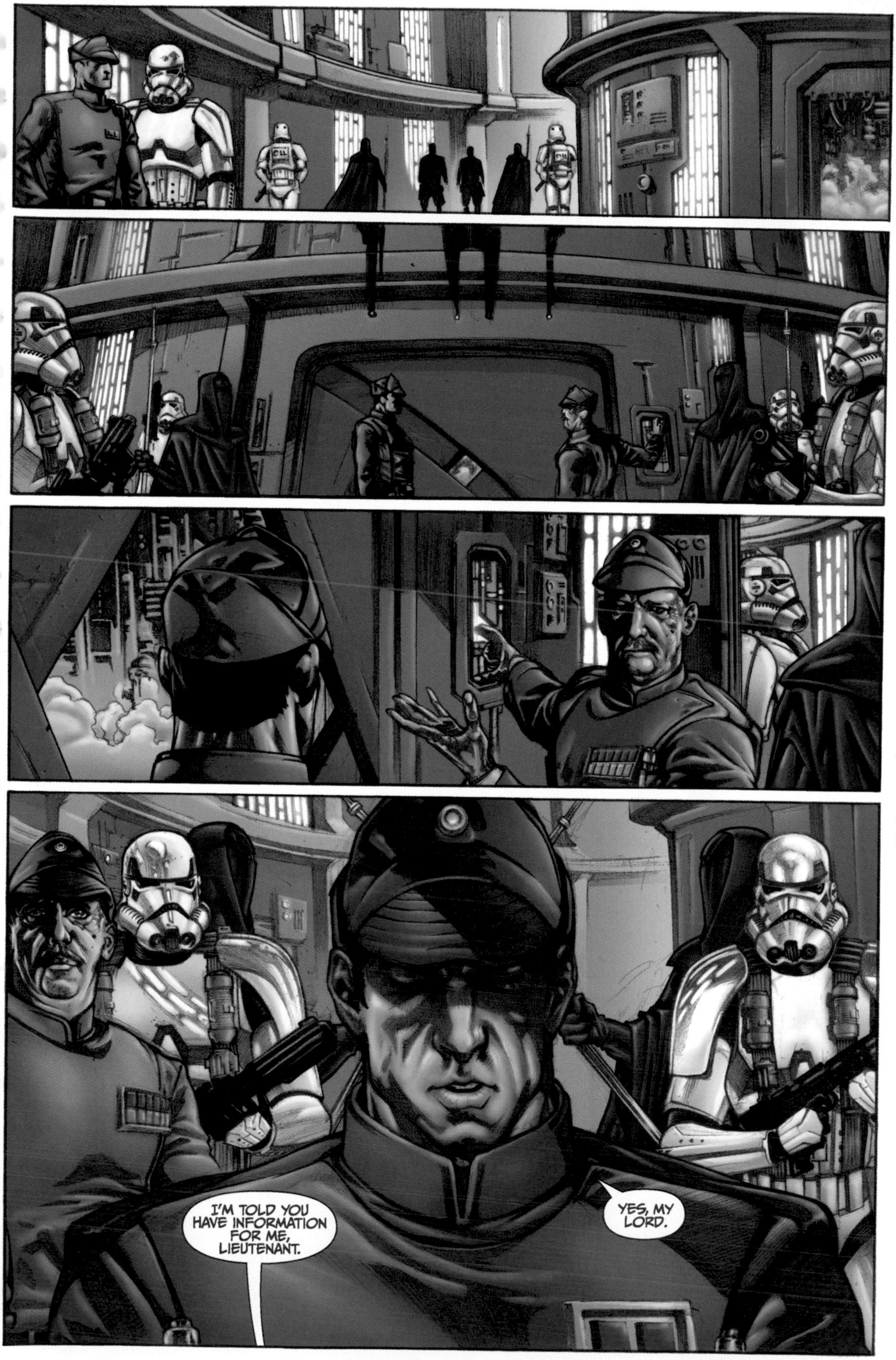
I'M TOLD YOU HAVE INFORMATION FOR ME, LIEUTENANT.
YES, MY LORD.

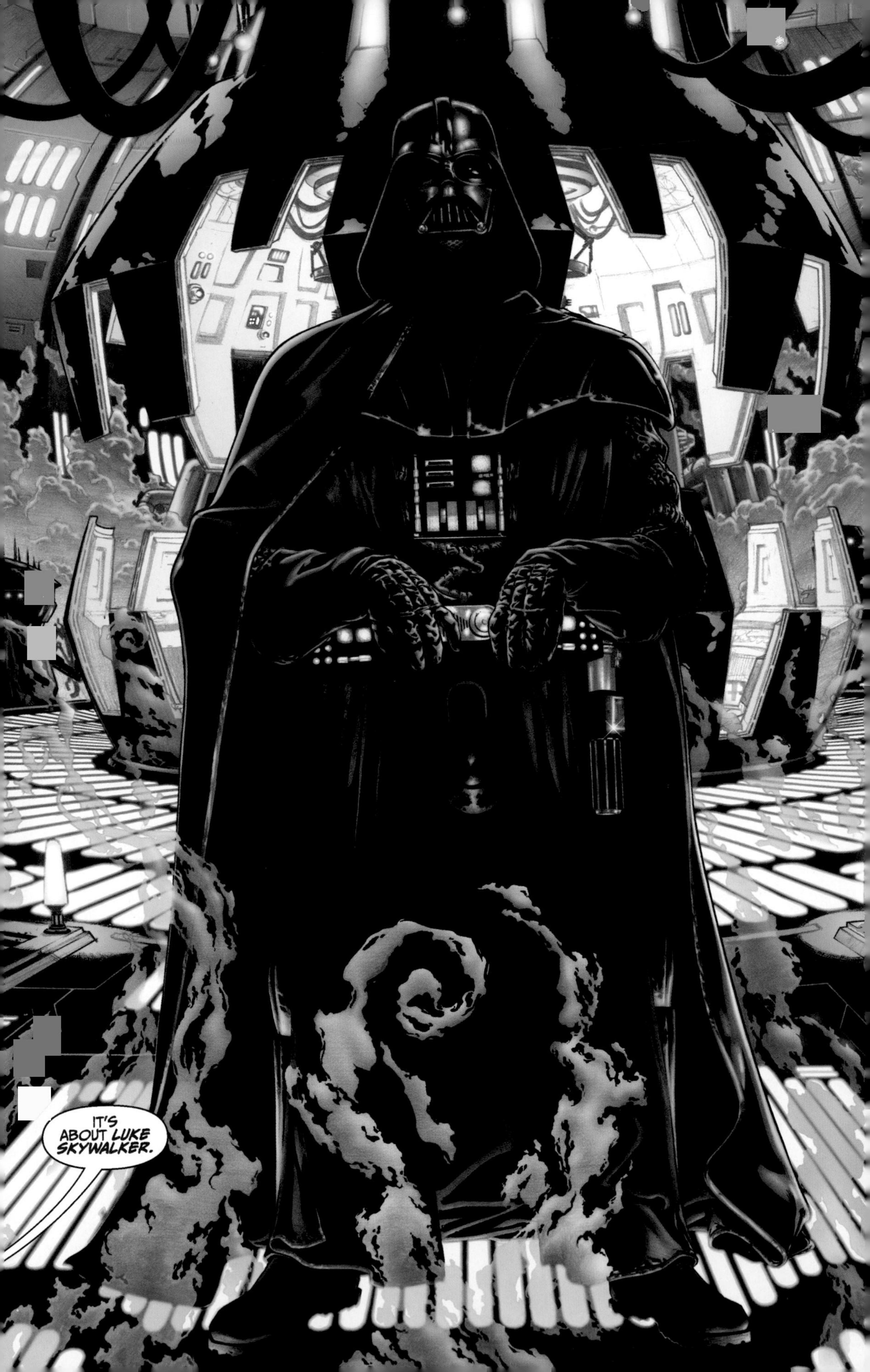
IT'S ABOUT LUKE SKYWALKER.

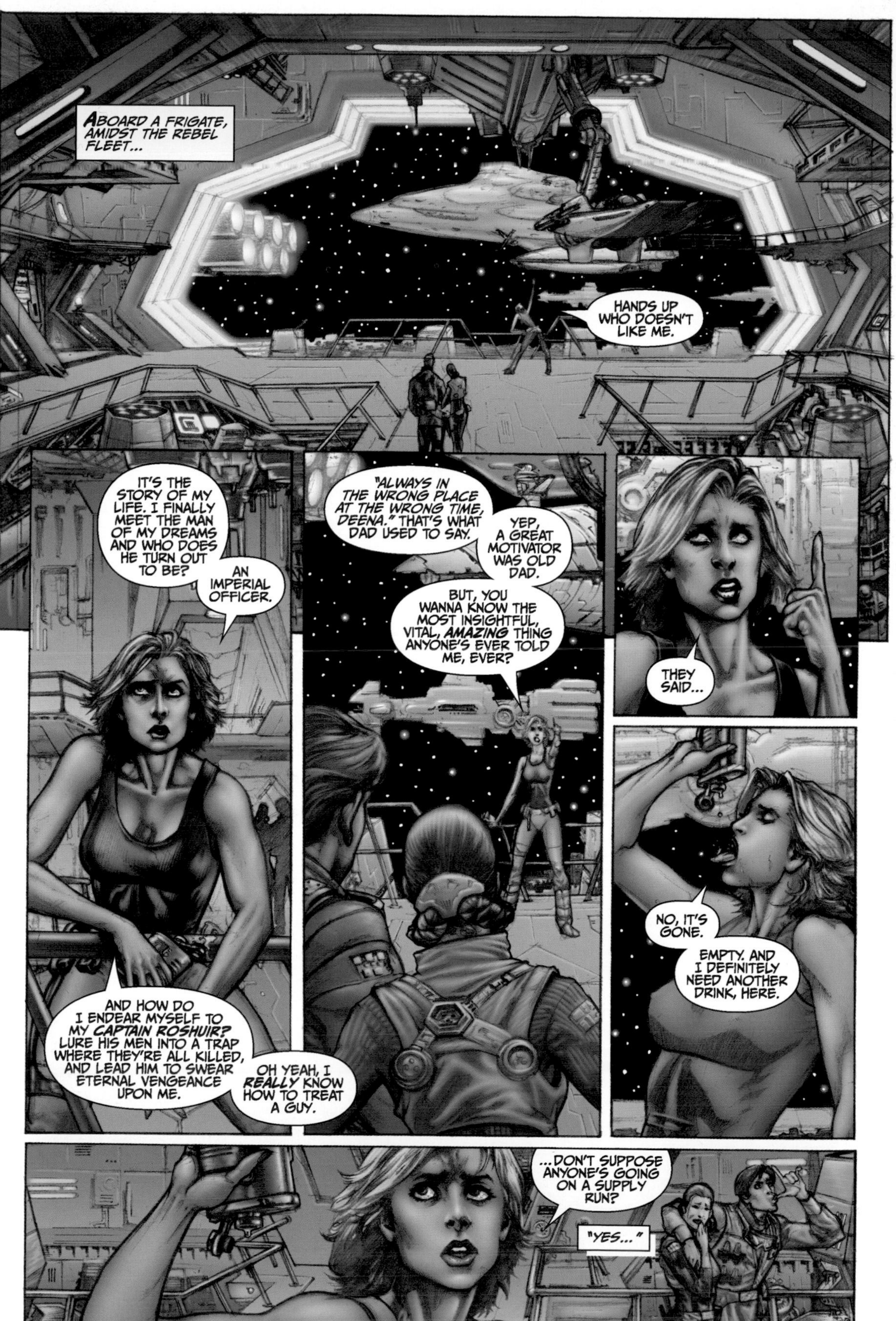
ABOARD A FRIGATE, AMIDST THE REBEL FLEET...
HANDS UP WHO DOESN'T LIKE ME.
IT'S THE STORY OF MY LIFE. I FINALLY MEET THE MAN OF MY DREAMS AND WHO DOES HE TURN OUT TO BE?
AN IMPERIAL OFFICER.
AND HOW DO I ENDEAR MYSELF TO MY CAPTAIN ROSHUIR? LURE HIS MEN INTO A TRAP WHERE THEY'RE ALL KILLED, AND LEAD HIM TO SWEAR ETERNAL VENGEANCE UPON ME.
OH YEAH, I REALLY KNOW HOW TO TREAT A GUY.
"ALWAYS IN THE WRONG PLACE AT THE WRONG TIME, DEENA." THAT'S WHAT DAD USED TO SAY.
YEP, A GREAT MOTIVATOR WAS OLD DAD.
BUT, YOU WANNA KNOW THE MOST INSIGHTFUL, VITAL, AMAZING THING ANYONE'S EVER TOLD ME, EVER?
THEY SAID...
NO, IT'S GONE.
EMPTY. AND I DEFINITELY NEED ANOTHER DRINK, HERE.
...DON'T SUPPOSE ANYONE'S GOING ON A SUPPLY RUN?
"YES..."

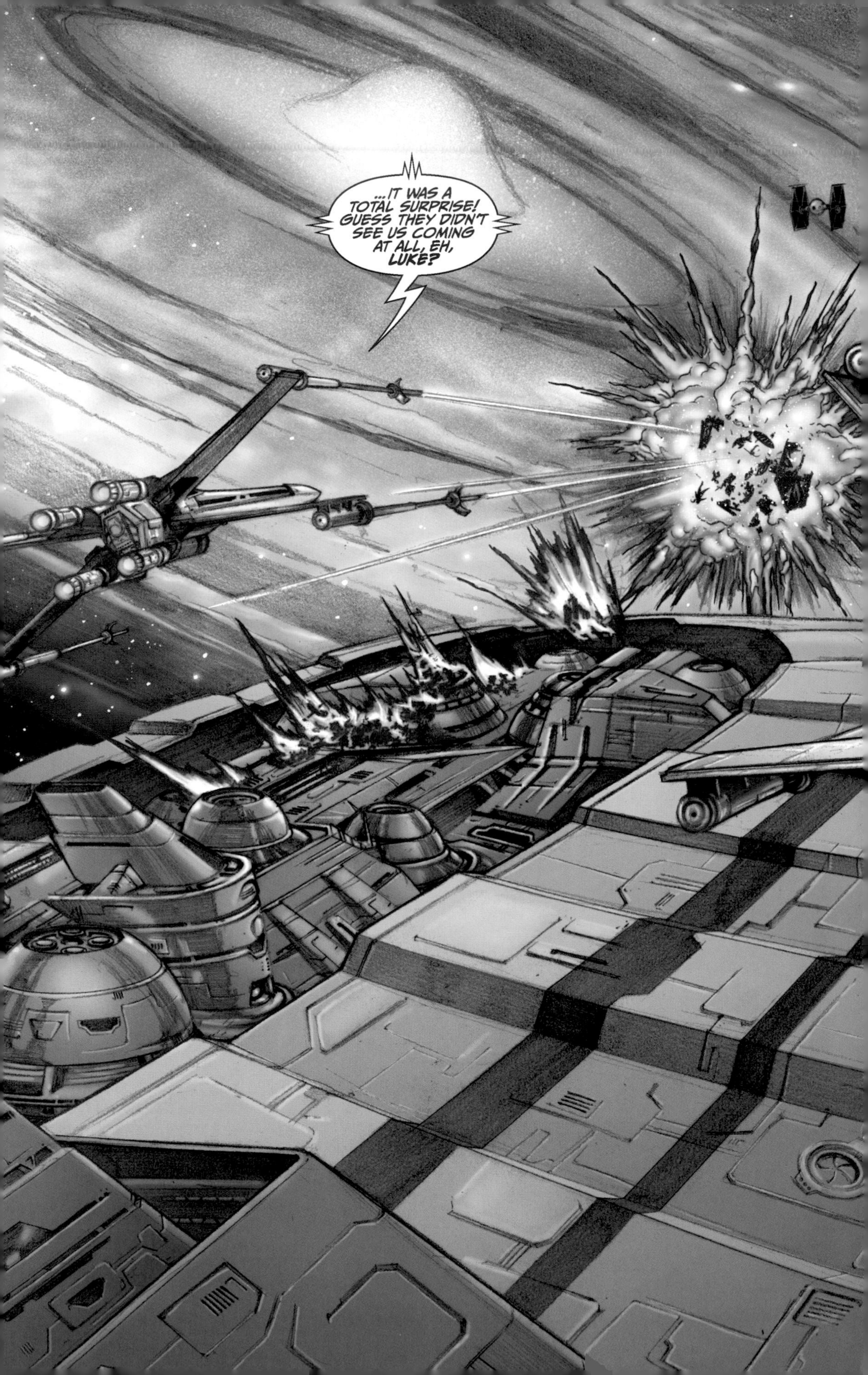
...IT WAS A TOTAL SURPRISE! GUESS THEY DIDN'T SEE US COMING AT ALL, EH, LUKE?

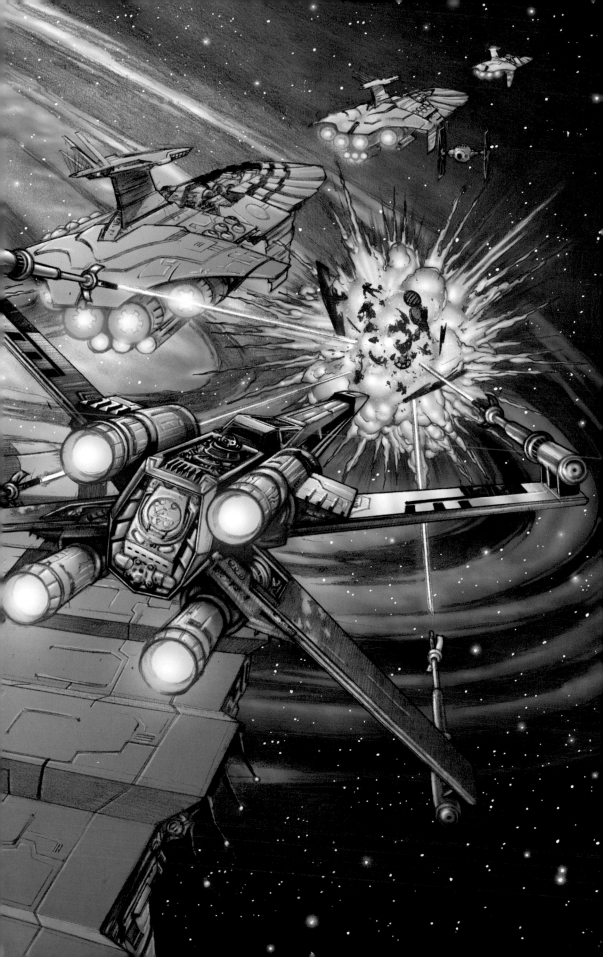

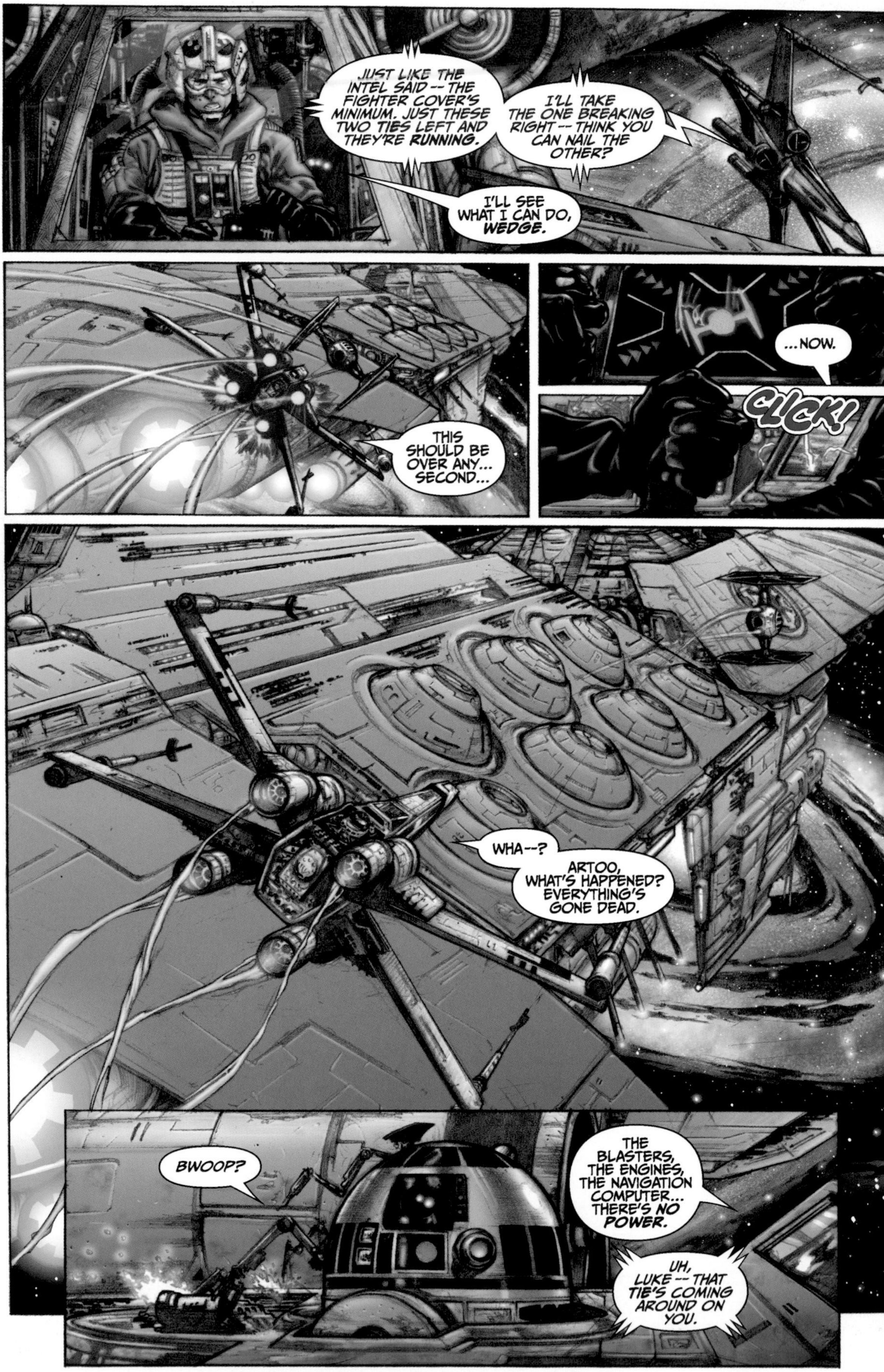
JUST LIKE THE INTEL SAID -- THE FIGHTER COVER'S MINIMUM. JUST THESE TWO TIES LEFT AND THEY'RE RUNNING.
I'LL TAKE THE ONE BREAKING RIGHT -- THINK YOU CAN NAIL THE OTHER?
I'LL SEE WHAT I CAN DO, WEDGE.
THIS SHOULD BE OVER ANY... SECOND...
...NOW.
CLICK!
WHA--?
ARTOO, WHAT'S HAPPENED? EVERYTHING'S GONE DEAD.
BWOOP?
THE BLASTERS, THE ENGINES, THE NAVIGATION COMPUTER... THERE'S NO POWER.
UH, LUKE -- THAT TIE'S COMING AROUND ON YOU.

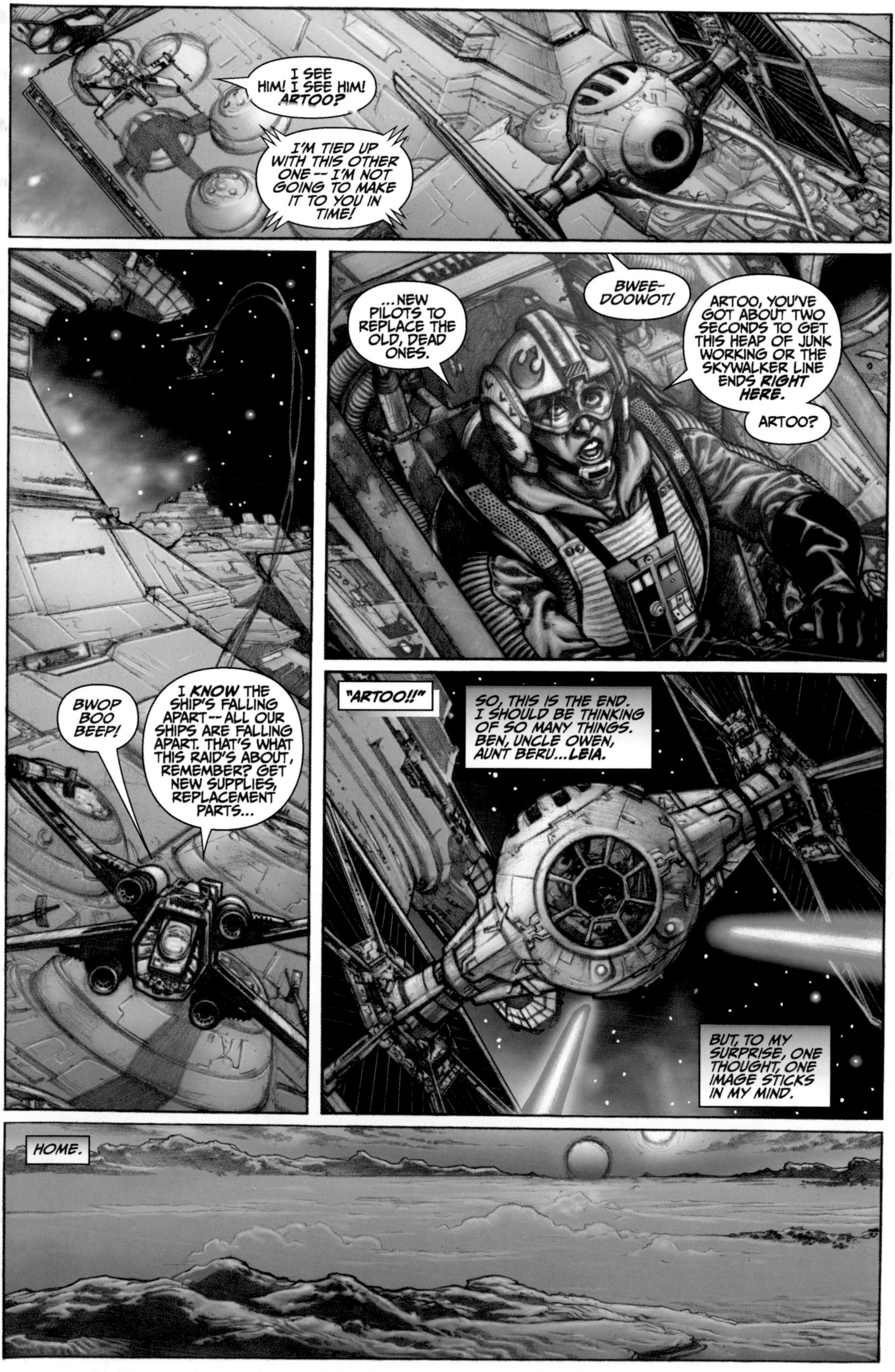
I SEE HIM! I SEE HIM! ARTOO?
I'M TIED UP WITH THIS OTHER ONE -- I'M NOT GOING TO MAKE IT TO YOU IN TIME!
BWOP BOO BEEP!
I KNOW THE SHIP'S FALLING APART -- ALL OUR SHIPS ARE FALLING APART. THAT'S WHAT THIS RAID'S ABOUT, REMEMBER? GET NEW SUPPLIES, REPLACEMENT PARTS...
...NEW PILOTS TO REPLACE THE OLD, DEAD ONES.
BWEE-DOOWOT!
ARTOO, YOU'VE GOT ABOUT TWO SECONDS TO GET THIS HEAP OF JUNK WORKING OR THE SKYWALKER LINE ENDS RIGHT HERE.
ARTOO?
"ARTOO!!"
SO, THIS IS THE END. I SHOULD BE THINKING OF SO MANY THINGS. BEN, UNCLE OWEN, AUNT BERU...LEIA.
BUT, TO MY SURPRISE, ONE THOUGHT, ONE IMAGE STICKS IN MY MIND.
HOME.

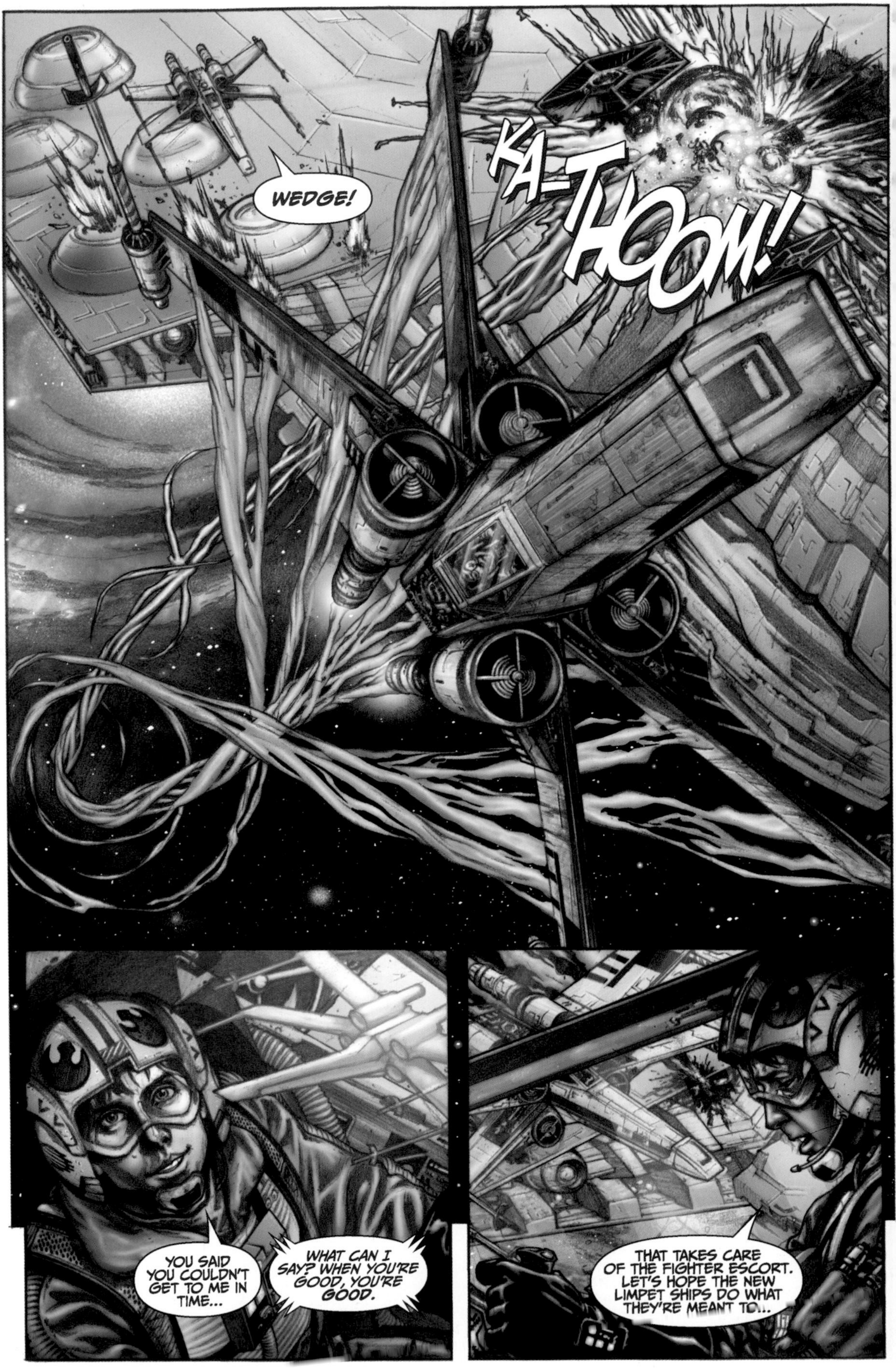
WEDGE!
KA-THOOM!
YOU SAID YOU COULDN'T GET TO ME IN TIME...
WHAT CAN I SAY? WHEN YOU'RE GOOD, YOU'RE GOOD.
THAT TAKES CARE OF THE FIGHTER ESCORT. LET'S HOPE THE NEW LIMPET SHIPS DO WHAT THEY'RE MEANT TO...

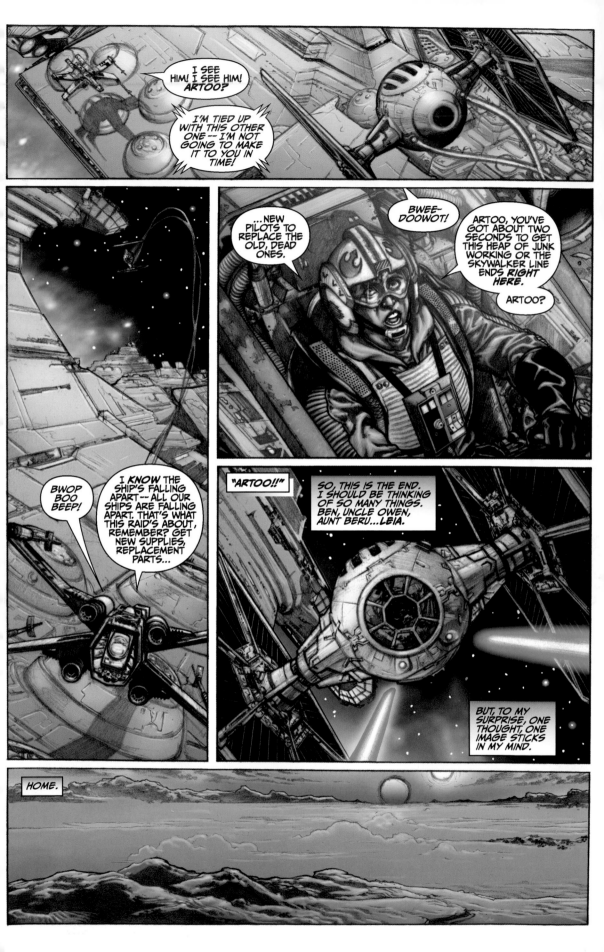

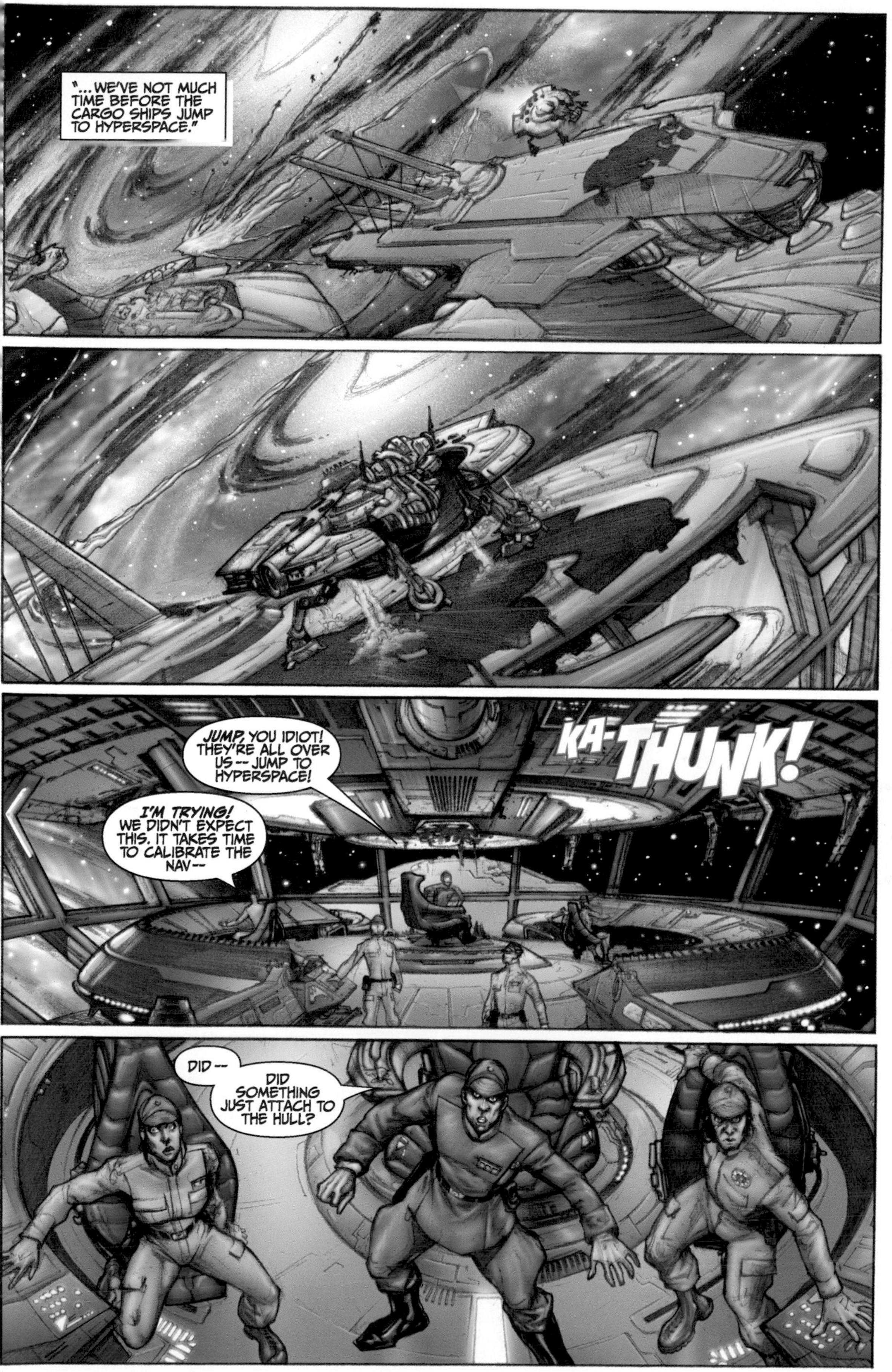
"...WE'VE NOT MUCH TIME BEFORE THE CARGO SHIPS JUMP TO HYPERSPACE."
JUMP, YOU IDIOT! THEY'RE ALL OVER US -- JUMP TO HYPERSPACE!
I'M TRYING! WE DIDN'T EXPECT THIS. IT TAKES TIME TO CALIBRATE THE NAV--
KA-THUNK!
DID --
DID SOMETHING JUST ATTACH TO THE HULL?

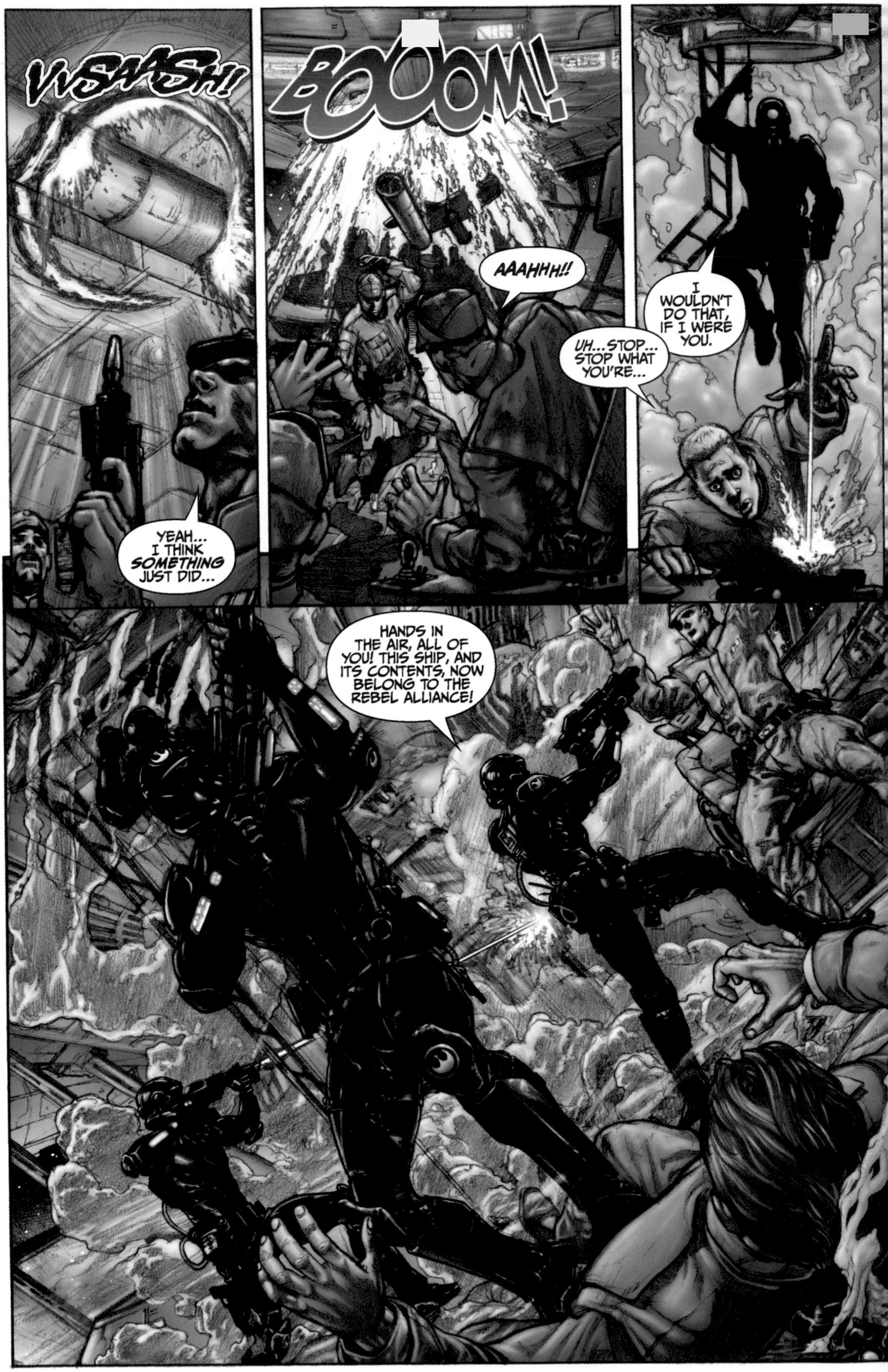
VVSSHH!
YEAH... I THINK SOMETHING JUST DID...
BOOOM!
AAAHHH!!
I WOULDN'T DO THAT, IF I WERE YOU.
UH...STOP... STOP WHAT YOU'RE...
HANDS IN THE AIR, ALL OF YOU! THIS SHIP, AND ITS CONTENTS, NOW BELONG TO THE REBEL ALLIANCE!

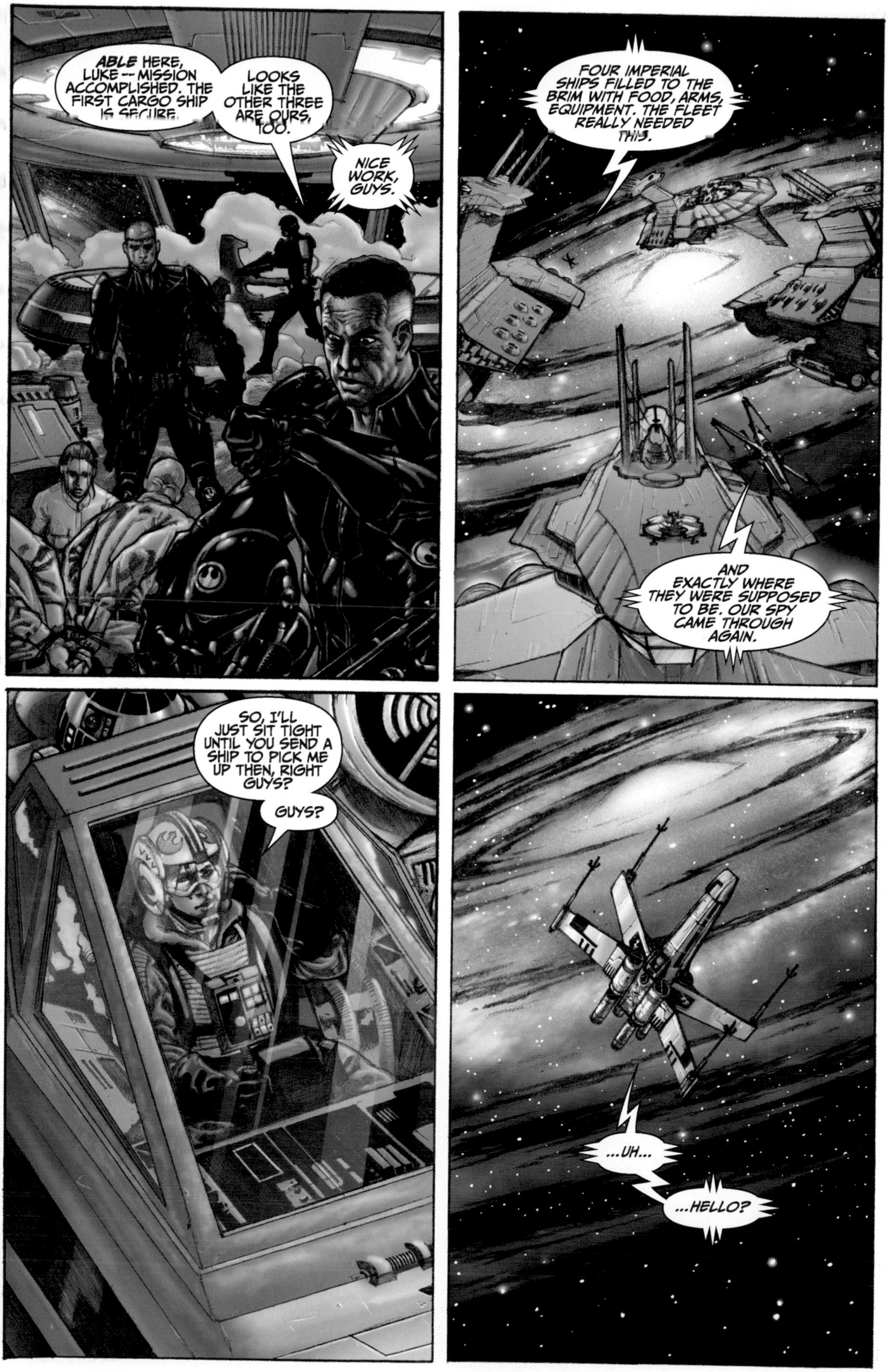
ABLE HERE, LUKE -- MISSION ACCOMPLISHED. THE FIRST CARGO SHIP IS SECURE.
LOOKS LIKE THE OTHER THREE ARE OURS, TOO.
NICE WORK, GUYS.
FOUR IMPERIAL SHIPS FILLED TO THE BRIM WITH FOOD, ARMS, EQUIPMENT. THE FLEET REALLY NEEDED THIS.
AND EXACTLY WHERE THEY WERE SUPPOSED TO BE. OUR SPY CAME THROUGH AGAIN.
SO, I'LL JUST SIT TIGHT UNTIL YOU SEND A SHIP TO PICK ME UP THEN, RIGHT GUYS?
GUYS?
...UH...
...HELLO?

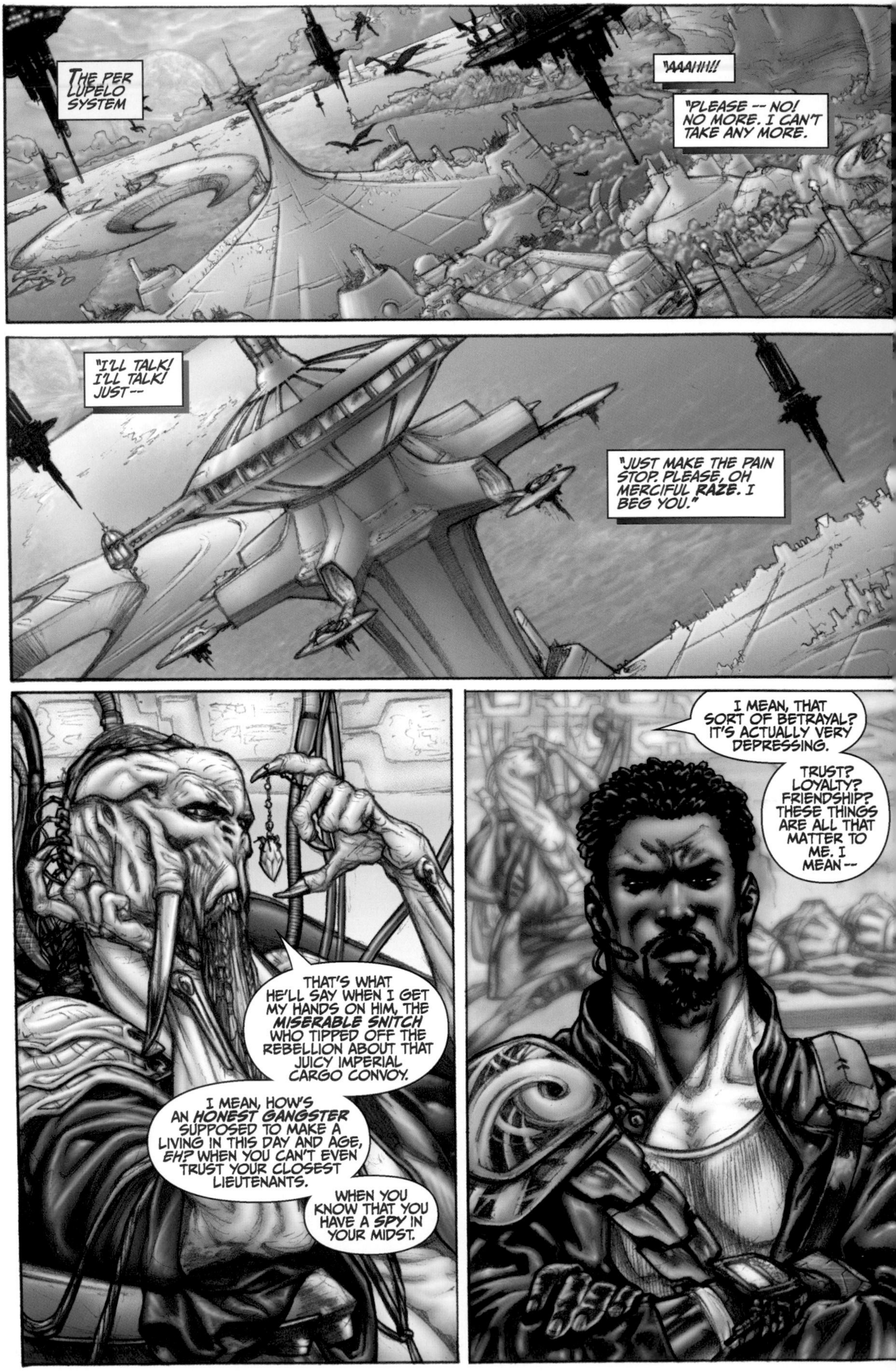
THE PER LUPELO SYSTEM
"AAAHH!!
"PLEASE -- NO! NO MORE. I CAN'T TAKE ANY MORE.
"I'LL TALK! I'LL TALK! JUST--
"JUST MAKE THE PAIN STOP. PLEASE, OH MERCIFUL RAZE. I BEG YOU."
THAT'S WHAT HE'LL SAY WHEN I GET MY HANDS ON HIM, THE MISERABLE SNITCH WHO TIPPED OFF THE REBELLION ABOUT THAT JUICY IMPERIAL CARGO CONVOY.
I MEAN, HOW'S AN HONEST GANGSTER SUPPOSED TO MAKE A LIVING IN THIS DAY AND AGE, EH? WHEN YOU CAN'T EVEN TRUST YOUR CLOSEST LIEUTENANTS.
WHEN YOU KNOW THAT YOU HAVE A SPY IN YOUR MIDST.
I MEAN, THAT SORT OF BETRAYAL? IT'S ACTUALLY VERY DEPRESSING.
TRUST? LOYALTY? FRIENDSHIP? THESE THINGS ARE ALL THAT MATTER TO ME. I MEAN --

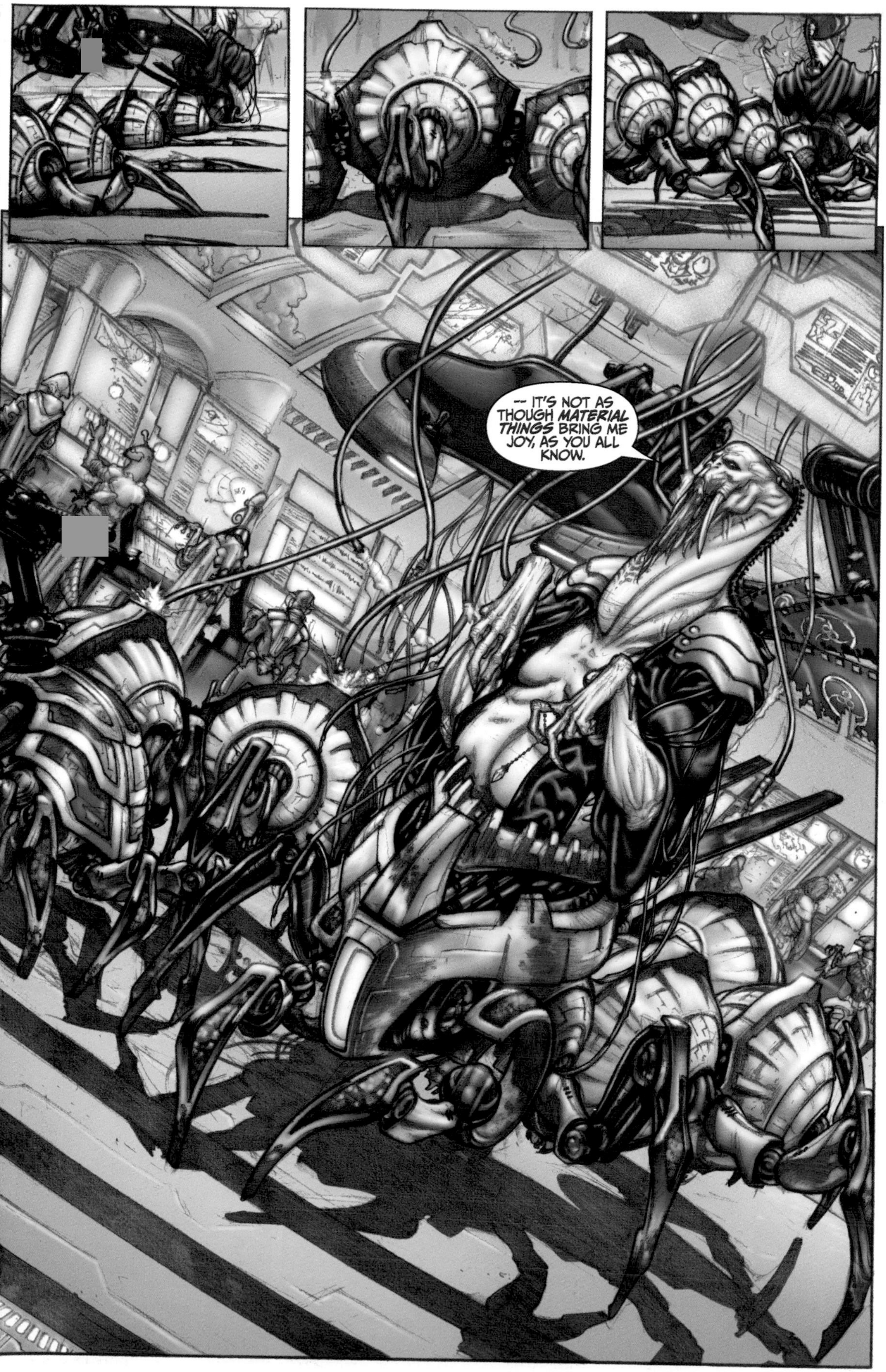
-- IT'S NOT AS THOUGH MATERIAL THINGS BRING ME JOY, AS YOU ALL KNOW.

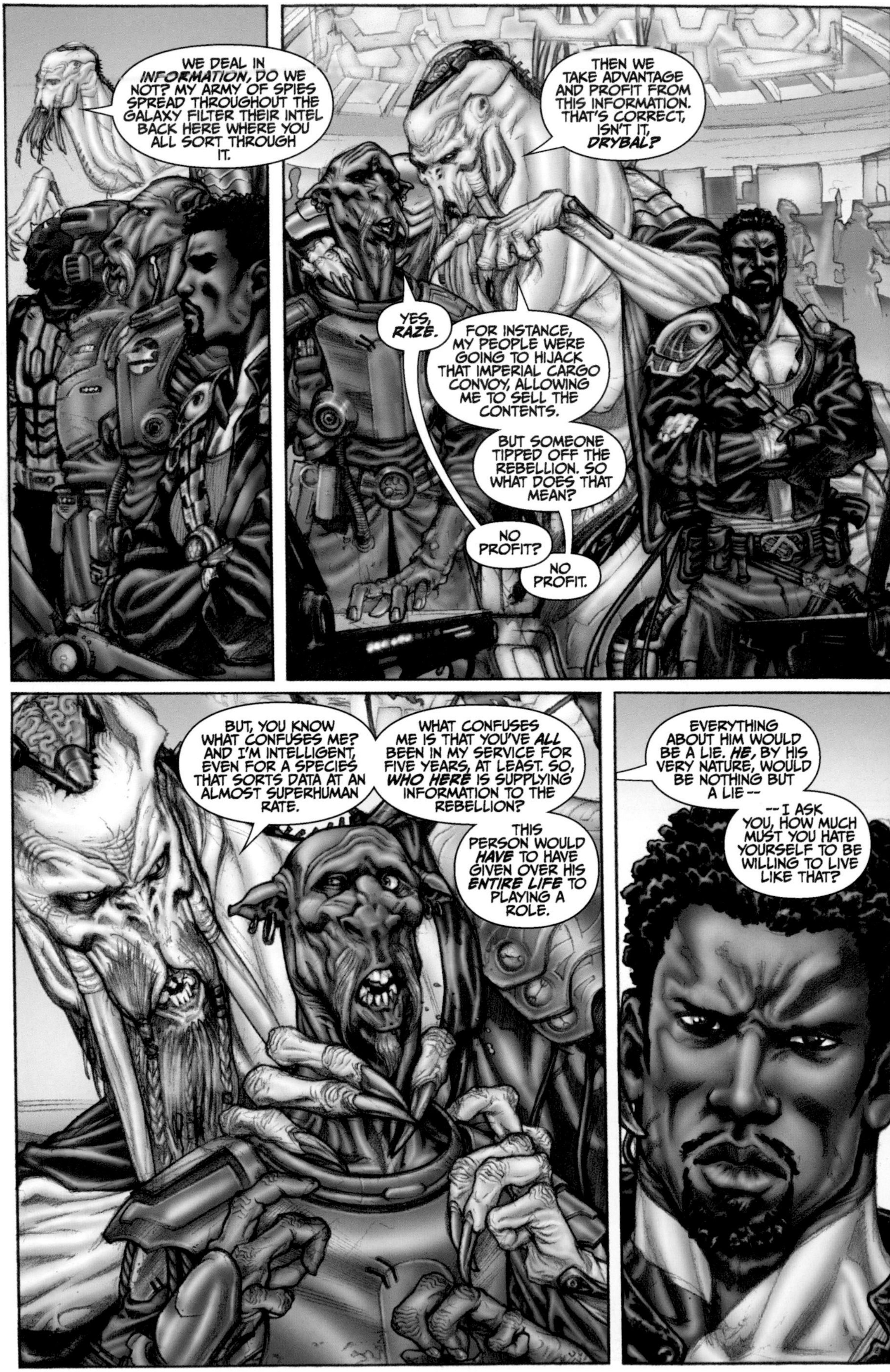
WE DEAL IN *INFORMATION*, DO WE NOT? MY ARMY OF SPIES SPREAD THROUGHOUT THE GALAXY FILTER THEIR INTEL BACK HERE WHERE YOU ALL SORT THROUGH IT.
THEN WE TAKE ADVANTAGE AND PROFIT FROM THIS INFORMATION. THAT'S CORRECT, ISN'T IT, ***DRYBAL?***
YES, ***RAZE***.
FOR INSTANCE, MY PEOPLE WERE GOING TO HIJACK THAT IMPERIAL CARGO CONVOY, ALLOWING ME TO SELL THE CONTENTS.
BUT SOMEONE TIPPED OFF THE REBELLION. SO WHAT DOES THAT MEAN?
NO PROFIT?
NO PROFIT.
BUT, YOU KNOW WHAT CONFUSES ME? AND I'M INTELLIGENT, EVEN FOR A SPECIES THAT SORTS DATA AT AN ALMOST SUPERHUMAN RATE.
WHAT CONFUSES ME IS THAT YOU'VE *ALL* BEEN IN MY SERVICE FOR FIVE YEARS, AT LEAST. SO, ***WHO HERE*** IS SUPPLYING INFORMATION TO THE REBELLION?
THIS PERSON WOULD *HAVE* TO HAVE GIVEN OVER HIS ***ENTIRE LIFE*** TO PLAYING A ROLE.
EVERYTHING ABOUT HIM WOULD BE A LIE. ***HE***, BY HIS VERY NATURE, WOULD BE NOTHING BUT A LIE --
-- I ASK YOU, HOW MUCH MUST YOU HATE YOURSELF TO BE WILLING TO LIVE LIKE THAT?

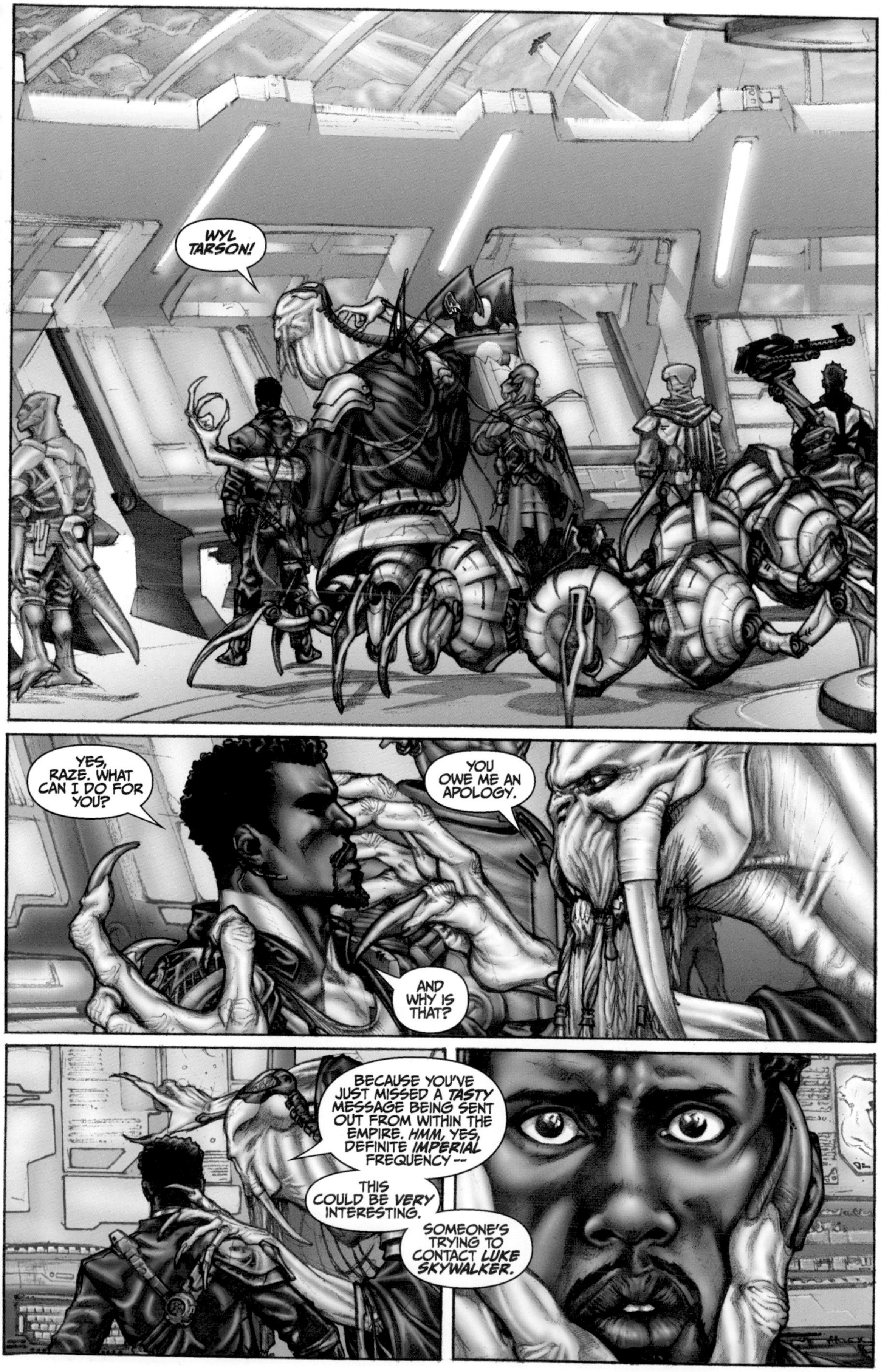
WYL TARSON!
YES, RAZE. WHAT CAN I DO FOR YOU?
YOU OWE ME AN APOLOGY.
AND WHY IS THAT?
BECAUSE YOU'VE JUST MISSED A TASTY MESSAGE BEING SENT OUT FROM WITHIN THE EMPIRE. HMM, YES, DEFINITE IMPERIAL FREQUENCY--
THIS COULD BE VERY INTERESTING.
SOMEONE'S TRYING TO CONTACT LUKE SKYWALKER.

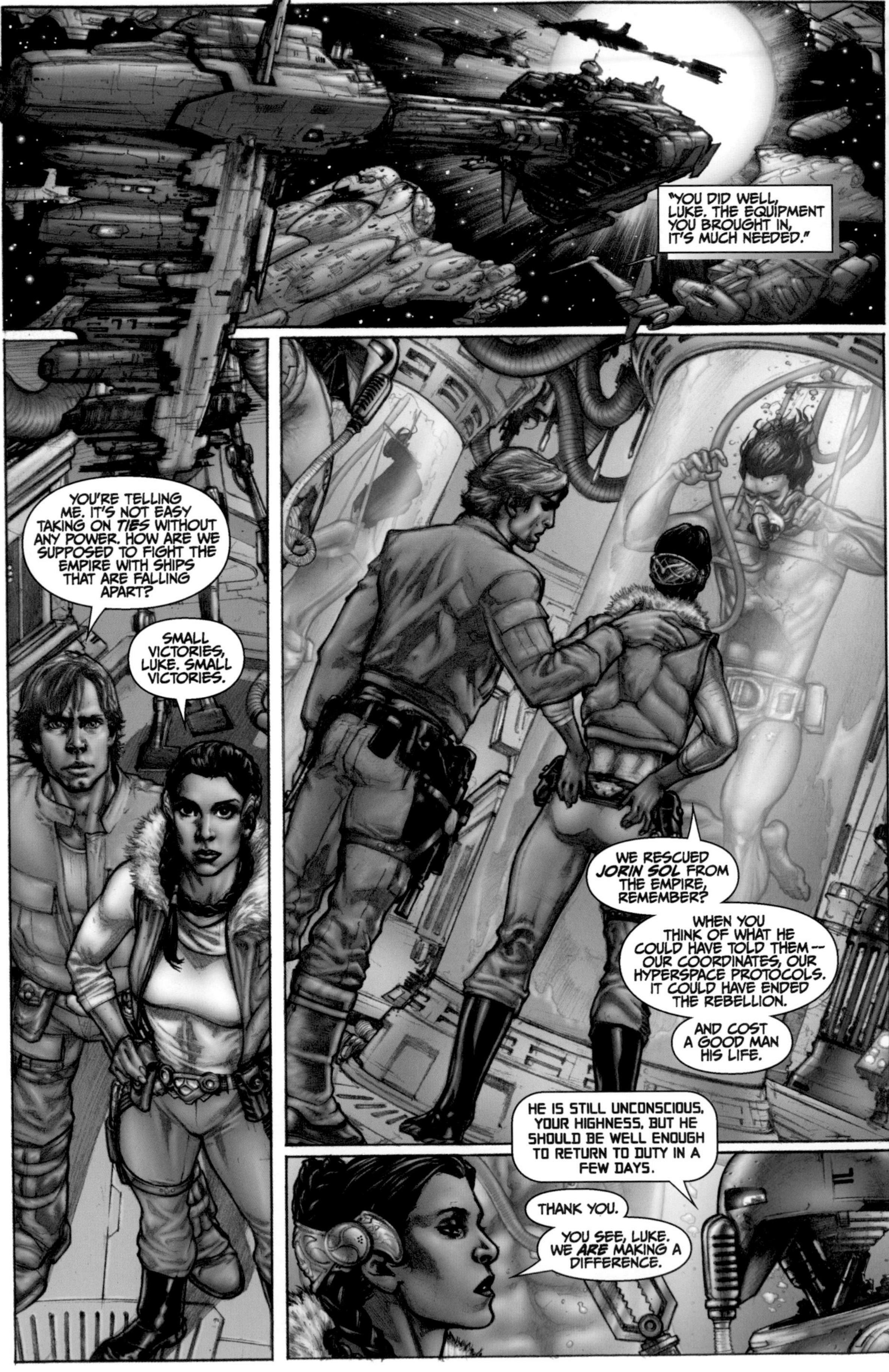
"YOU DID WELL, LUKE. THE EQUIPMENT YOU BROUGHT IN, IT'S MUCH NEEDED."
YOU'RE TELLING ME. IT'S NOT EASY TAKING ON *TIES* WITHOUT ANY POWER. HOW ARE WE SUPPOSED TO FIGHT THE EMPIRE WITH SHIPS THAT ARE FALLING APART?
SMALL VICTORIES, LUKE. SMALL VICTORIES.
WE RESCUED *JORIN SOL* FROM THE EMPIRE, REMEMBER?
WHEN YOU THINK OF WHAT HE COULD HAVE TOLD THEM -- OUR COORDINATES, OUR HYPERSPACE PROTOCOLS. IT COULD HAVE ENDED THE REBELLION.
AND COST A GOOD MAN HIS LIFE.
HE IS STILL UNCONSCIOUS, YOUR HIGHNESS, BUT HE SHOULD BE WELL ENOUGH TO RETURN TO DUTY IN A FEW DAYS.
THANK YOU.
YOU SEE, LUKE. WE *ARE* MAKING A DIFFERENCE.

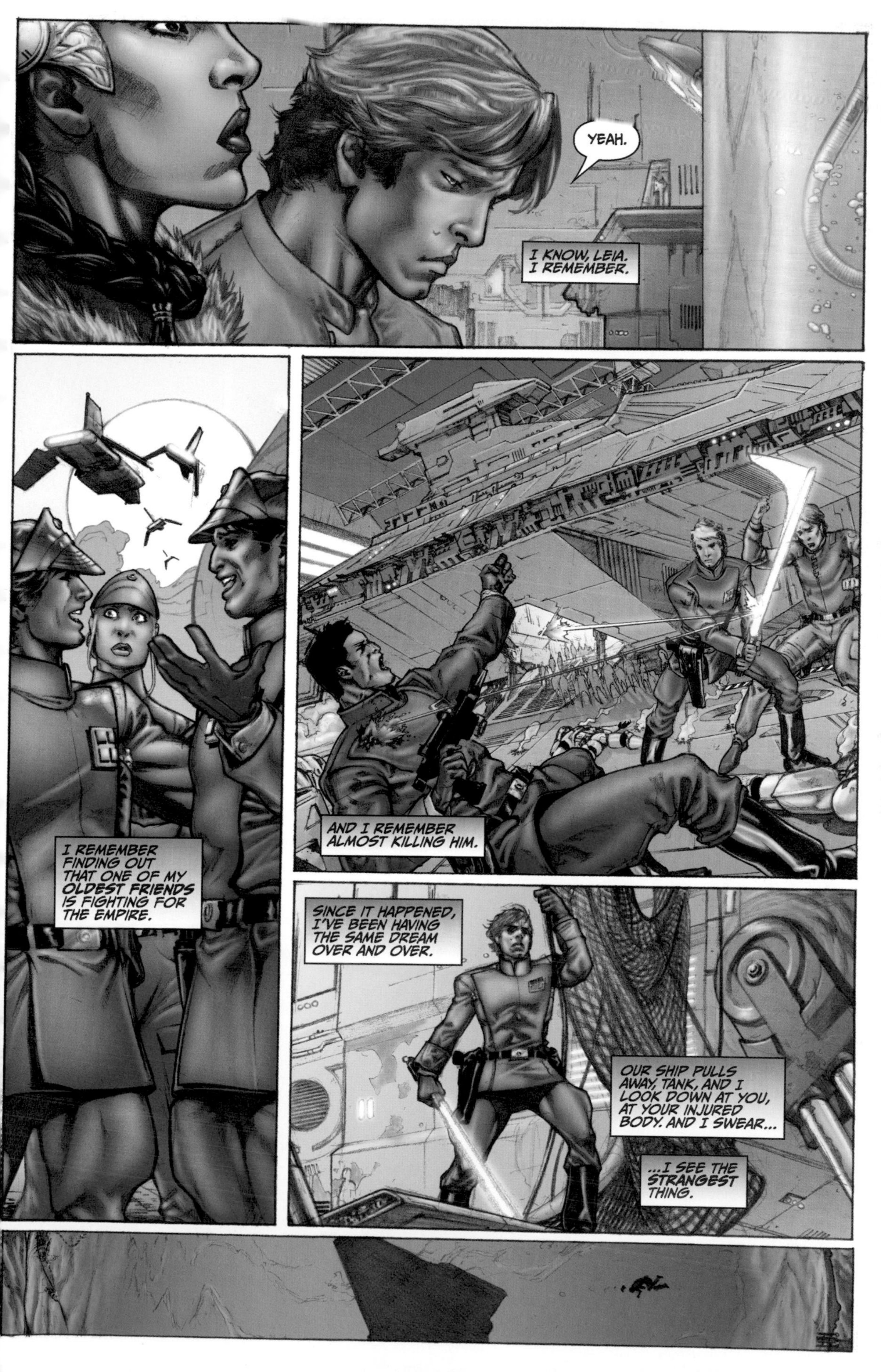
YEAH.
I KNOW, LEIA. I REMEMBER.
I REMEMBER FINDING OUT THAT ONE OF MY OLDEST FRIENDS IS FIGHTING FOR THE EMPIRE.
AND I REMEMBER ALMOST KILLING HIM.
SINCE IT HAPPENED, I'VE BEEN HAVING THE SAME DREAM OVER AND OVER.
OUR SHIP PULLS AWAY, TANK, AND I LOOK DOWN AT YOU, AT YOUR INJURED BODY. AND I SWEAR...
...I SEE THE STRANGEST THING.

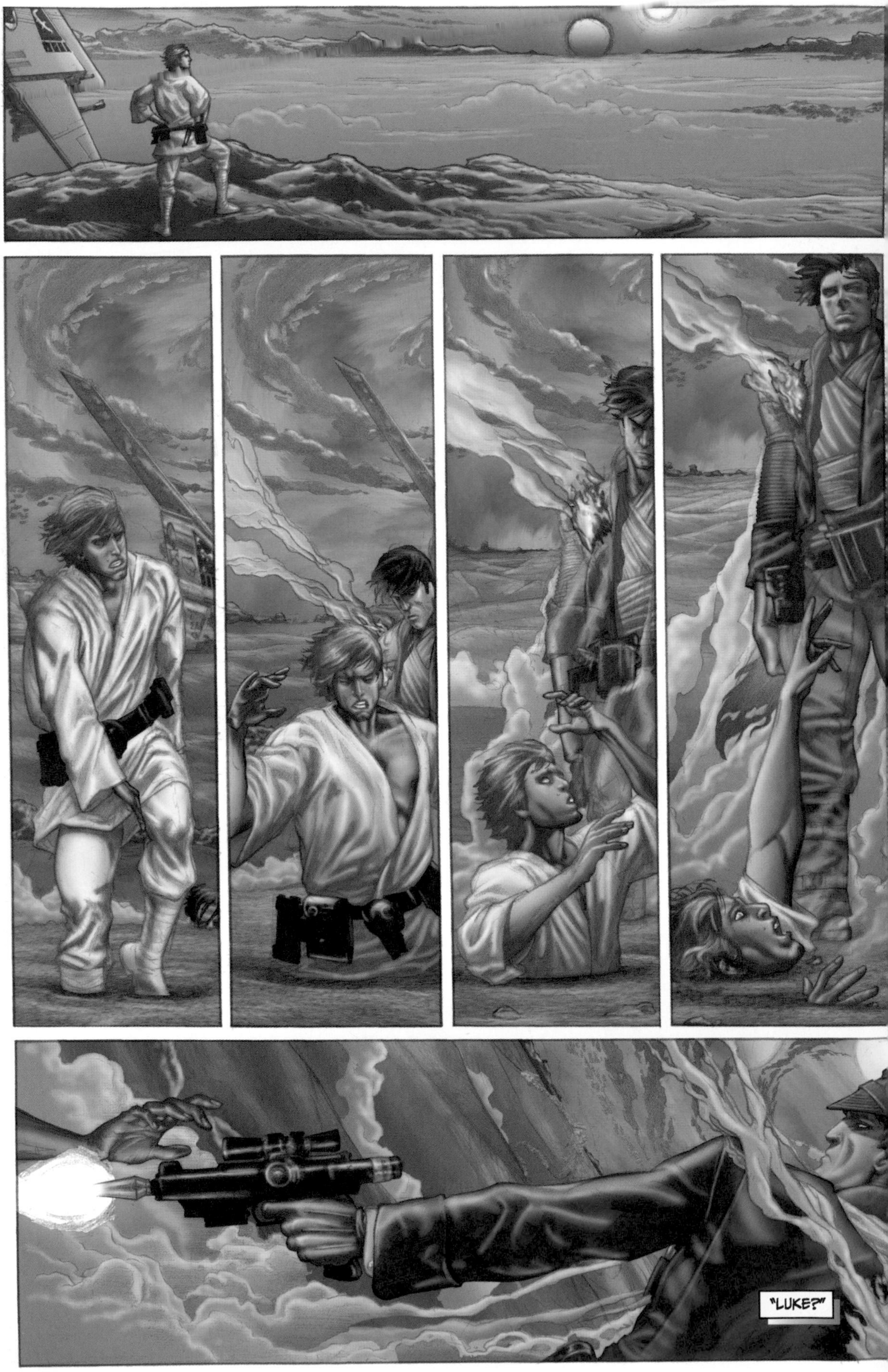
"LUKE?"

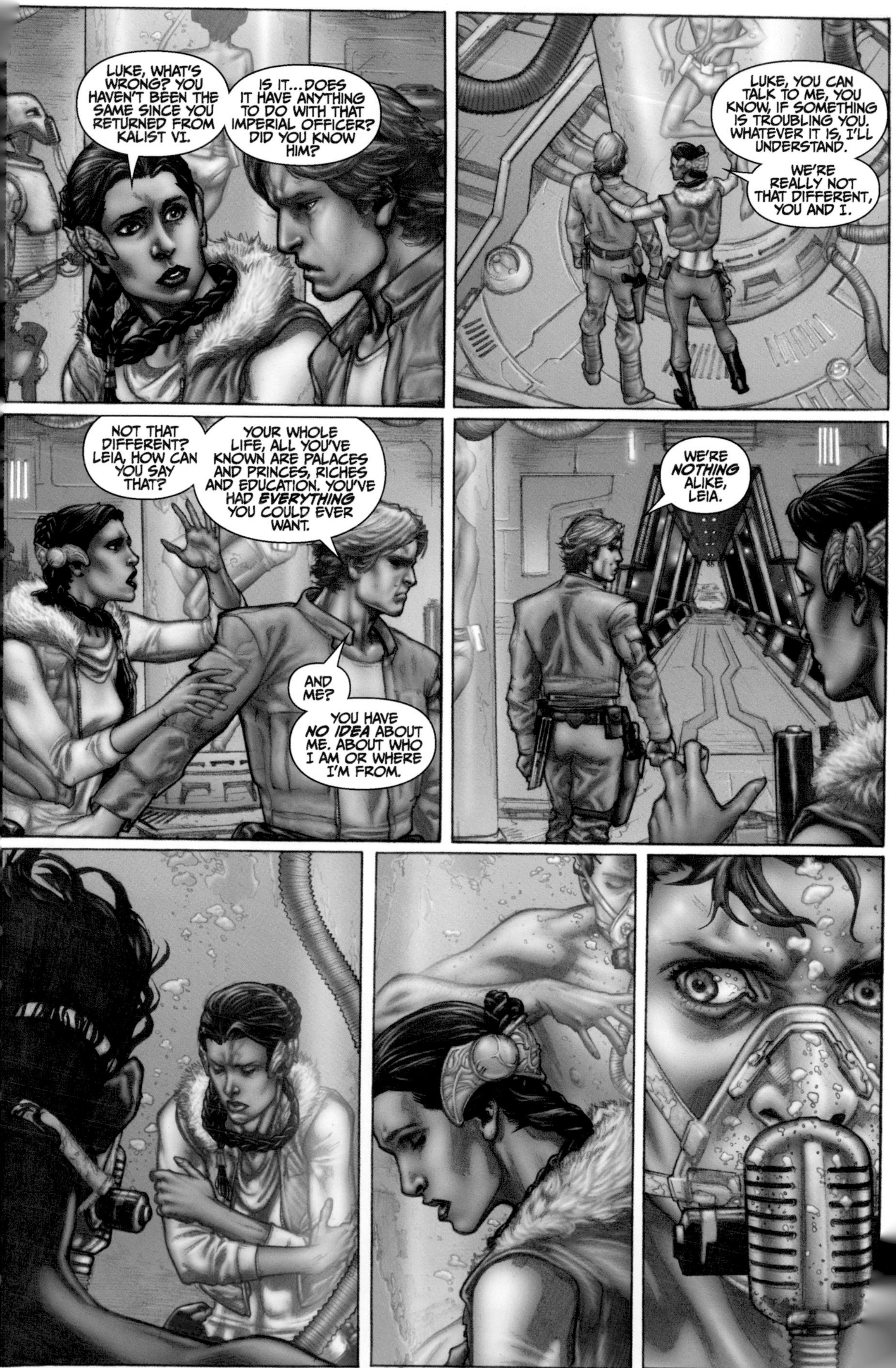
LUKE, WHAT'S WRONG? YOU HAVEN'T BEEN THE SAME SINCE YOU RETURNED FROM KALIST VI.
IS IT...DOES IT HAVE ANYTHING TO DO WITH THAT IMPERIAL OFFICER? DID YOU KNOW HIM?
LUKE, YOU CAN TALK TO ME, YOU KNOW, IF SOMETHING IS TROUBLING YOU. WHATEVER IT IS, I'LL UNDERSTAND.
WE'RE REALLY NOT THAT DIFFERENT, YOU AND I.
NOT THAT DIFFERENT? LEIA, HOW CAN YOU SAY THAT?
YOUR WHOLE LIFE, ALL YOU'VE KNOWN ARE PALACES AND PRINCES, RICHES AND EDUCATION. YOU'VE HAD *EVERYTHING* YOU COULD EVER WANT.
AND ME?
YOU HAVE ***NO IDEA*** ABOUT ME. ABOUT WHO I AM OR WHERE I'M FROM.
WE'RE ***NOTHING*** ALIKE, LEIA.

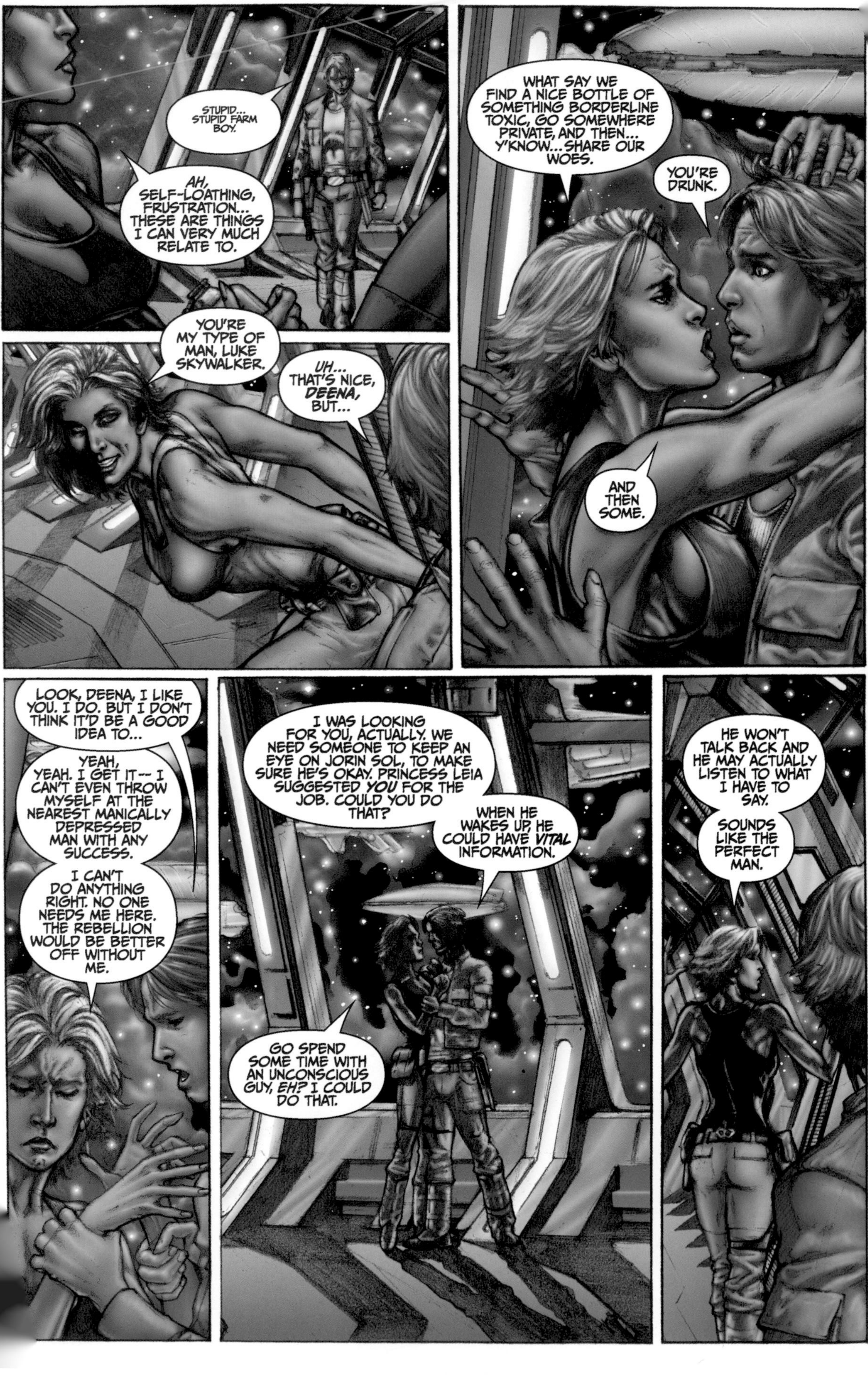
STUPID... STUPID FARM BOY.
AH, SELF-LOATHING, FRUSTRATION... THESE ARE THINGS I CAN VERY MUCH RELATE TO.
WHAT SAY WE FIND A NICE BOTTLE OF SOMETHING BORDERLINE TOXIC, GO SOMEWHERE PRIVATE, AND THEN... Y'KNOW... SHARE OUR WOES.
YOU'RE DRUNK.
YOU'RE MY TYPE OF MAN, LUKE SKYWALKER.
UH... THAT'S NICE, DEENA, BUT...
AND THEN SOME.
LOOK, DEENA, I LIKE YOU. I DO. BUT I DON'T THINK IT'D BE A GOOD IDEA TO...
YEAH, YEAH. I GET IT-- I CAN'T EVEN THROW MYSELF AT THE NEAREST MANICALLY DEPRESSED MAN WITH ANY SUCCESS.
I CAN'T DO ANYTHING RIGHT. NO ONE NEEDS ME HERE. THE REBELLION WOULD BE BETTER OFF WITHOUT ME.
I WAS LOOKING FOR YOU, ACTUALLY. WE NEED SOMEONE TO KEEP AN EYE ON JORIN SOL, TO MAKE SURE HE'S OKAY. PRINCESS LEIA SUGGESTED YOU FOR THE JOB. COULD YOU DO THAT?
WHEN HE WAKES UP, HE COULD HAVE VITAL INFORMATION.
GO SPEND SOME TIME WITH AN UNCONSCIOUS GUY, EH? I COULD DO THAT.
HE WON'T TALK BACK AND HE MAY ACTUALLY LISTEN TO WHAT I HAVE TO SAY.
SOUNDS LIKE THE PERFECT MAN.

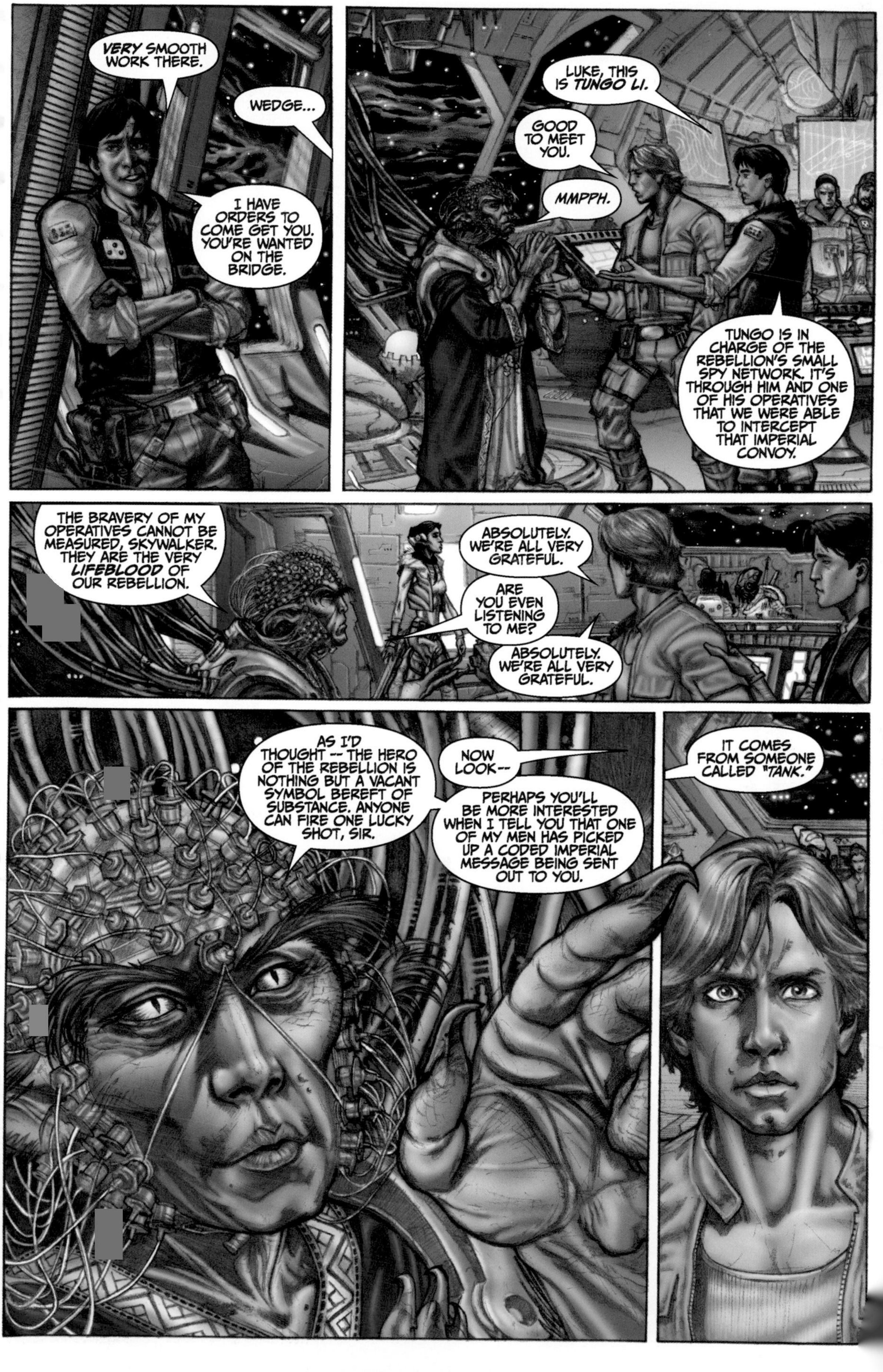
VERY SMOOTH WORK THERE.
WEDGE...
I HAVE ORDERS TO COME GET YOU. YOU'RE WANTED ON THE BRIDGE.
LUKE, THIS IS TUNGO LI.
GOOD TO MEET YOU.
MMPPH.
TUNGO IS IN CHARGE OF THE REBELLION'S SMALL SPY NETWORK. IT'S THROUGH HIM AND ONE OF HIS OPERATIVES THAT WE WERE ABLE TO INTERCEPT THAT IMPERIAL CONVOY.
THE BRAVERY OF MY OPERATIVES CANNOT BE MEASURED, SKYWALKER. THEY ARE THE VERY LIFEBLOOD OF OUR REBELLION.
ABSOLUTELY. WE'RE ALL VERY GRATEFUL.
ARE YOU EVEN LISTENING TO ME?
ABSOLUTELY. WE'RE ALL VERY GRATEFUL.
AS I'D THOUGHT -- THE HERO OF THE REBELLION IS NOTHING BUT A VACANT SYMBOL BEREFT OF SUBSTANCE. ANYONE CAN FIRE ONE LUCKY SHOT, SIR.
NOW LOOK--
PERHAPS YOU'LL BE MORE INTERESTED WHEN I TELL YOU THAT ONE OF MY MEN HAS PICKED UP A CODED IMPERIAL MESSAGE BEING SENT OUT TO YOU.
IT COMES FROM SOMEONE CALLED "TANK."

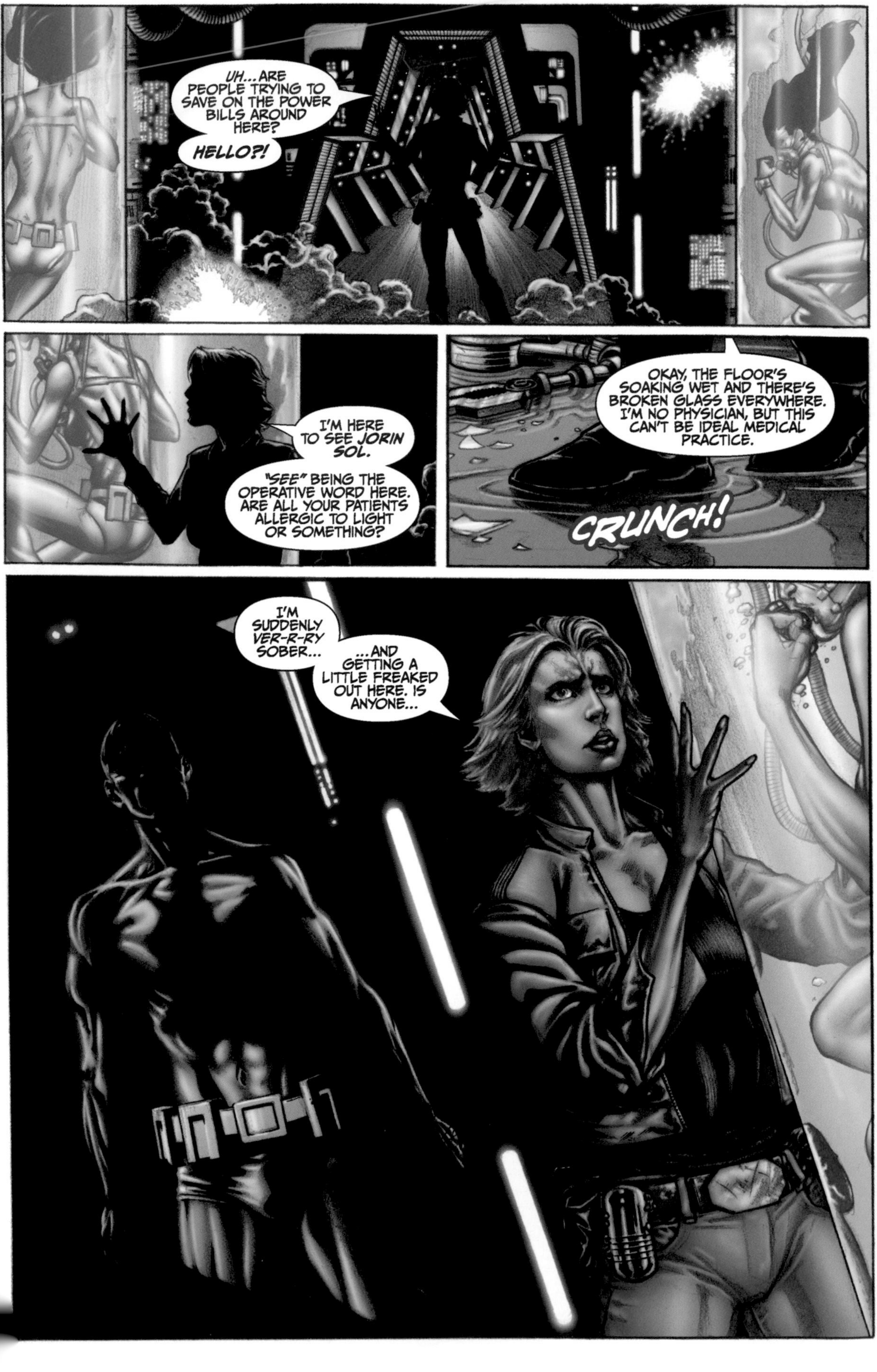
UH...ARE PEOPLE TRYING TO SAVE ON THE POWER BILLS AROUND HERE?
HELLO?!
I'M HERE TO SEE JORIN SOL.
"SEE" BEING THE OPERATIVE WORD HERE. ARE ALL YOUR PATIENTS ALLERGIC TO LIGHT OR SOMETHING?
OKAY, THE FLOOR'S SOAKING WET AND THERE'S BROKEN GLASS EVERYWHERE. I'M NO PHYSICIAN, BUT THIS CAN'T BE IDEAL MEDICAL PRACTICE.
CRUNCH!
I'M SUDDENLY VER-R-RY SOBER...
...AND GETTING A LITTLE FREAKED OUT HERE. IS ANYONE...

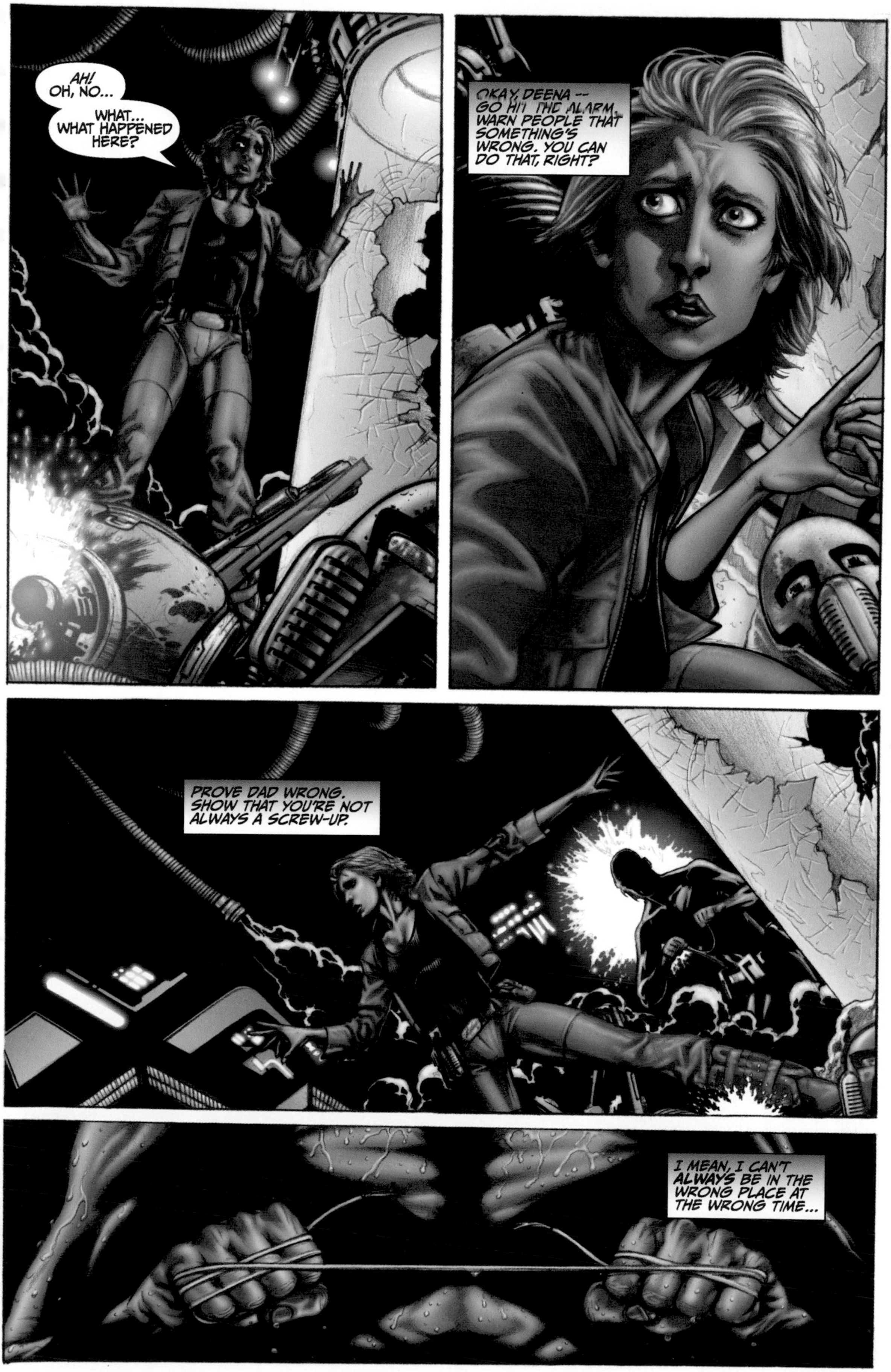
AH! OH, NO...
WHAT... WHAT HAPPENED HERE?
OKAY, DEENA -- GO HIT THE ALARM. WARN PEOPLE THAT SOMETHING'S WRONG. YOU CAN DO THAT, RIGHT?
PROVE DAD WRONG. SHOW THAT YOU'RE NOT ALWAYS A SCREW-UP.
I MEAN, I CAN'T ALWAYS BE IN THE WRONG PLACE AT THE WRONG TIME...

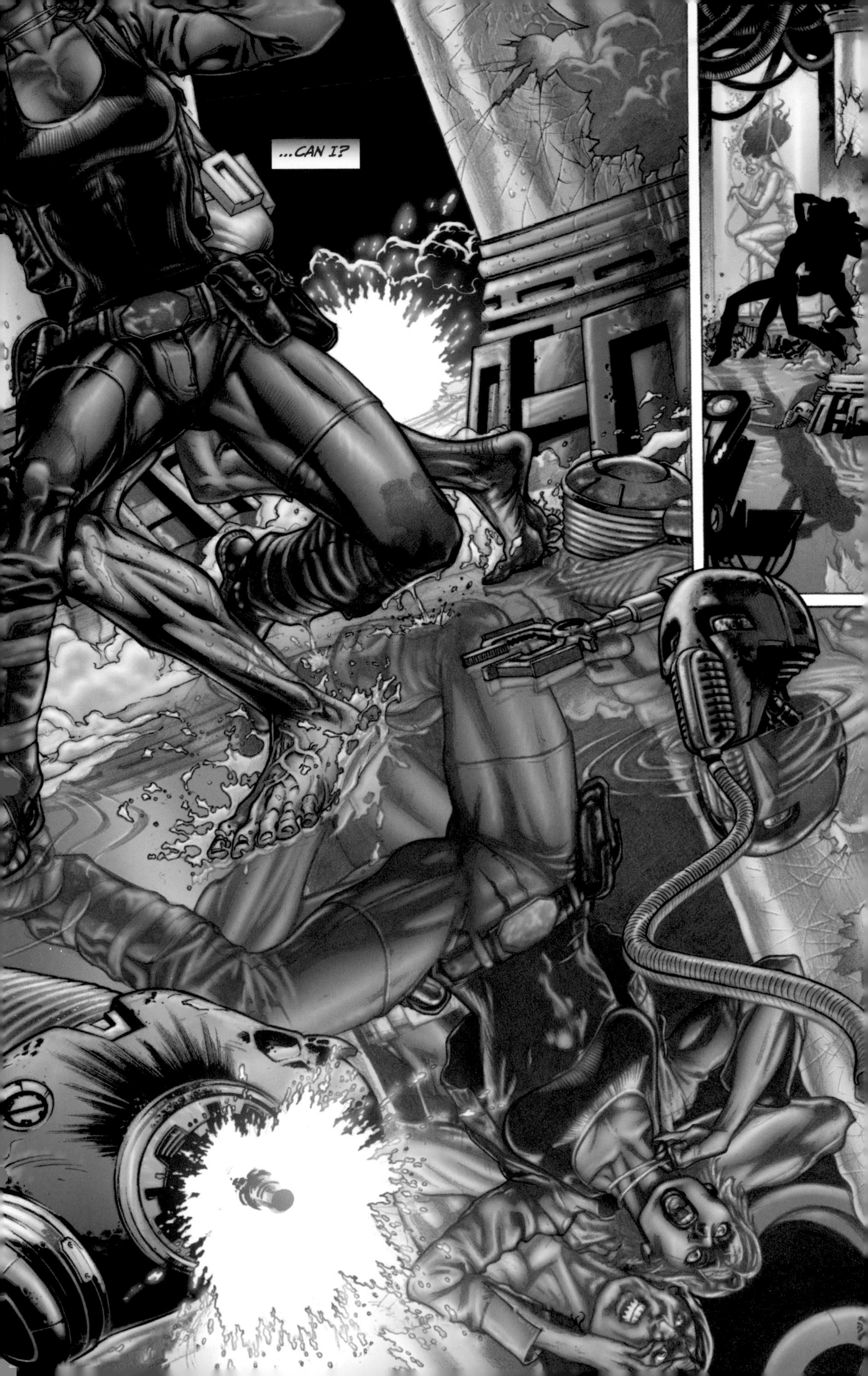
...CAN I?

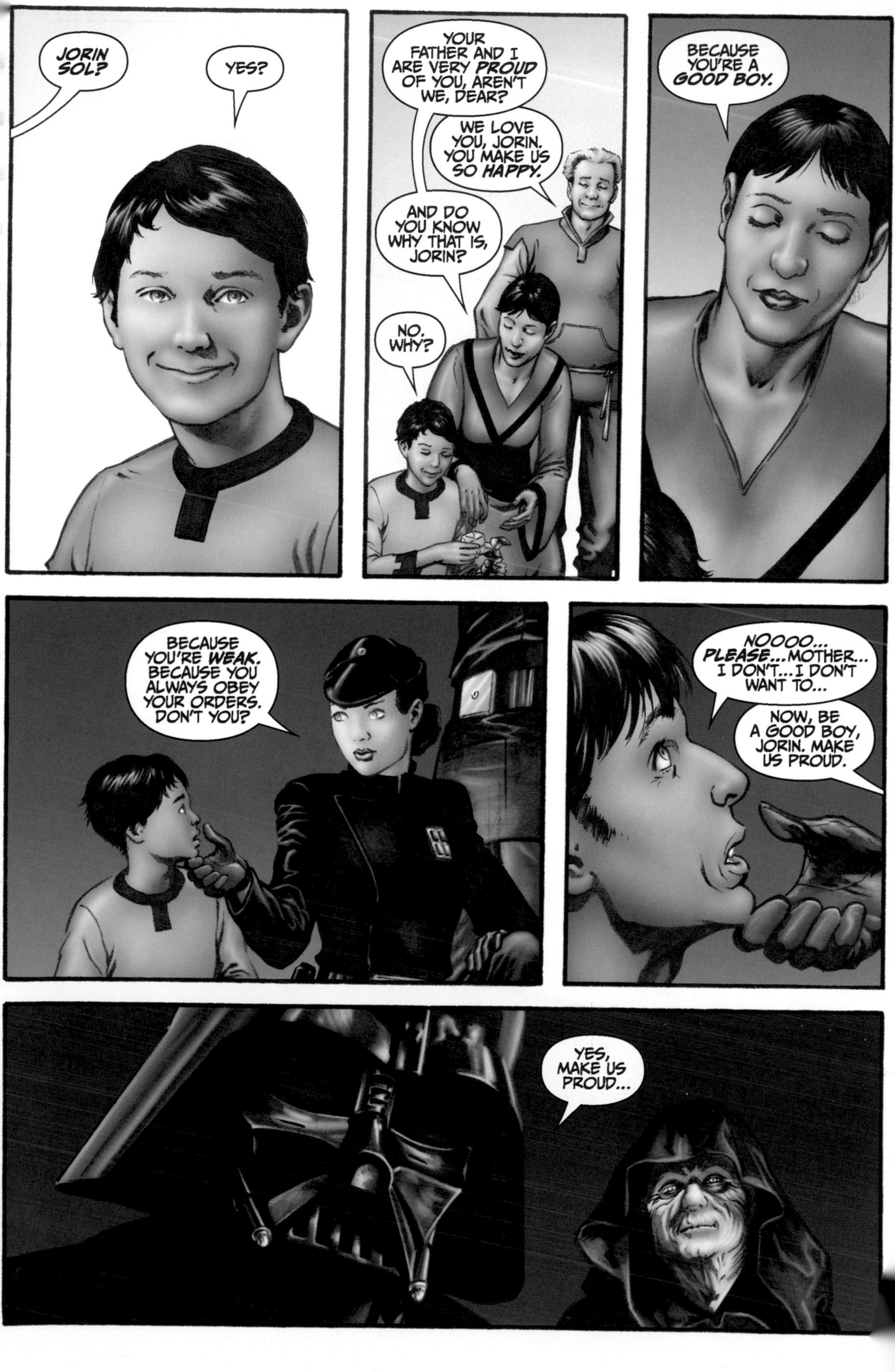
JORIN SOL?
YES?
YOUR FATHER AND I ARE VERY PROUD OF YOU, AREN'T WE, DEAR?
WE LOVE YOU, JORIN. YOU MAKE US SO HAPPY.
AND DO YOU KNOW WHY THAT IS, JORIN?
NO. WHY?
BECAUSE YOU'RE A GOOD BOY.
BECAUSE YOU'RE WEAK. BECAUSE YOU ALWAYS OBEY YOUR ORDERS. DON'T YOU?
NOOOO... PLEASE...MOTHER... I DON'T...I DON'T WANT TO...
NOW, BE A GOOD BOY, JORIN. MAKE US PROUD.
YES, MAKE US PROUD...

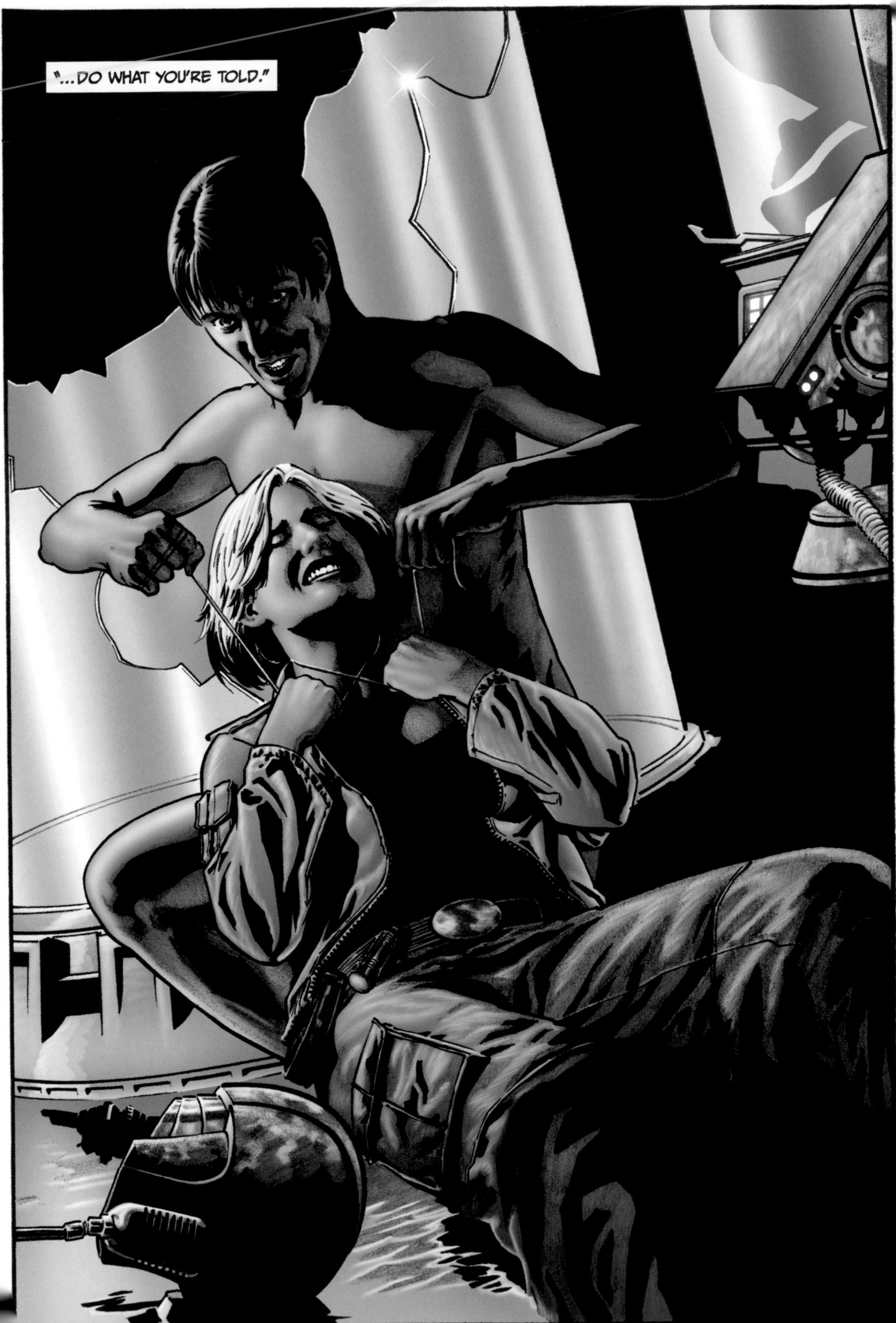
"...DO WHAT YOU'RE TOLD."

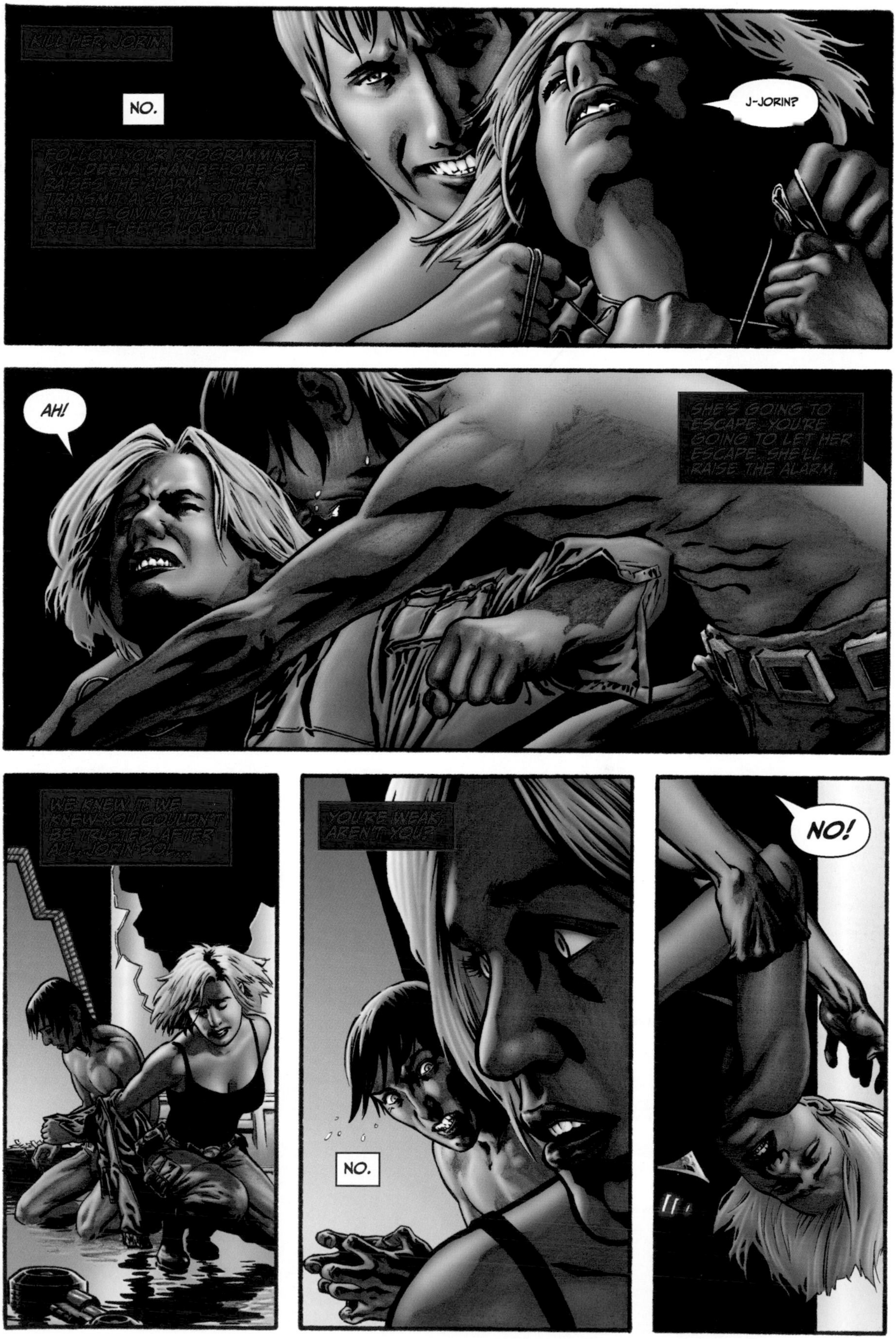
KILL HER, JORIN.
NO.
FOLLOW YOUR PROGRAMMING. KILL DEENA SHAN BEFORE SHE RAISES THE ALARM -- THEN TRANSMIT A SIGNAL TO THE EMPIRE, GIVING THEM THE REBEL FLEET'S LOCATION.
J-JORIN?
AH!
SHE'S GOING TO ESCAPE. YOU'RE GOING TO LET HER ESCAPE. SHE'LL RAISE THE ALARM.
WE KNEW IT. WE KNEW YOU COULDN'T BE TRUSTED AFTER ALL, JORIN SOL...
YOU'RE WEAK, AREN'T YOU?
NO.
NO!

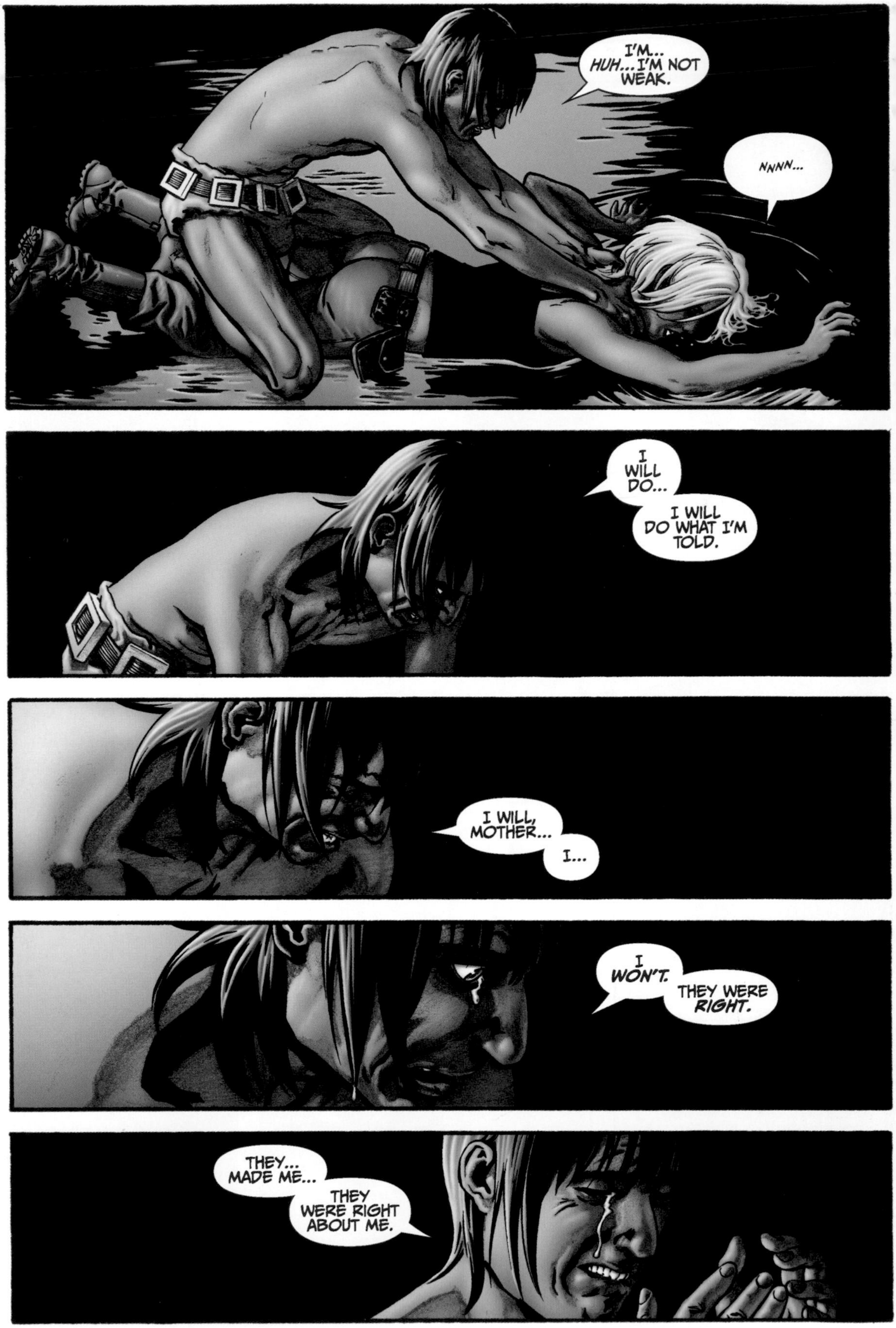
I'M... *HUH*... I'M NOT WEAK.
NNNN...
I WILL DO...
I WILL DO WHAT I'M TOLD.
I WILL, MOTHER...
I...
I *WON'T.*
THEY WERE *RIGHT.*
THEY... MADE ME...
THEY WERE RIGHT ABOUT ME.

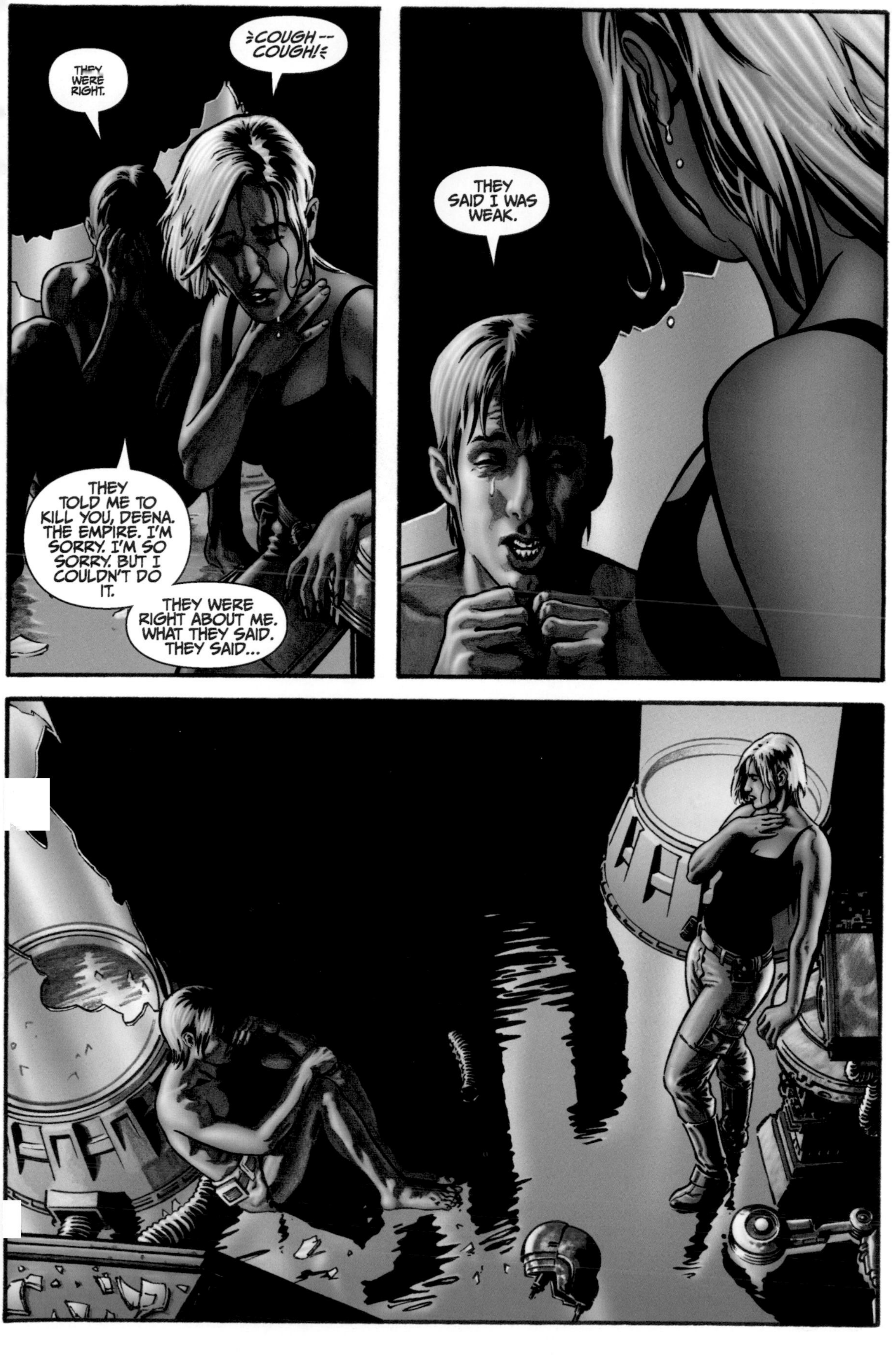THEY WERE RIGHT.
COUGH -- COUGH!
THEY TOLD ME TO KILL YOU, DEENA. THE EMPIRE. I'M SORRY. I'M SO SORRY. BUT I COULDN'T DO IT.
THEY WERE RIGHT ABOUT ME. WHAT THEY SAID. THEY SAID...
THEY SAID I WAS WEAK.

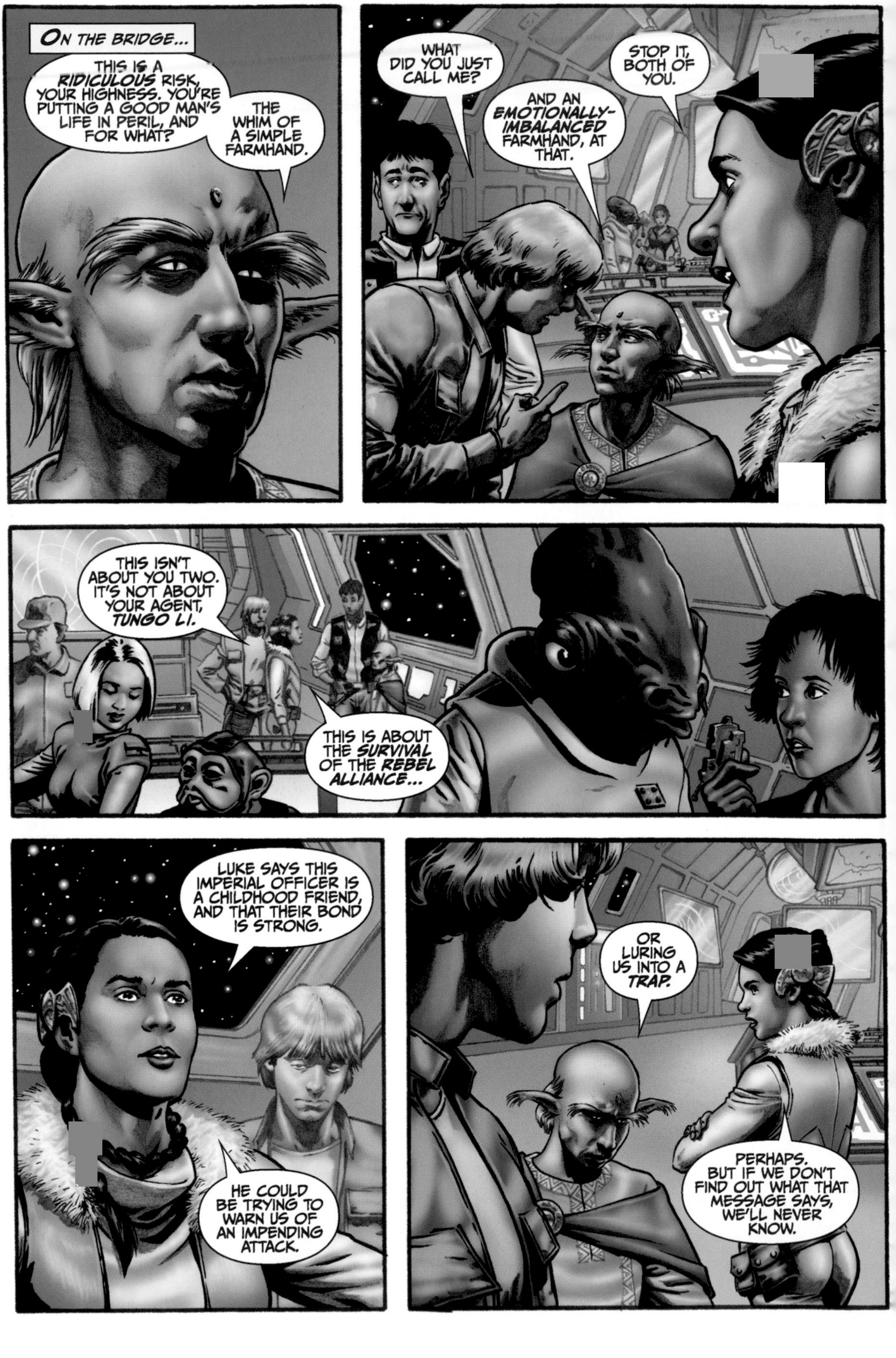
ON THE BRIDGE...
THIS IS A RIDICULOUS RISK, YOUR HIGHNESS. YOU'RE PUTTING A GOOD MAN'S LIFE IN PERIL, AND FOR WHAT?
THE WHIM OF A SIMPLE FARMHAND.
WHAT DID YOU JUST CALL ME?
AND AN EMOTIONALLY-IMBALANCED FARMHAND, AT THAT.
STOP IT, BOTH OF YOU.
THIS ISN'T ABOUT YOU TWO. IT'S NOT ABOUT YOUR AGENT, TUNGO LI.
THIS IS ABOUT THE SURVIVAL OF THE REBEL ALLIANCE...
LUKE SAYS THIS IMPERIAL OFFICER IS A CHILDHOOD FRIEND, AND THAT THEIR BOND IS STRONG.
HE COULD BE TRYING TO WARN US OF AN IMPENDING ATTACK.
OR LURING US INTO A TRAP.
PERHAPS. BUT IF WE DON'T FIND OUT WHAT THAT MESSAGE SAYS, WE'LL NEVER KNOW.

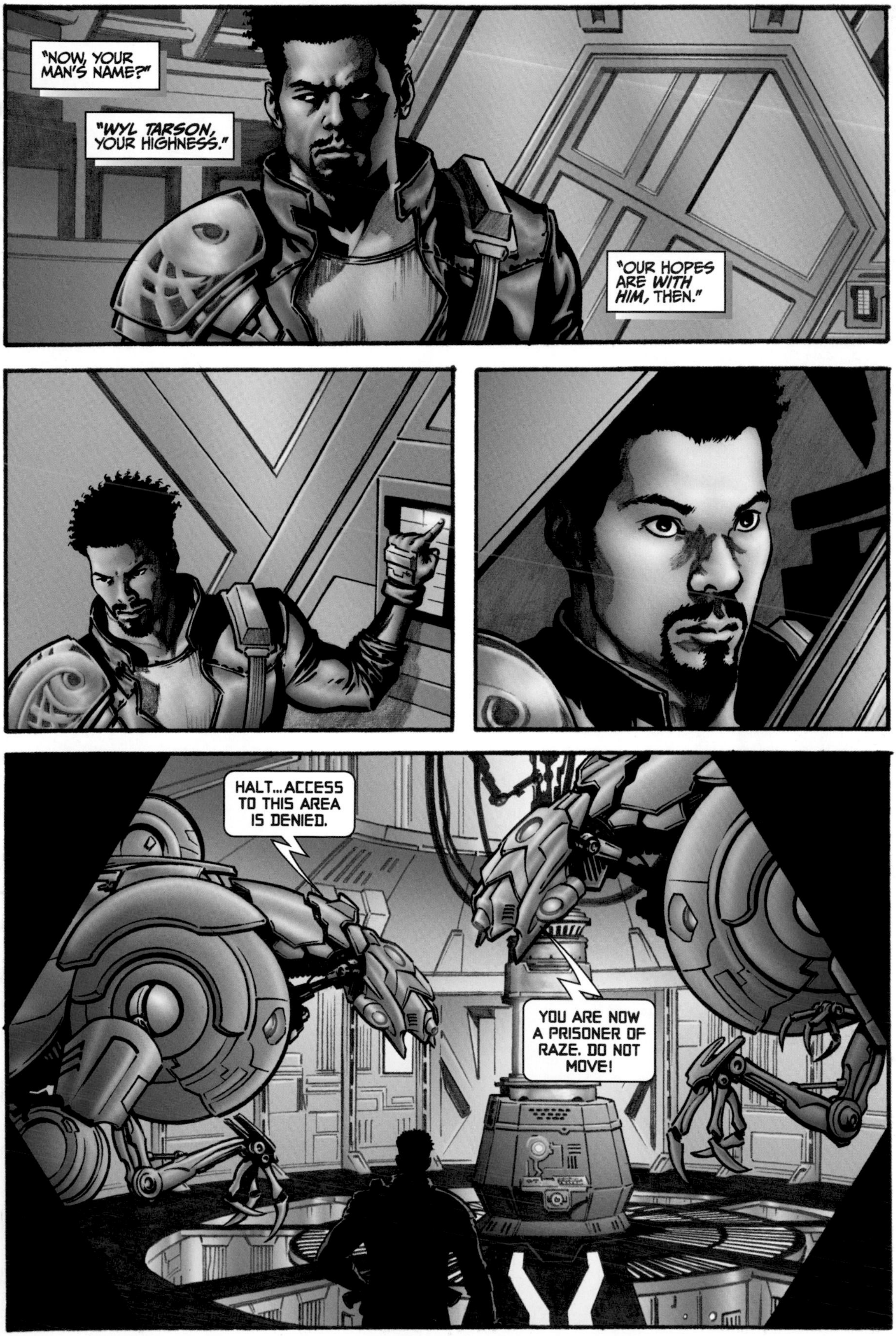
"NOW, YOUR MAN'S NAME?"
"WYL TARSON, YOUR HIGHNESS."
"OUR HOPES ARE WITH HIM, THEN."
HALT...ACCESS TO THIS AREA IS DENIED.
YOU ARE NOW A PRISONER OF RAZE. DO NOT MOVE!

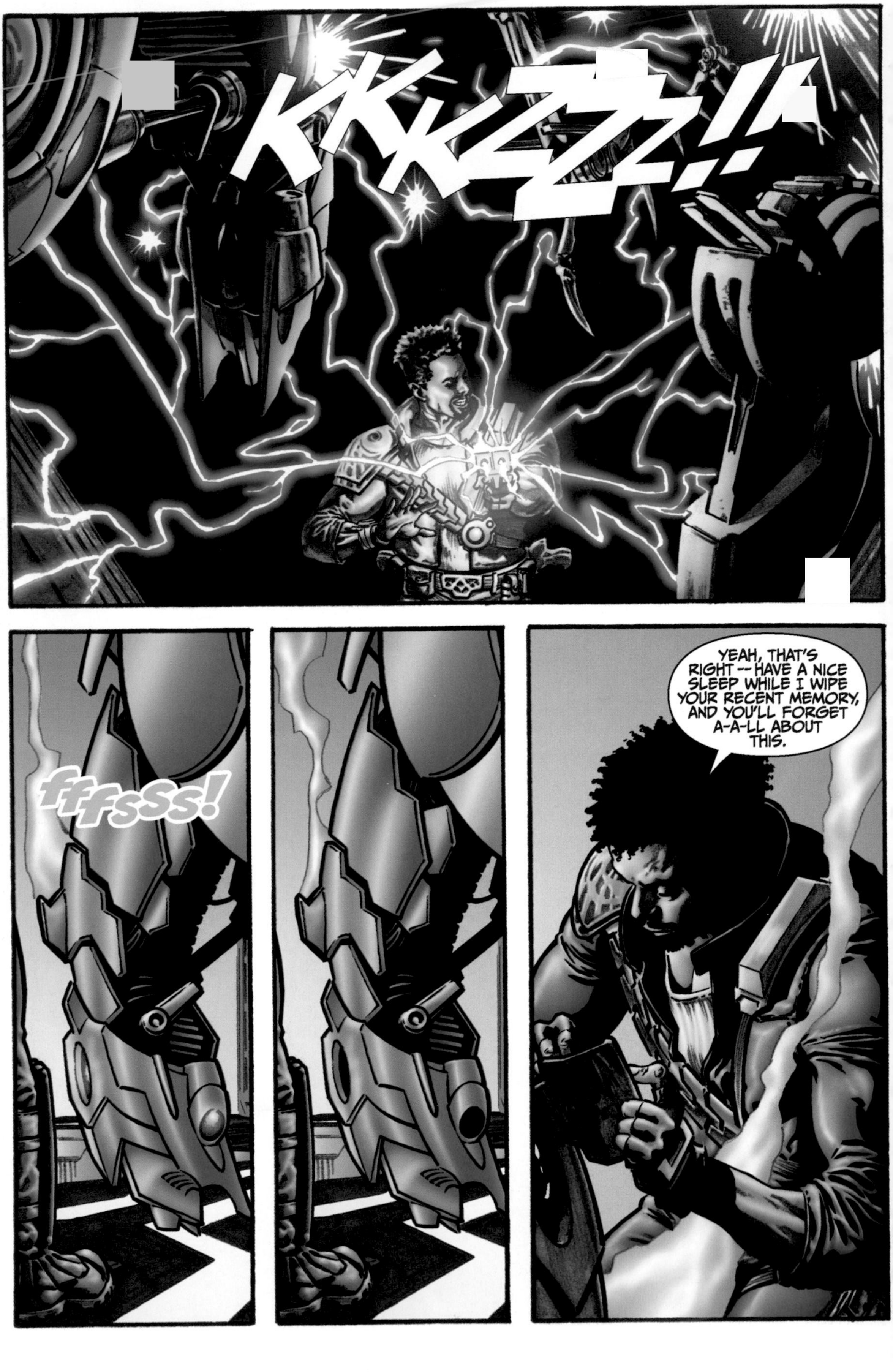
KKKZZZ!!
fffsss!
YEAH, THAT'S RIGHT -- HAVE A NICE SLEEP WHILE I WIPE YOUR RECENT MEMORY, AND YOU'LL FORGET A-A-LL ABOUT THIS.

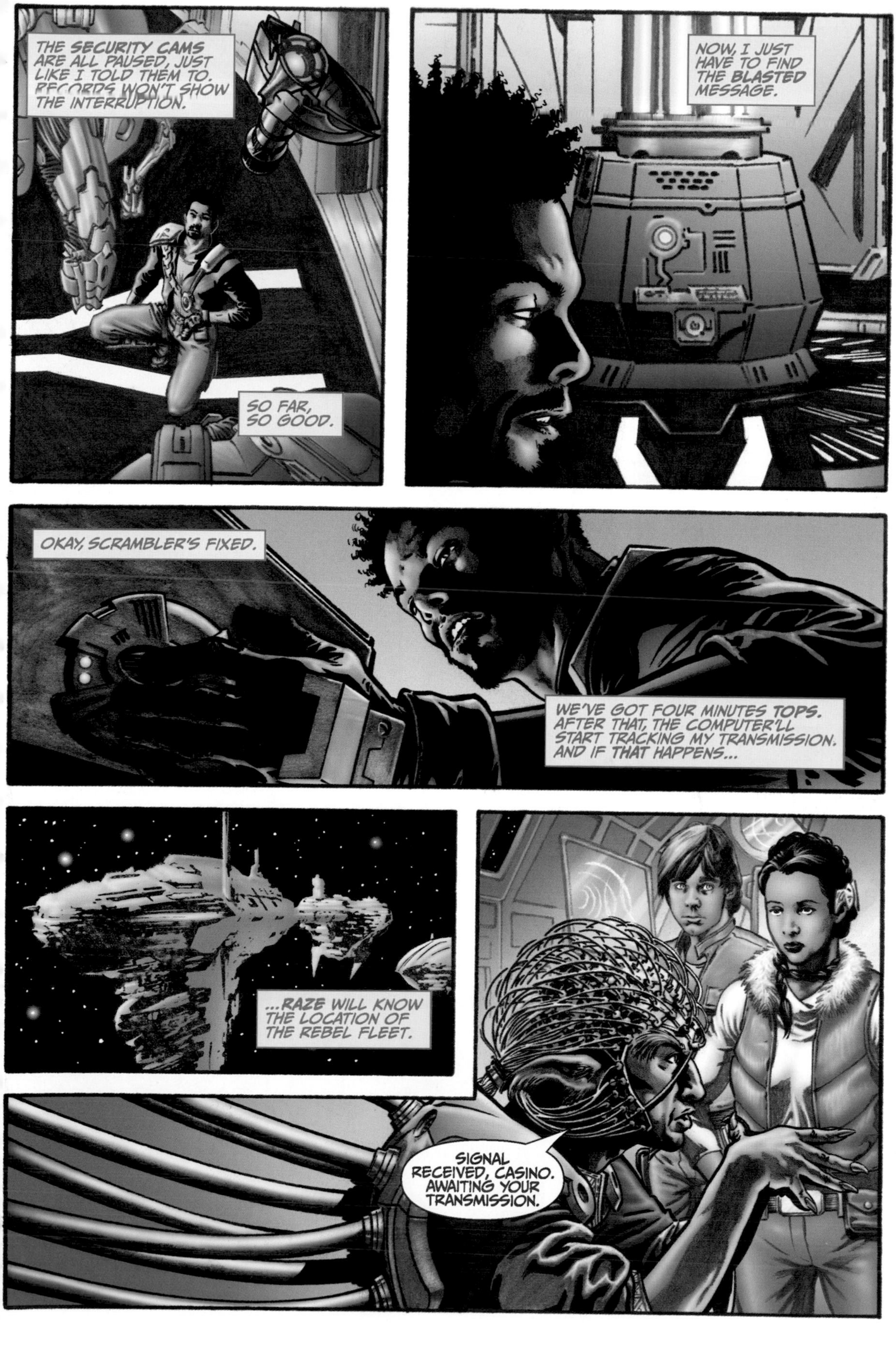
THE SECURITY CAMS ARE ALL PAUSED, JUST LIKE I TOLD THEM TO. RECORDS WON'T SHOW THE INTERRUPTION.
SO FAR, SO GOOD.
NOW, I JUST HAVE TO FIND THE BLASTED MESSAGE.
OKAY, SCRAMBLER'S FIXED.
WE'VE GOT FOUR MINUTES TOPS. AFTER THAT, THE COMPUTER'LL START TRACKING MY TRANSMISSION. AND IF THAT HAPPENS...
...RAZE WILL KNOW THE LOCATION OF THE REBEL FLEET.
SIGNAL RECEIVED, CASINO. AWAITING YOUR TRANSMISSION.

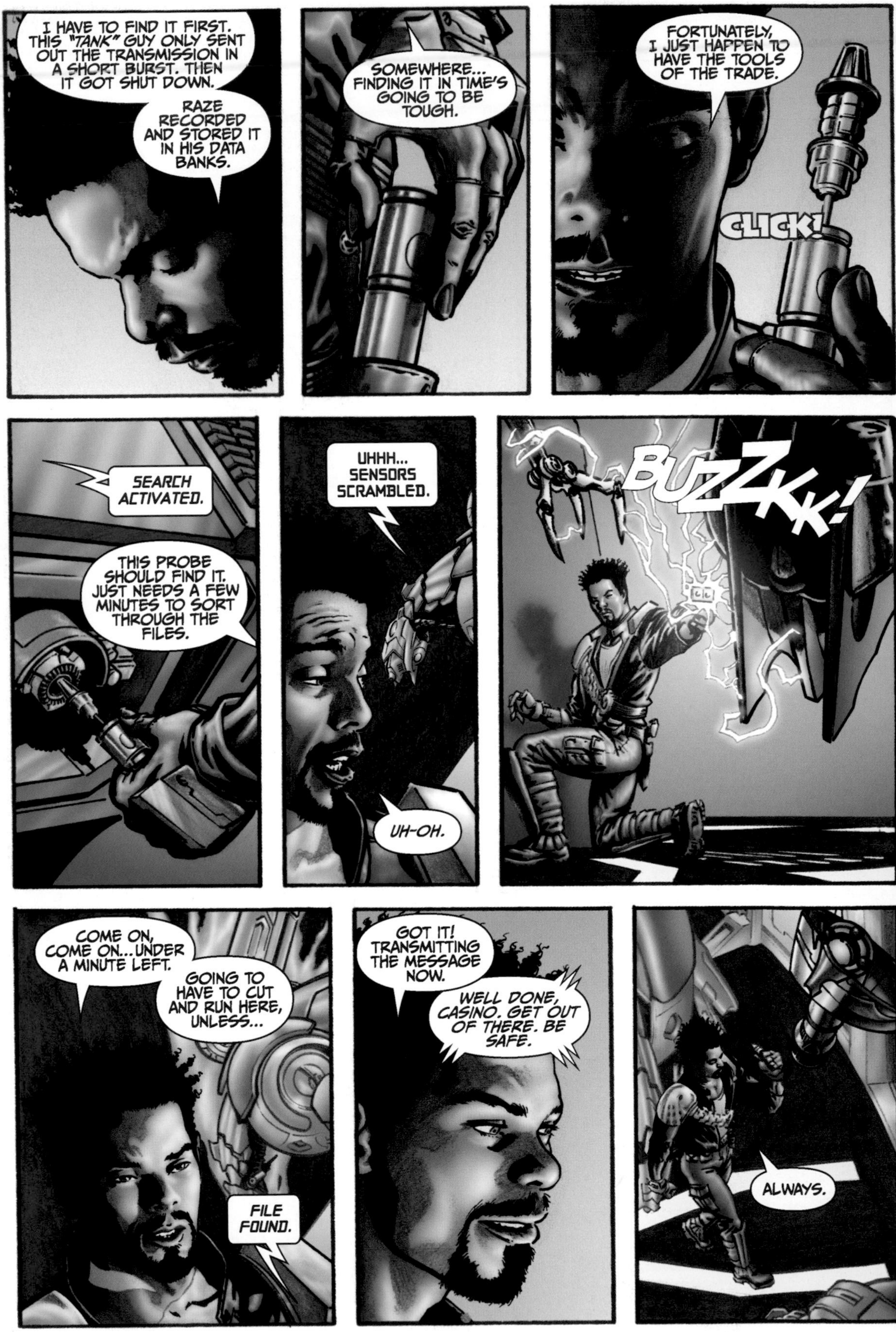
I HAVE TO FIND IT FIRST. THIS "TANK" GUY ONLY SENT OUT THE TRANSMISSION IN A SHORT BURST. THEN IT GOT SHUT DOWN.
RAZE RECORDED AND STORED IT IN HIS DATA BANKS.
SOMEWHERE... FINDING IT IN TIME'S GOING TO BE TOUGH.
FORTUNATELY, I JUST HAPPEN TO HAVE THE TOOLS OF THE TRADE.
CLICK!
SEARCH ACTIVATED.
THIS PROBE SHOULD FIND IT. JUST NEEDS A FEW MINUTES TO SORT THROUGH THE FILES.
UHHH... SENSORS SCRAMBLED.
UH-OH.
BUZZKK!
COME ON, COME ON... UNDER A MINUTE LEFT.
GOING TO HAVE TO CUT AND RUN HERE, UNLESS...
FILE FOUND.
GOT IT! TRANSMITTING THE MESSAGE NOW.
WELL DONE, CASINO. GET OUT OF THERE. BE SAFE.
ALWAYS.

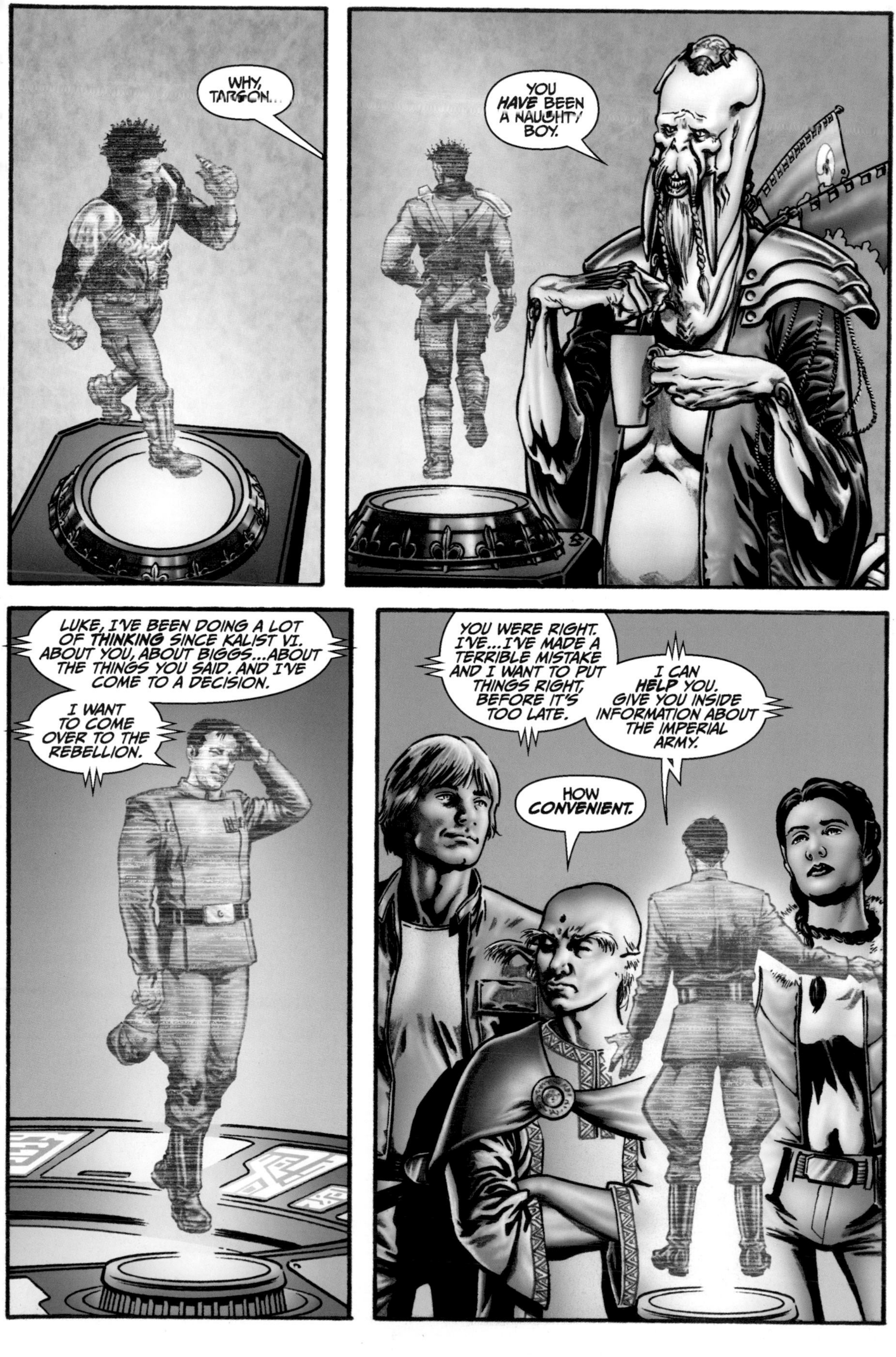
WHY, TARSON...
YOU HAVE BEEN A NAUGHTY BOY.
LUKE, I'VE BEEN DOING A LOT OF THINKING SINCE KALIST VI. ABOUT YOU, ABOUT BIGGS...ABOUT THE THINGS YOU SAID. AND I'VE COME TO A DECISION.
I WANT TO COME OVER TO THE REBELLION.
YOU WERE RIGHT. I'VE...I'VE MADE A TERRIBLE MISTAKE AND I WANT TO PUT THINGS RIGHT, BEFORE IT'S TOO LATE.
I CAN HELP YOU. GIVE YOU INSIDE INFORMATION ABOUT THE IMPERIAL ARMY.
HOW CONVENIENT.

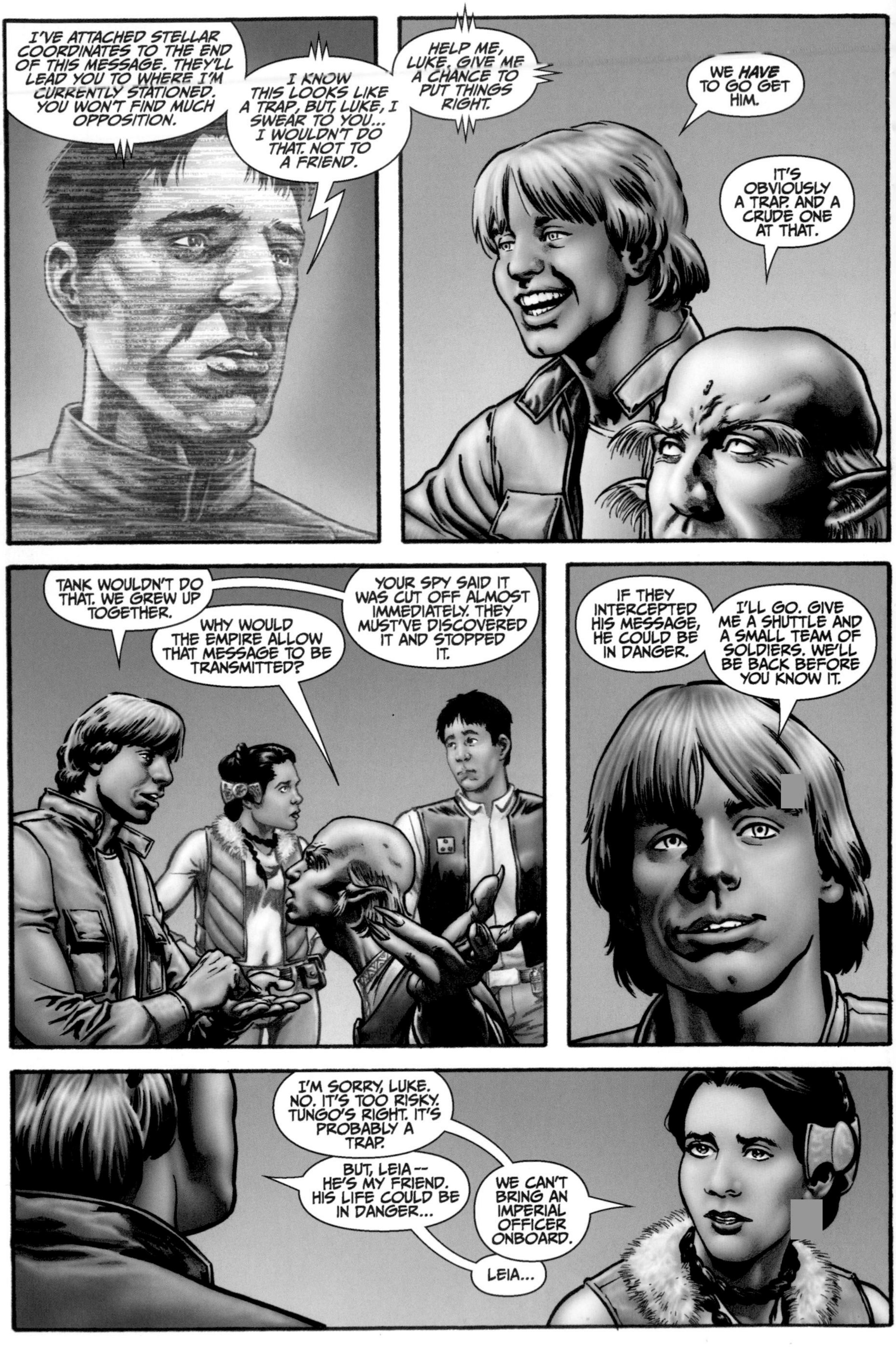
I'VE ATTACHED STELLAR COORDINATES TO THE END OF THIS MESSAGE. THEY'LL LEAD YOU TO WHERE I'M CURRENTLY STATIONED. YOU WON'T FIND MUCH OPPOSITION.
I KNOW THIS LOOKS LIKE A TRAP, BUT, LUKE, I SWEAR TO YOU... I WOULDN'T DO THAT. NOT TO A FRIEND.
HELP ME, LUKE. GIVE ME A CHANCE TO PUT THINGS RIGHT.
WE HAVE TO GO GET HIM.
IT'S OBVIOUSLY A TRAP. AND A CRUDE ONE AT THAT.
TANK WOULDN'T DO THAT. WE GREW UP TOGETHER.
YOUR SPY SAID IT WAS CUT OFF ALMOST IMMEDIATELY. THEY MUST'VE DISCOVERED IT AND STOPPED IT.
WHY WOULD THE EMPIRE ALLOW THAT MESSAGE TO BE TRANSMITTED?
IF THEY INTERCEPTED HIS MESSAGE, HE COULD BE IN DANGER.
I'LL GO. GIVE ME A SHUTTLE AND A SMALL TEAM OF SOLDIERS. WE'LL BE BACK BEFORE YOU KNOW IT.
I'M SORRY, LUKE. NO. IT'S TOO RISKY. TUNGO'S RIGHT. IT'S PROBABLY A TRAP.
BUT, LEIA -- HE'S MY FRIEND. HIS LIFE COULD BE IN DANGER...
WE CAN'T BRING AN IMPERIAL OFFICER ONBOARD.
LEIA...

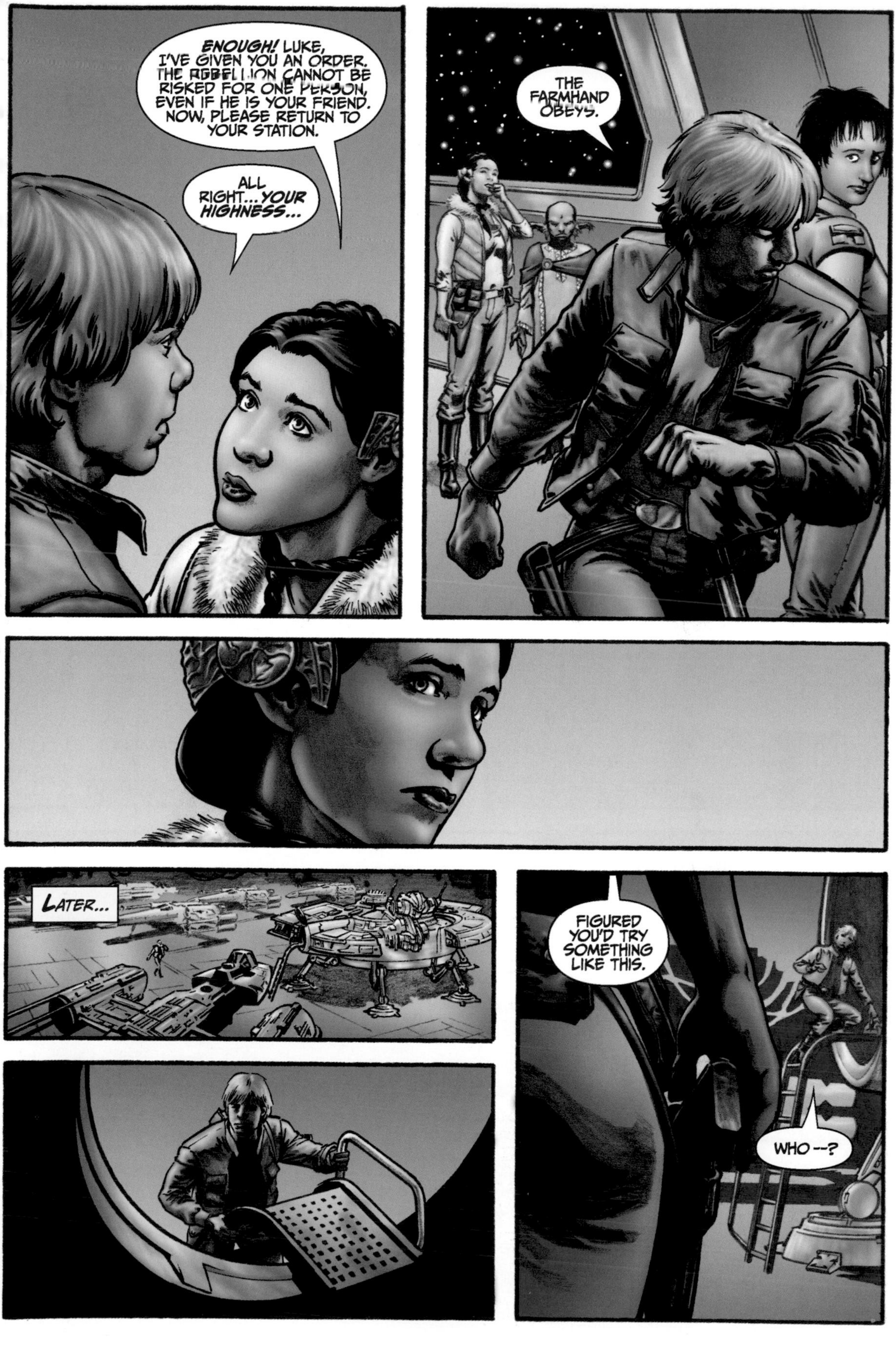
ENOUGH! LUKE, I'VE GIVEN YOU AN ORDER. THE REBELLION CANNOT BE RISKED FOR ONE PERSON, EVEN IF HE IS YOUR FRIEND. NOW, PLEASE RETURN TO YOUR STATION.
ALL RIGHT... YOUR HIGHNESS...
THE FARMHAND OBEYS.
LATER...
FIGURED YOU'D TRY SOMETHING LIKE THIS.
WHO --?

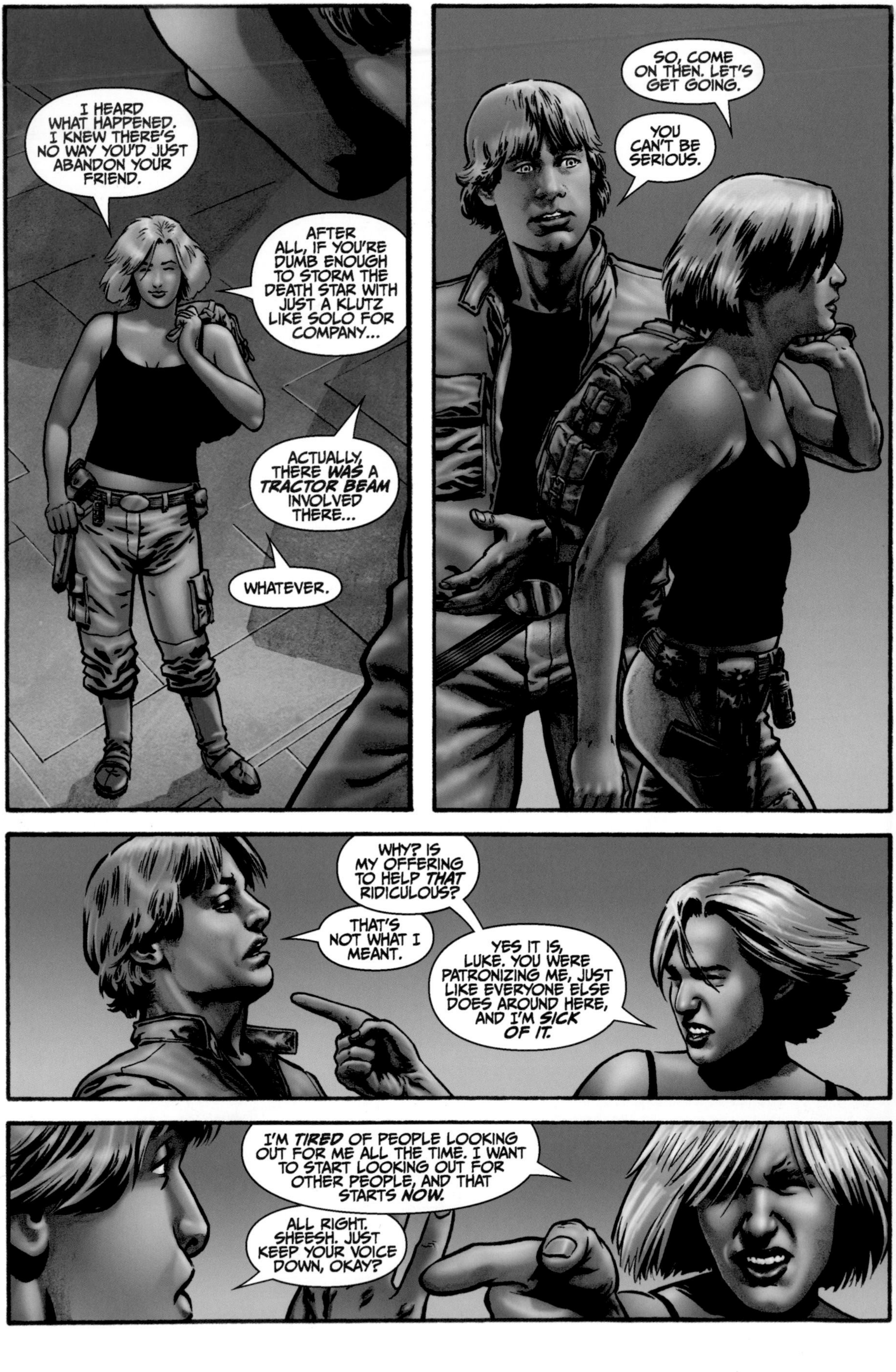
I HEARD WHAT HAPPENED. I KNEW THERE'S NO WAY YOU'D JUST ABANDON YOUR FRIEND.
AFTER ALL, IF YOU'RE DUMB ENOUGH TO STORM THE DEATH STAR WITH JUST A KLUTZ LIKE SOLO FOR COMPANY...
ACTUALLY, THERE *WAS* A *TRACTOR BEAM* INVOLVED THERE...
WHATEVER.
SO, COME ON THEN. LET'S GET GOING.
YOU CAN'T BE SERIOUS.
WHY? IS MY OFFERING TO HELP *THAT* RIDICULOUS?
THAT'S NOT WHAT I MEANT.
YES IT IS, LUKE. YOU WERE PATRONIZING ME, JUST LIKE EVERYONE ELSE DOES AROUND HERE, AND I'M *SICK OF IT.*
I'M *TIRED* OF PEOPLE LOOKING OUT FOR ME ALL THE TIME. I WANT TO START LOOKING OUT FOR OTHER PEOPLE, AND THAT STARTS *NOW.*
ALL RIGHT. SHEESH. JUST KEEP YOUR VOICE DOWN, OKAY?

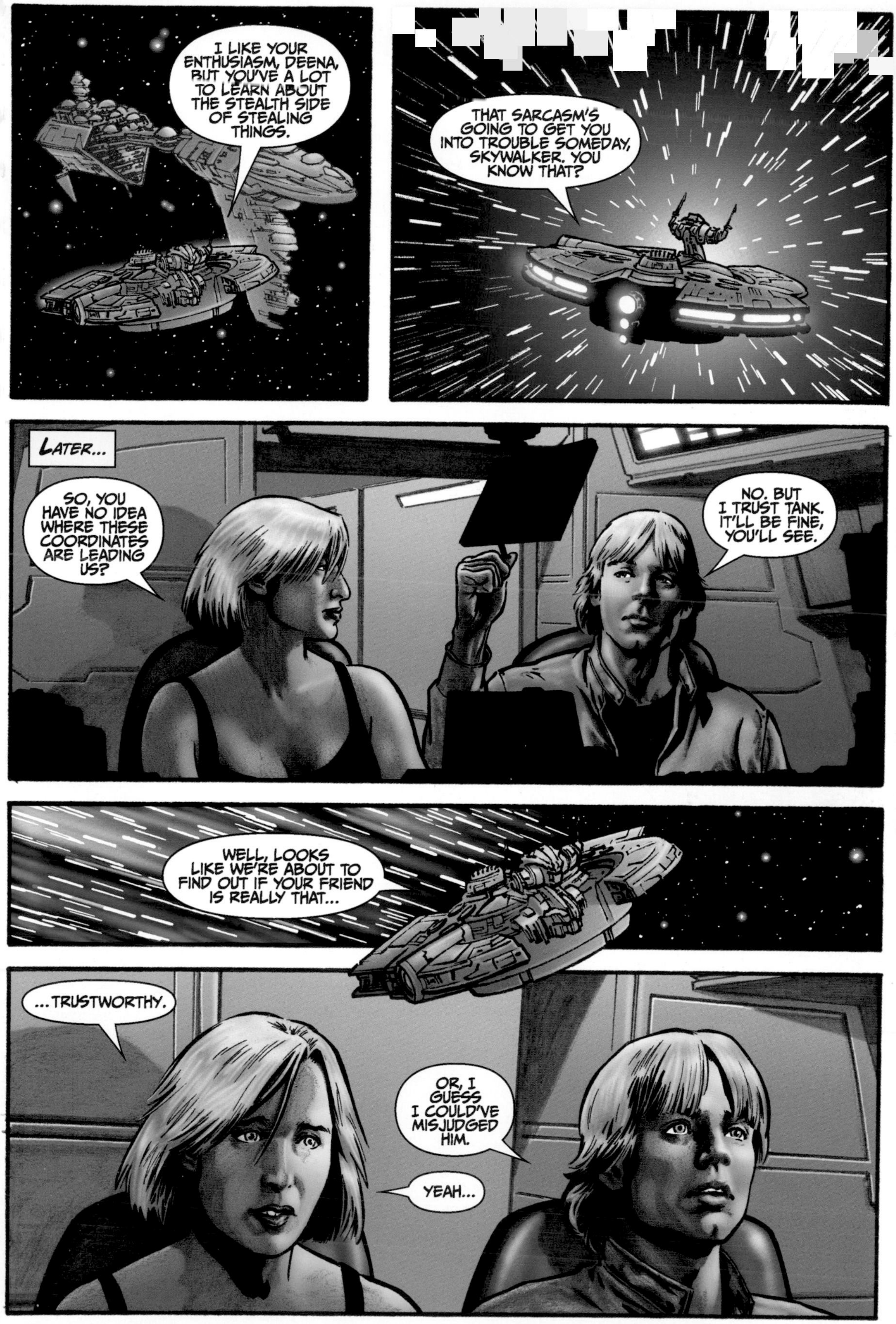
I LIKE YOUR ENTHUSIASM, DEENA, BUT YOU'VE A LOT TO LEARN ABOUT THE STEALTH SIDE OF STEALING THINGS.
THAT SARCASM'S GOING TO GET YOU INTO TROUBLE SOMEDAY, SKYWALKER. YOU KNOW THAT?
LATER...
SO, YOU HAVE NO IDEA WHERE THESE COORDINATES ARE LEADING US?
NO. BUT I TRUST TANK. IT'LL BE FINE, YOU'LL SEE.
WELL, LOOKS LIKE WE'RE ABOUT TO FIND OUT IF YOUR FRIEND IS REALLY THAT...
...TRUSTWORTHY.
OR, I GUESS I COULD'VE MISJUDGED HIM.
YEAH...

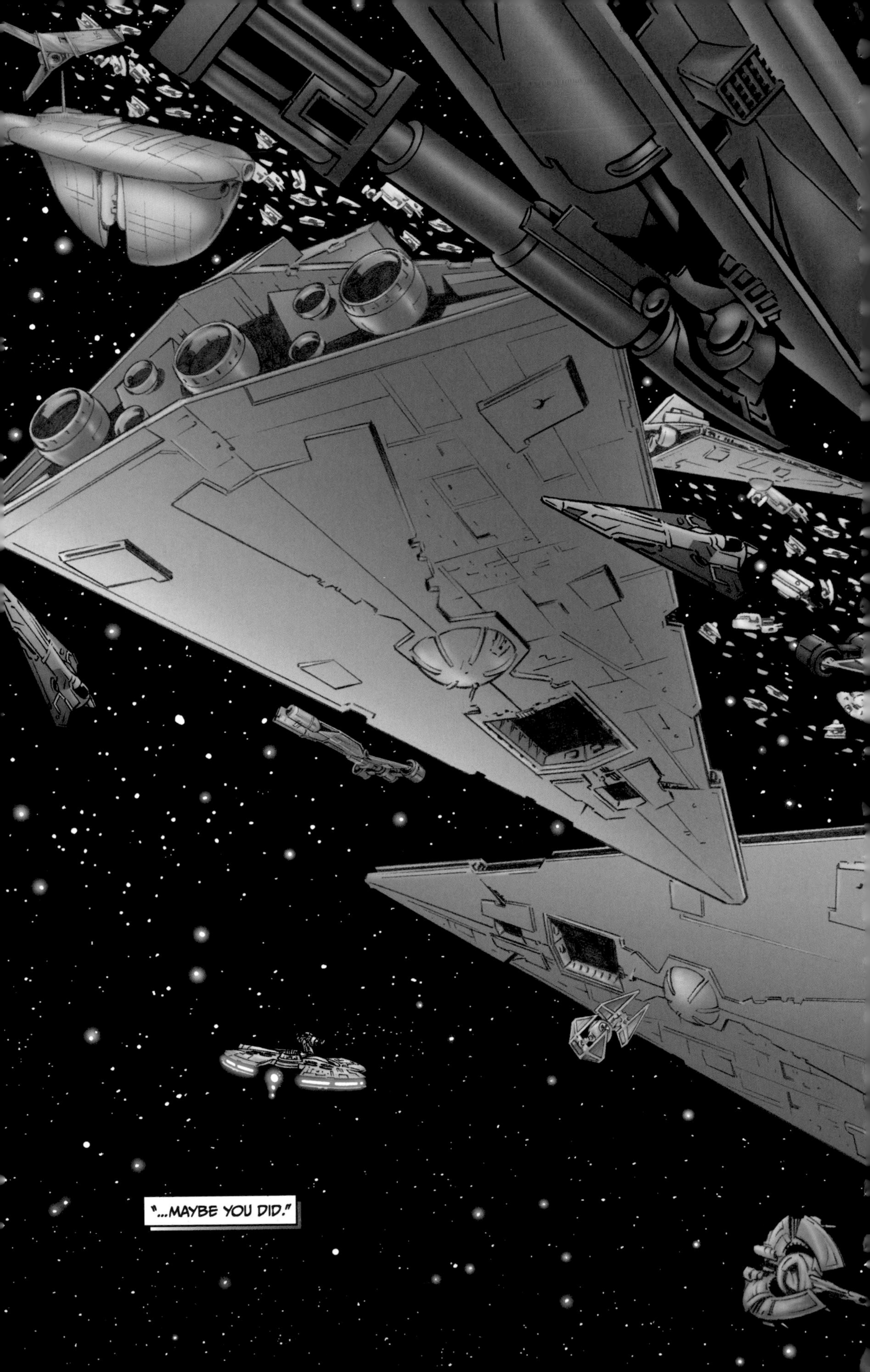
"...MAYBE YOU DID."

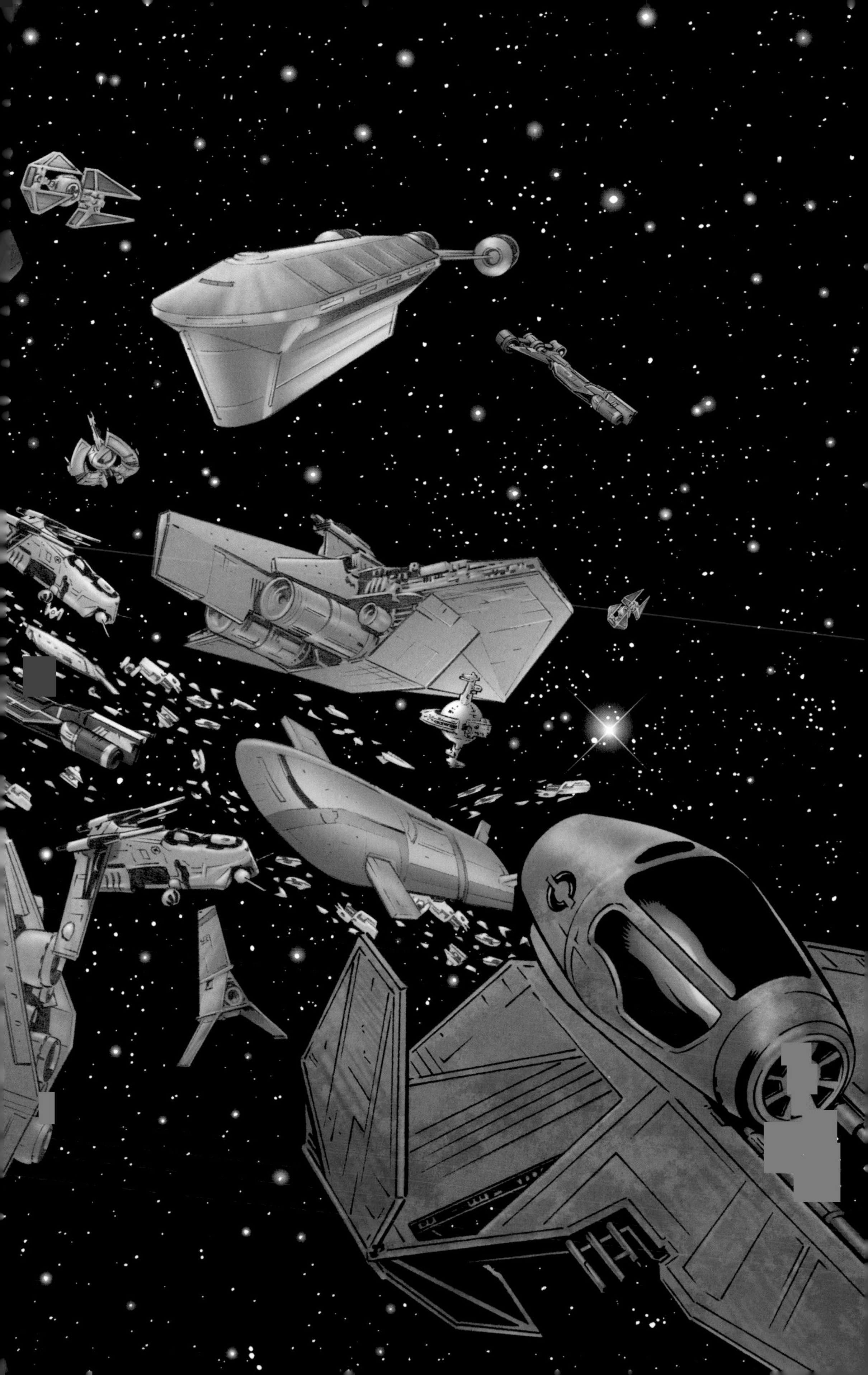

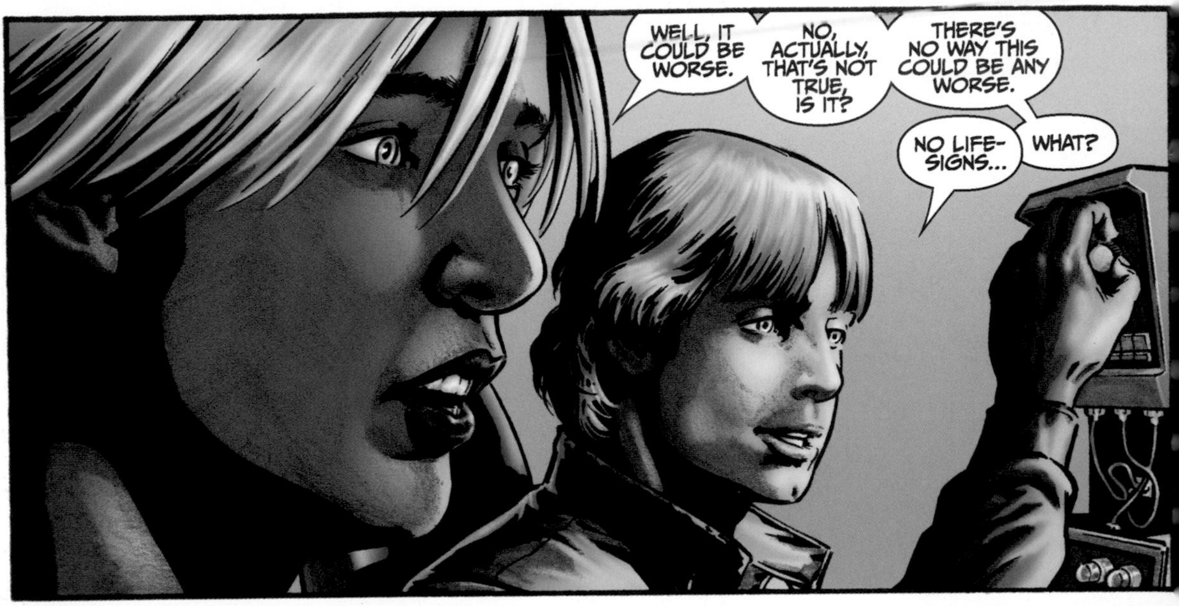
WELL, IT COULD BE WORSE.
NO, ACTUALLY, THAT'S NOT TRUE, IS IT?
THERE'S NO WAY THIS COULD BE ANY WORSE.
NO LIFE-SIGNS...
WHAT?

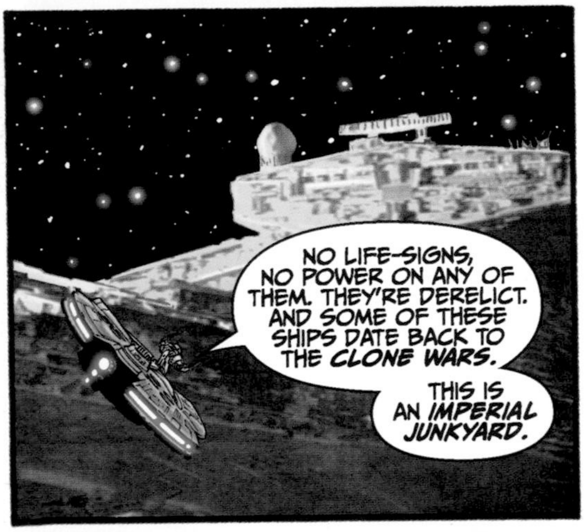
NO LIFE-SIGNS, NO POWER ON ANY OF THEM. THEY'RE DERELICT. AND SOME OF THESE SHIPS DATE BACK TO THE CLONE WARS.
THIS IS AN IMPERIAL JUNKYARD.

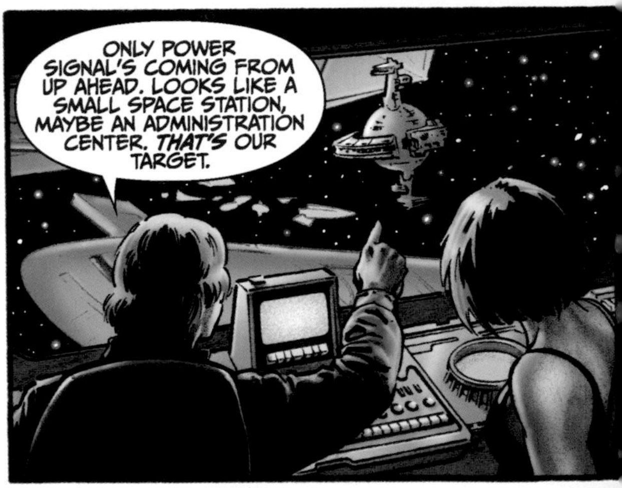
ONLY POWER SIGNAL'S COMING FROM UP AHEAD. LOOKS LIKE A SMALL SPACE STATION, MAYBE AN ADMINISTRATION CENTER. THAT'S OUR TARGET.

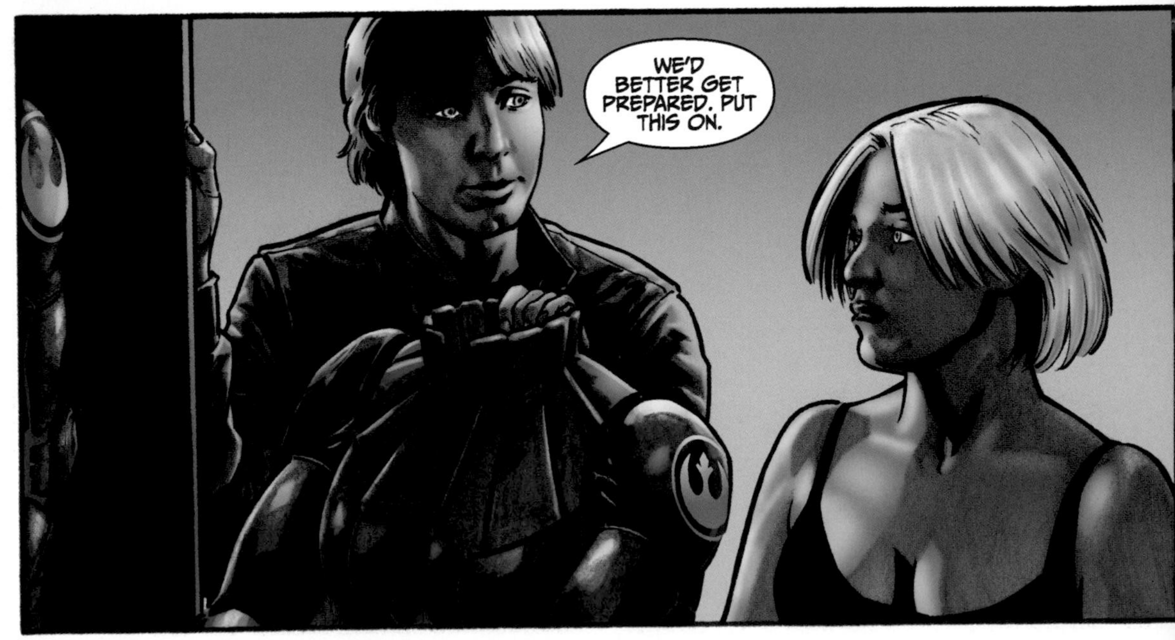
WE'D BETTER GET PREPARED. PUT THIS ON.

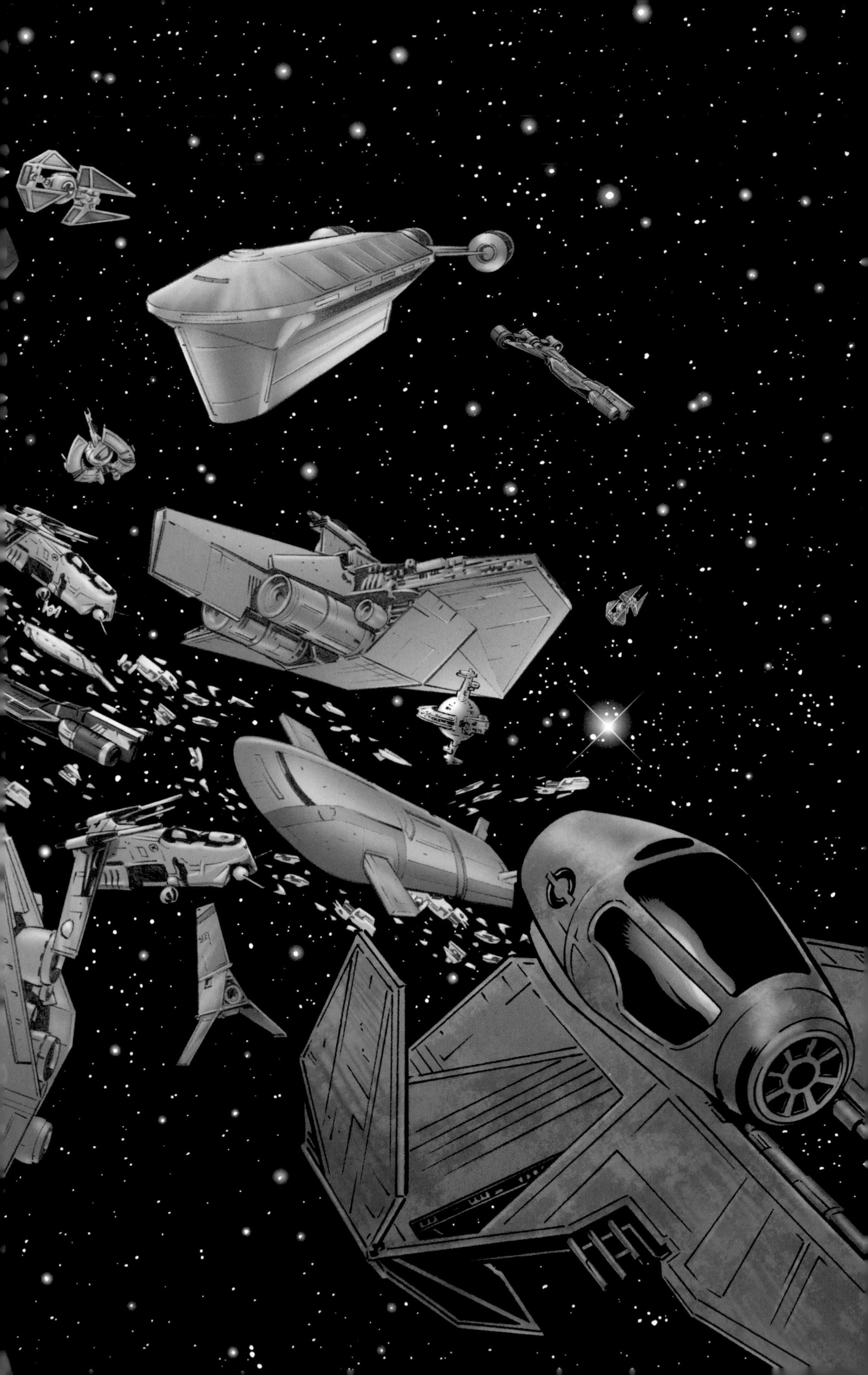

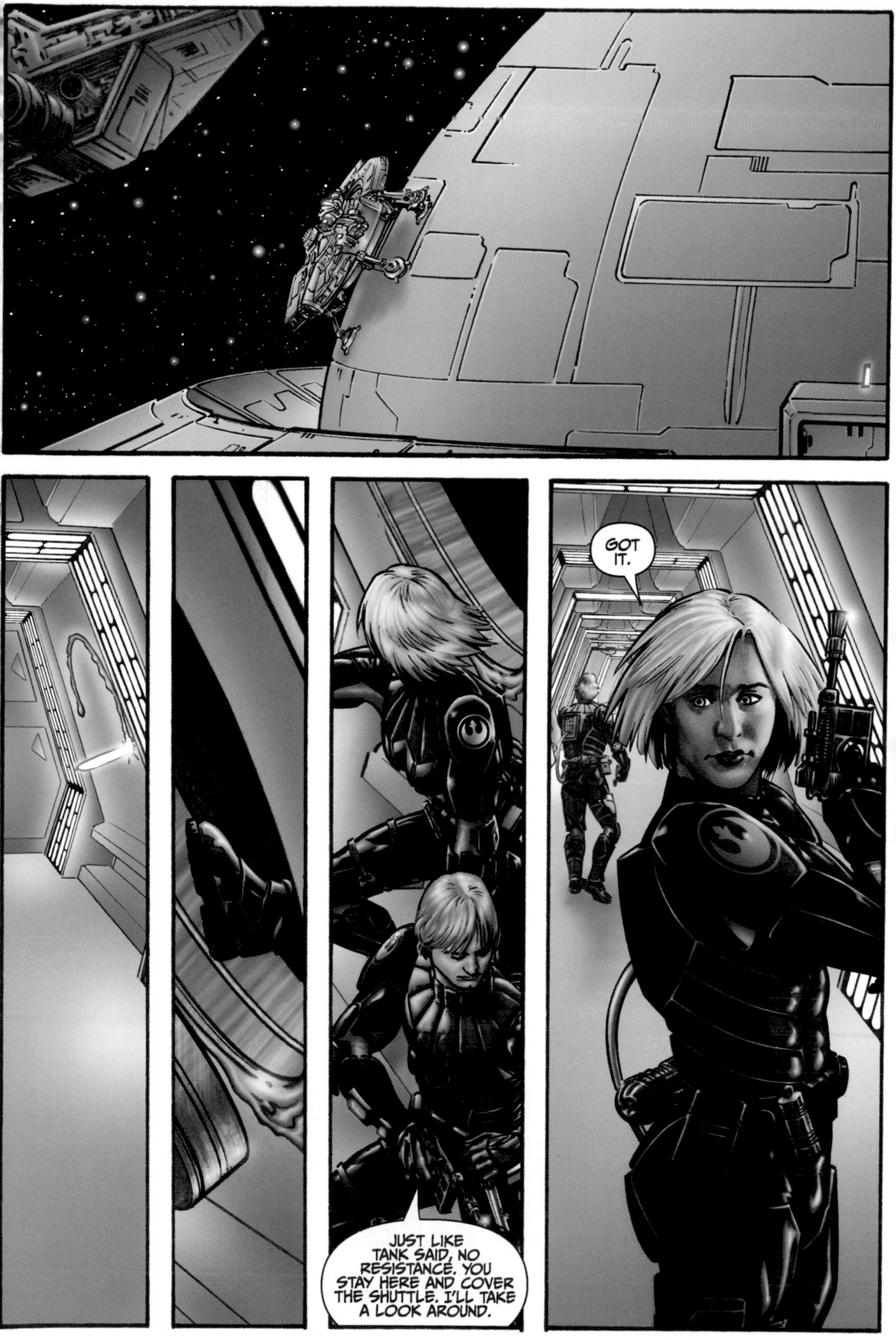
JUST LIKE TANK SAID, NO RESISTANCE. YOU STAY HERE AND COVER THE SHUTTLE. I'LL TAKE A LOOK AROUND.
GOT IT.

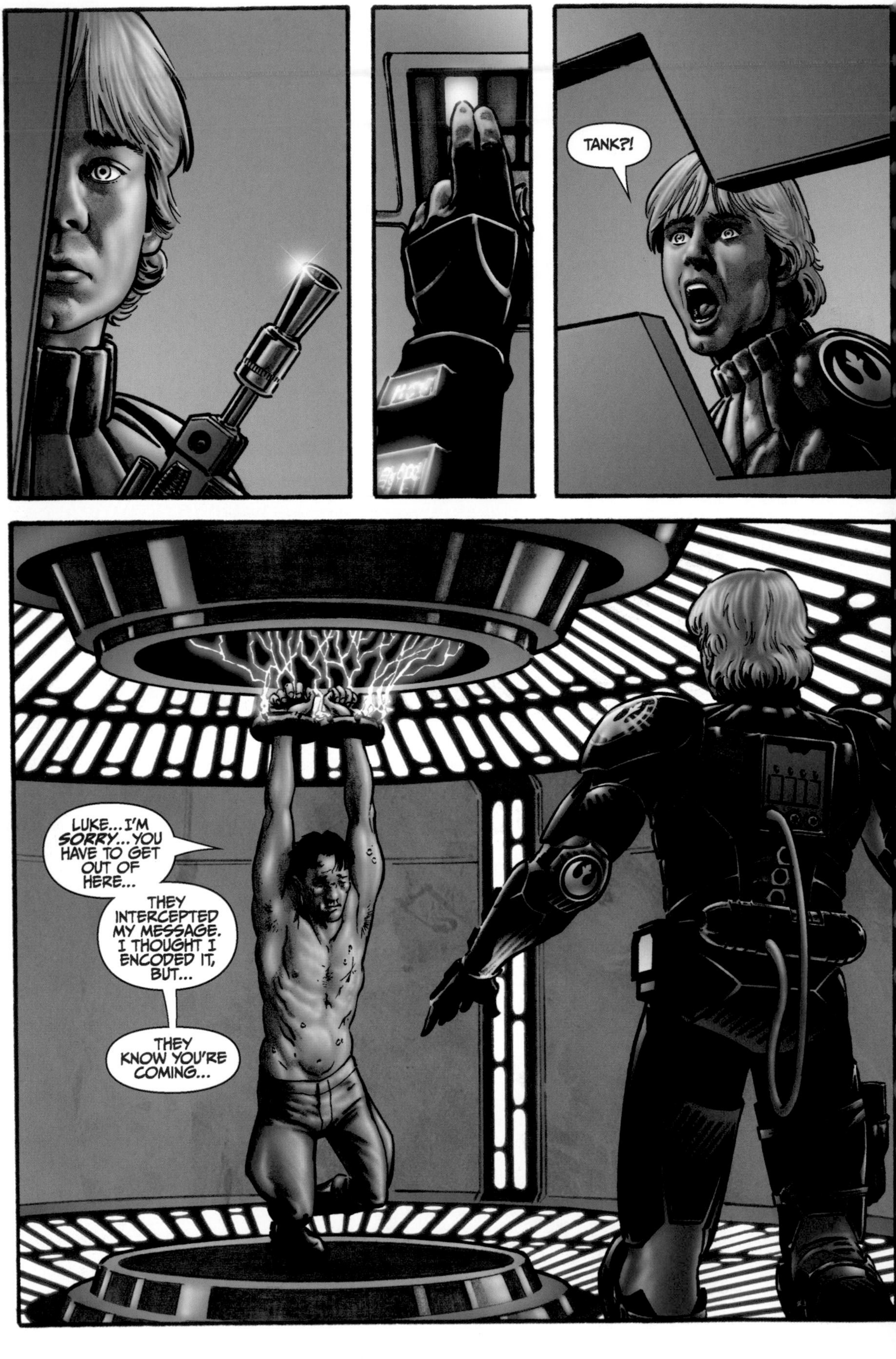
TANK?!
LUKE... I'M *SORRY*... YOU HAVE TO GET OUT OF HERE...
THEY INTERCEPTED MY MESSAGE. I THOUGHT I ENCODED IT, BUT...
THEY KNOW YOU'RE COMING...

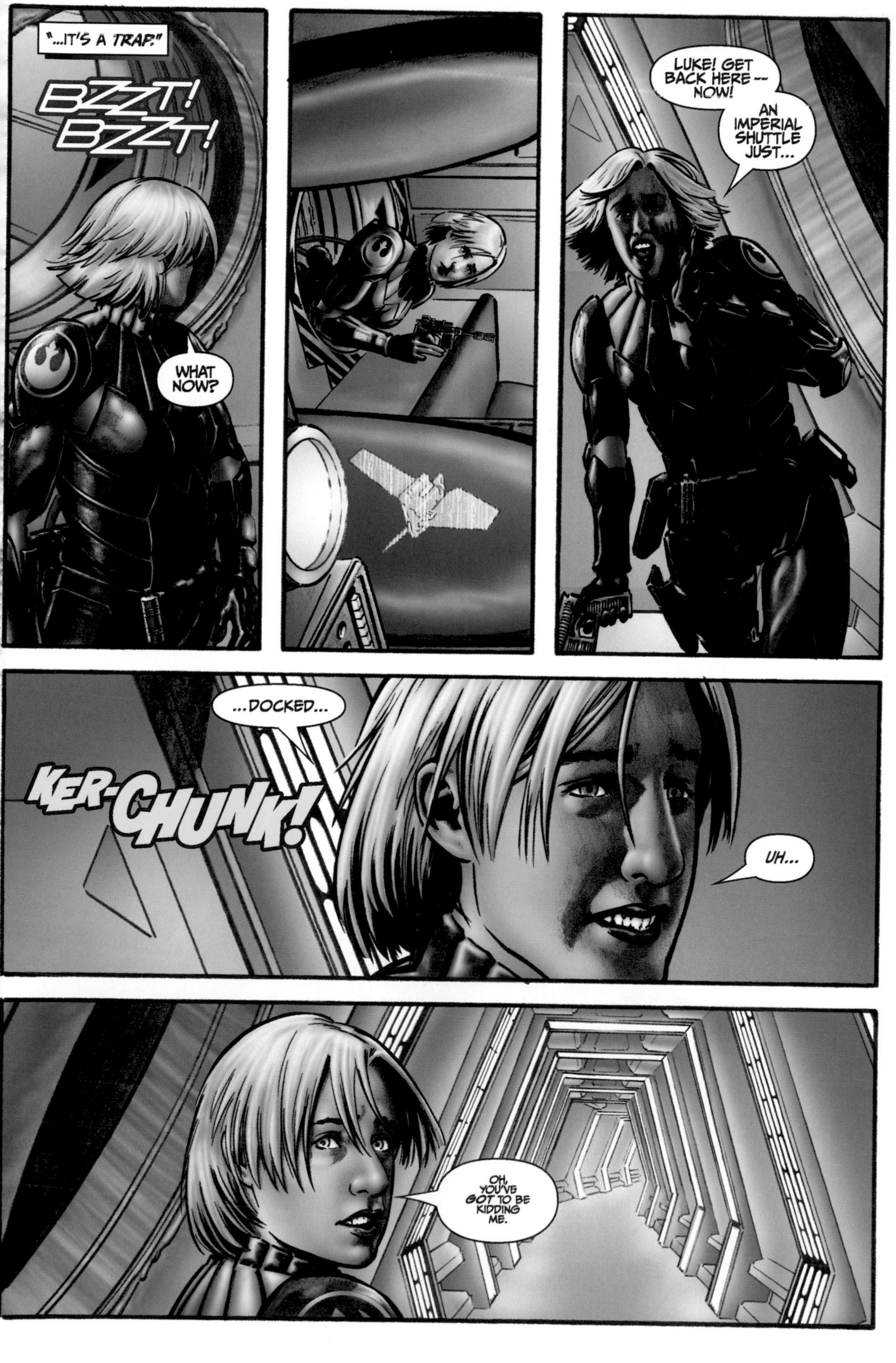
"...IT'S A TRAP."
BZZT! BZZT!
WHAT NOW?
LUKE! GET BACK HERE -- NOW!
AN IMPERIAL SHUTTLE JUST...
...DOCKED...
KER-CHUNK!
UH...
OH, YOU'VE GOT TO BE KIDDING ME.

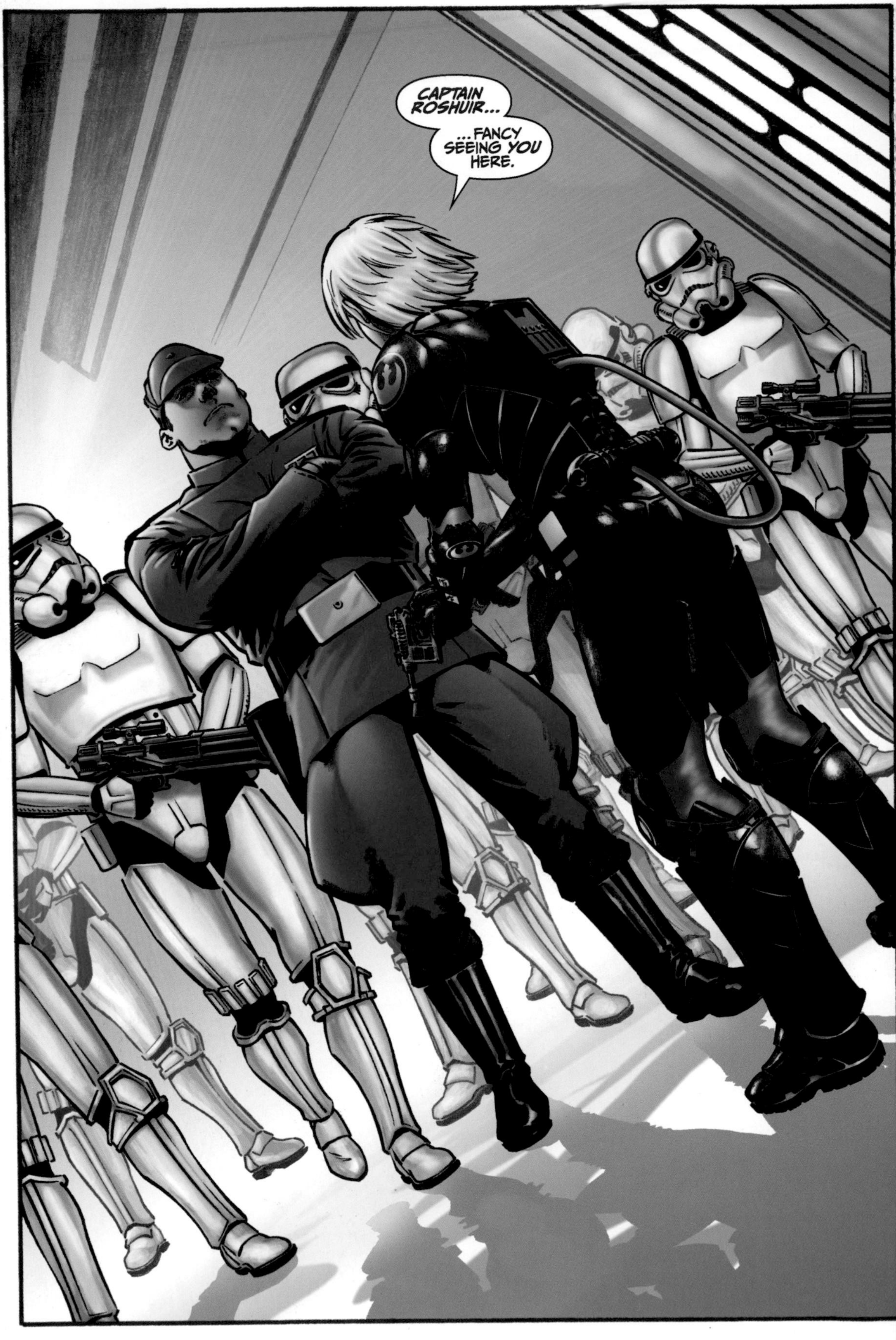
CAPTAIN ROSHUIR...
...FANCY SEEING YOU HERE.

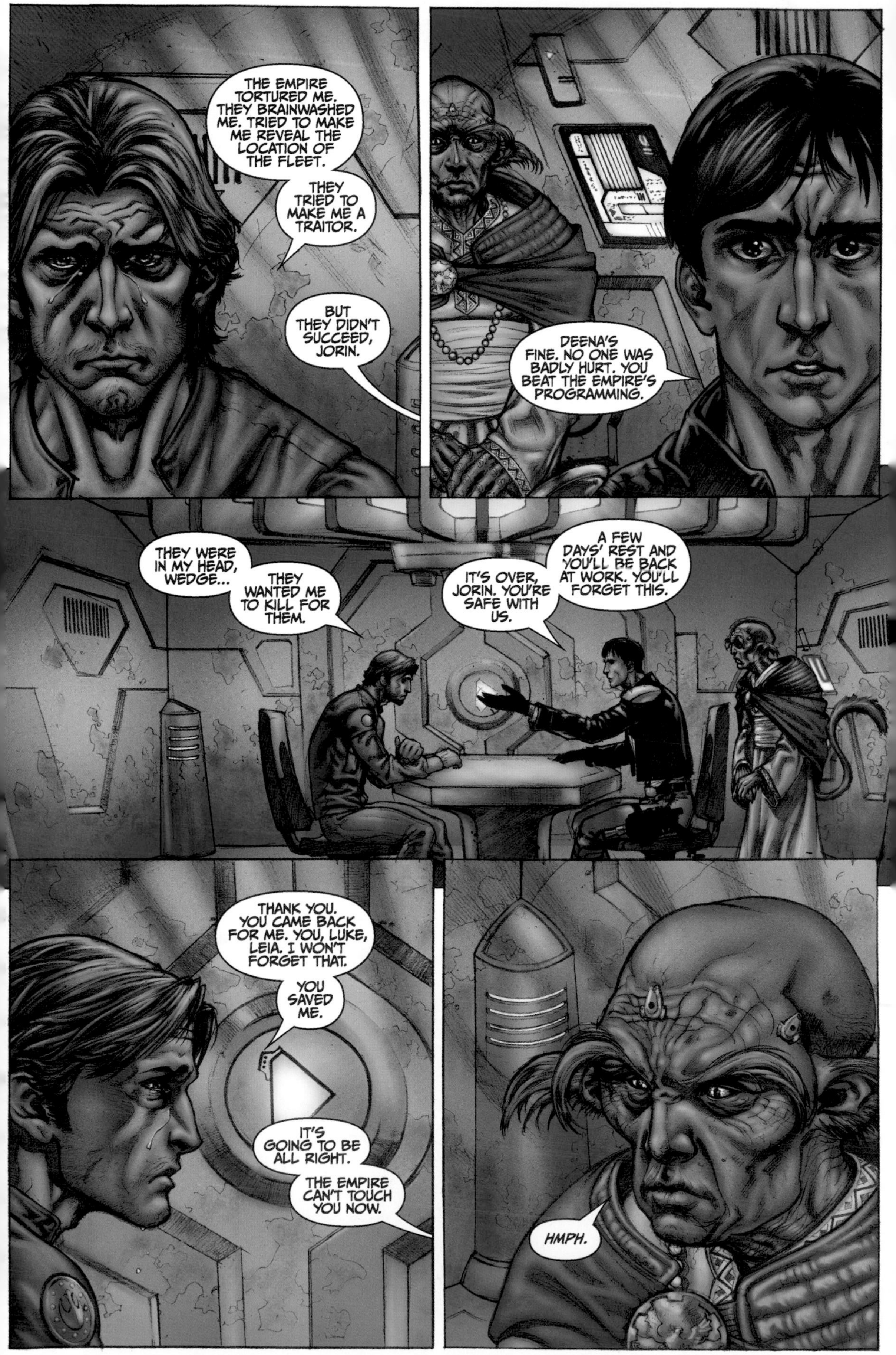
THE EMPIRE TORTURED ME. THEY BRAINWASHED ME. TRIED TO MAKE ME REVEAL THE LOCATION OF THE FLEET.
THEY TRIED TO MAKE ME A TRAITOR.
BUT THEY DIDN'T SUCCEED, JORIN.
DEENA'S FINE. NO ONE WAS BADLY HURT. YOU BEAT THE EMPIRE'S PROGRAMMING.
THEY WERE IN MY HEAD, WEDGE...
THEY WANTED ME TO KILL FOR THEM.
IT'S OVER, JORIN. YOU'RE SAFE WITH US.
A FEW DAYS' REST AND YOU'LL BE BACK AT WORK. YOU'LL FORGET THIS.
THANK YOU. YOU CAME BACK FOR ME. YOU, LUKE, LEIA. I WON'T FORGET THAT.
YOU SAVED ME.
IT'S GOING TO BE ALL RIGHT.
THE EMPIRE CAN'T TOUCH YOU NOW.
HMPH.

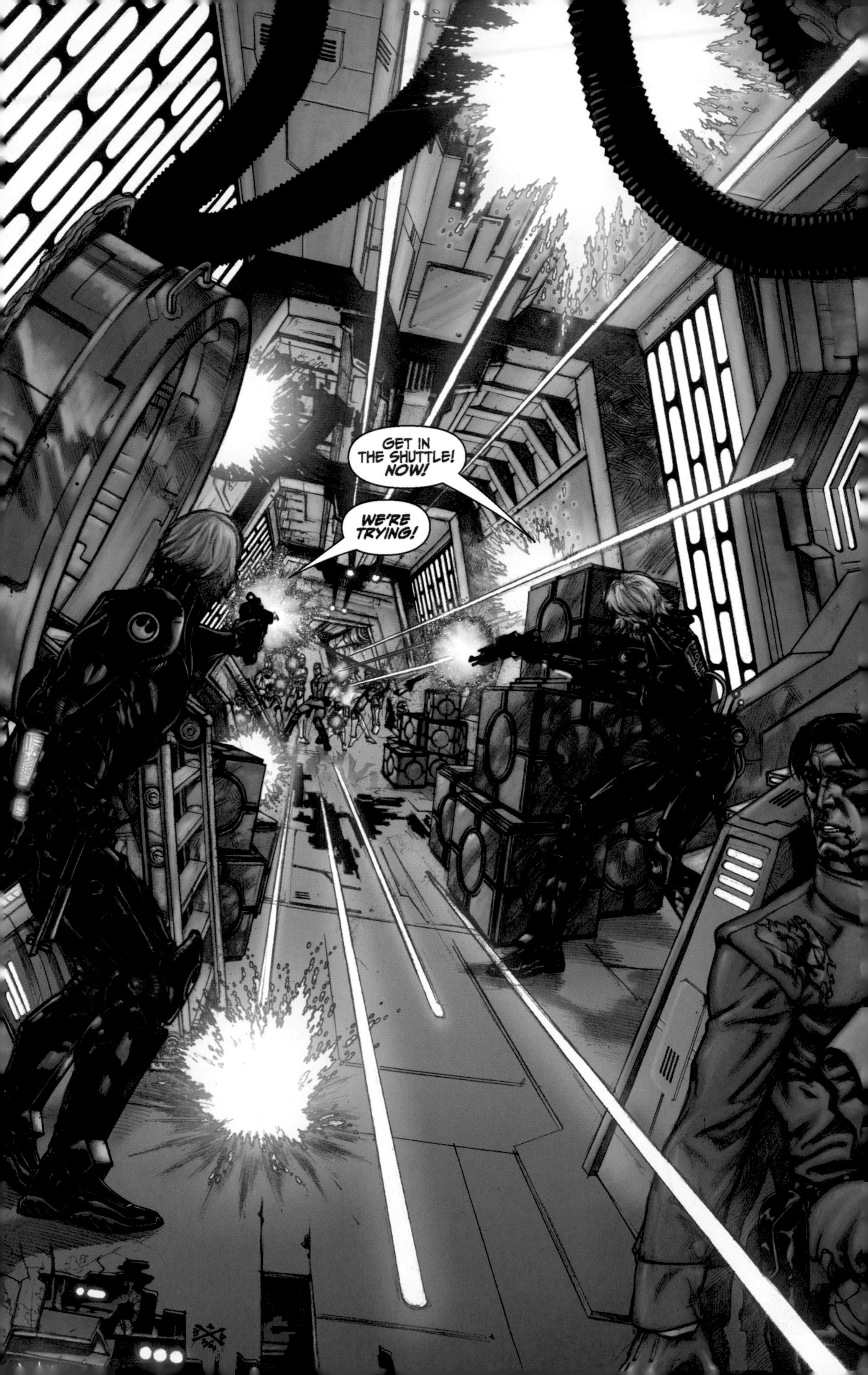
GET IN THE SHUTTLE! NOW!
WE'RE TRYING!

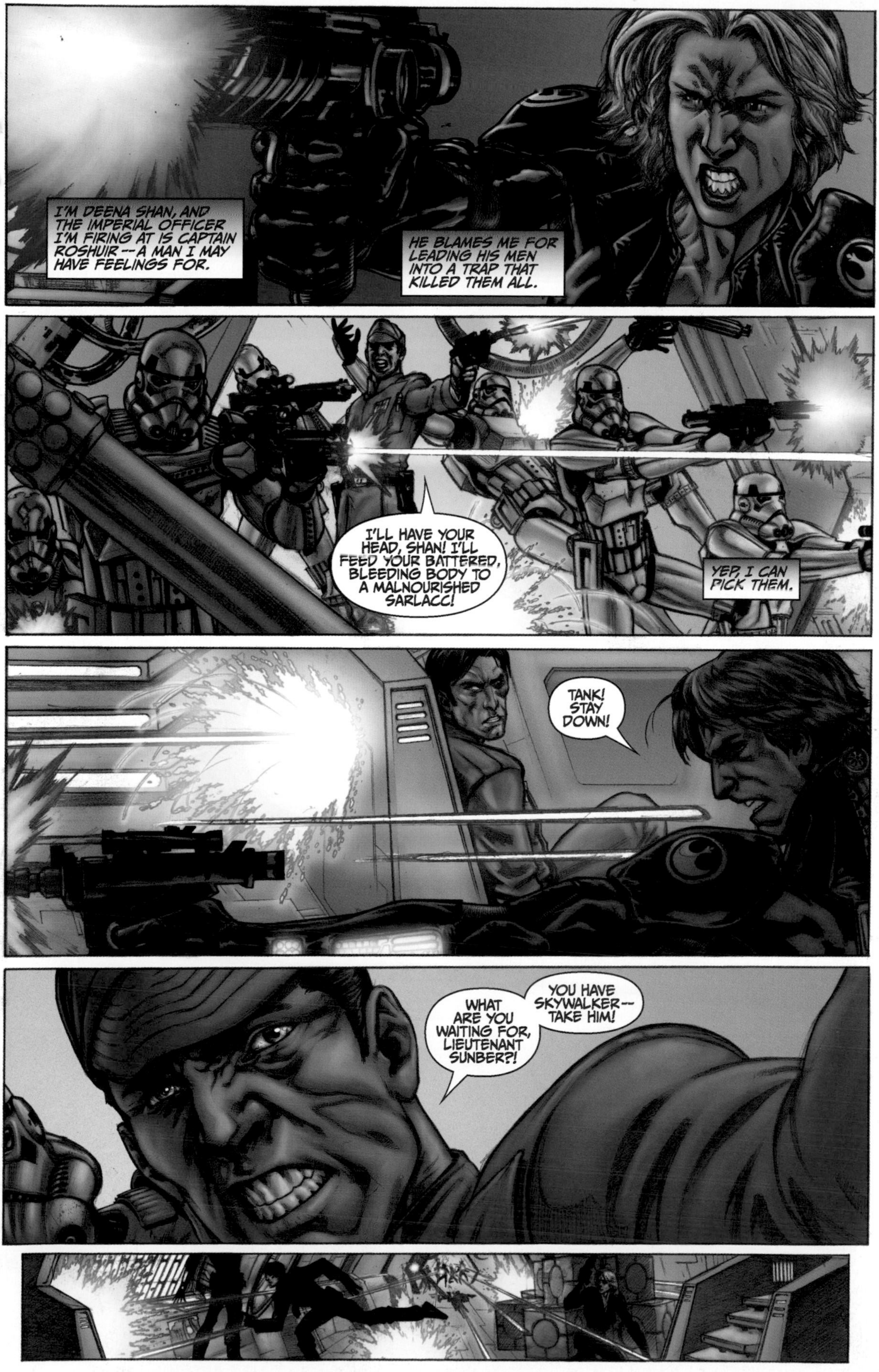
I'M DEENA SHAN, AND THE IMPERIAL OFFICER I'M FIRING AT IS CAPTAIN ROSHUIR -- A MAN I MAY HAVE FEELINGS FOR.
HE BLAMES ME FOR LEADING HIS MEN INTO A TRAP THAT KILLED THEM ALL.
I'LL HAVE YOUR HEAD, SHAN! I'LL FEED YOUR BATTERED, BLEEDING BODY TO A MALNOURISHED SARLACC!
YEP, I CAN PICK THEM.
TANK! STAY DOWN!
WHAT ARE YOU WAITING FOR, LIEUTENANT SUNBER?!
YOU HAVE SKYWALKER-- TAKE HIM!

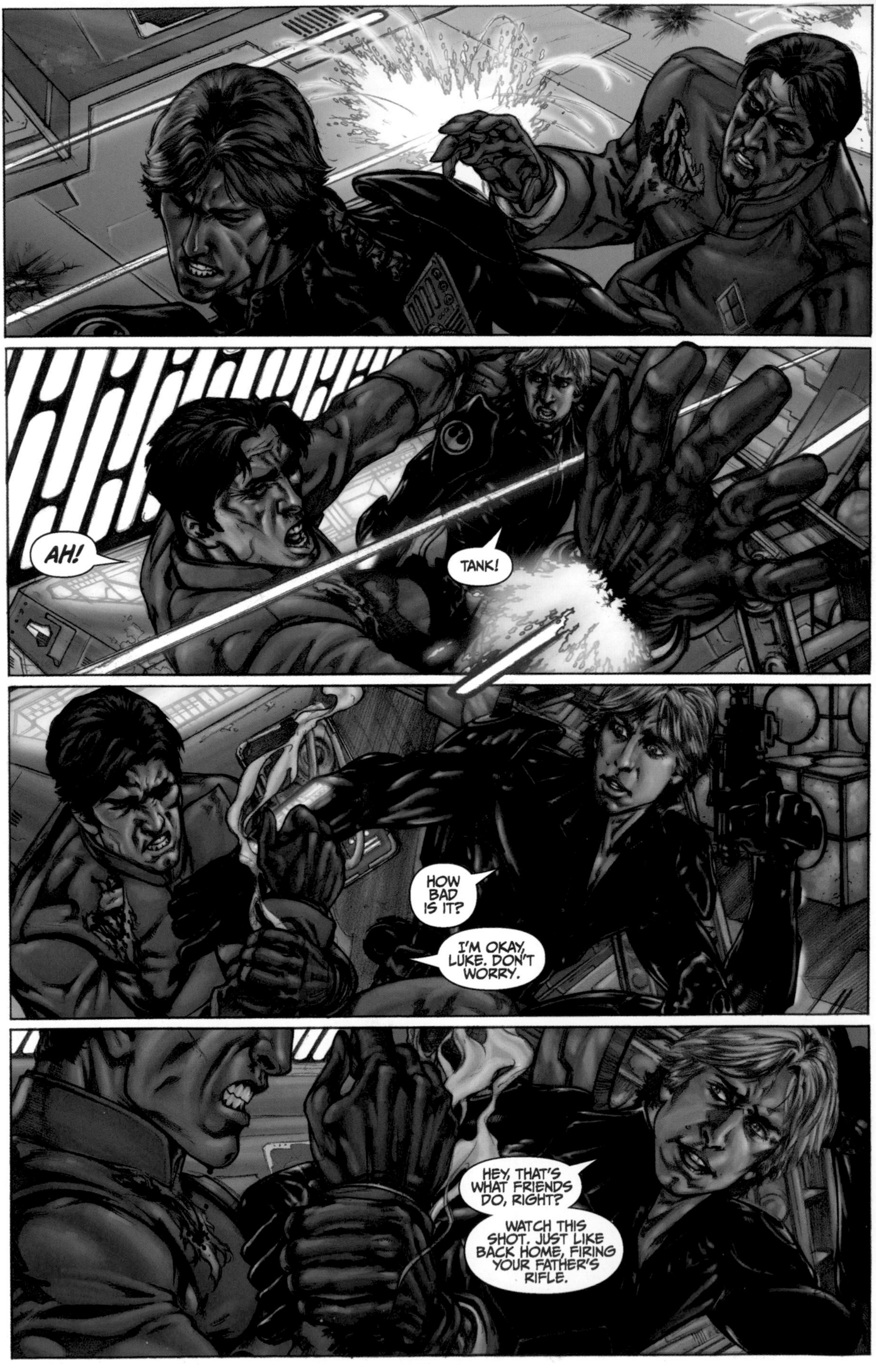
AH!
TANK!
HOW BAD IS IT?
I'M OKAY, LUKE. DON'T WORRY.
HEY, THAT'S WHAT FRIENDS DO, RIGHT?
WATCH THIS SHOT. JUST LIKE BACK HOME, FIRING YOUR FATHER'S RIFLE.

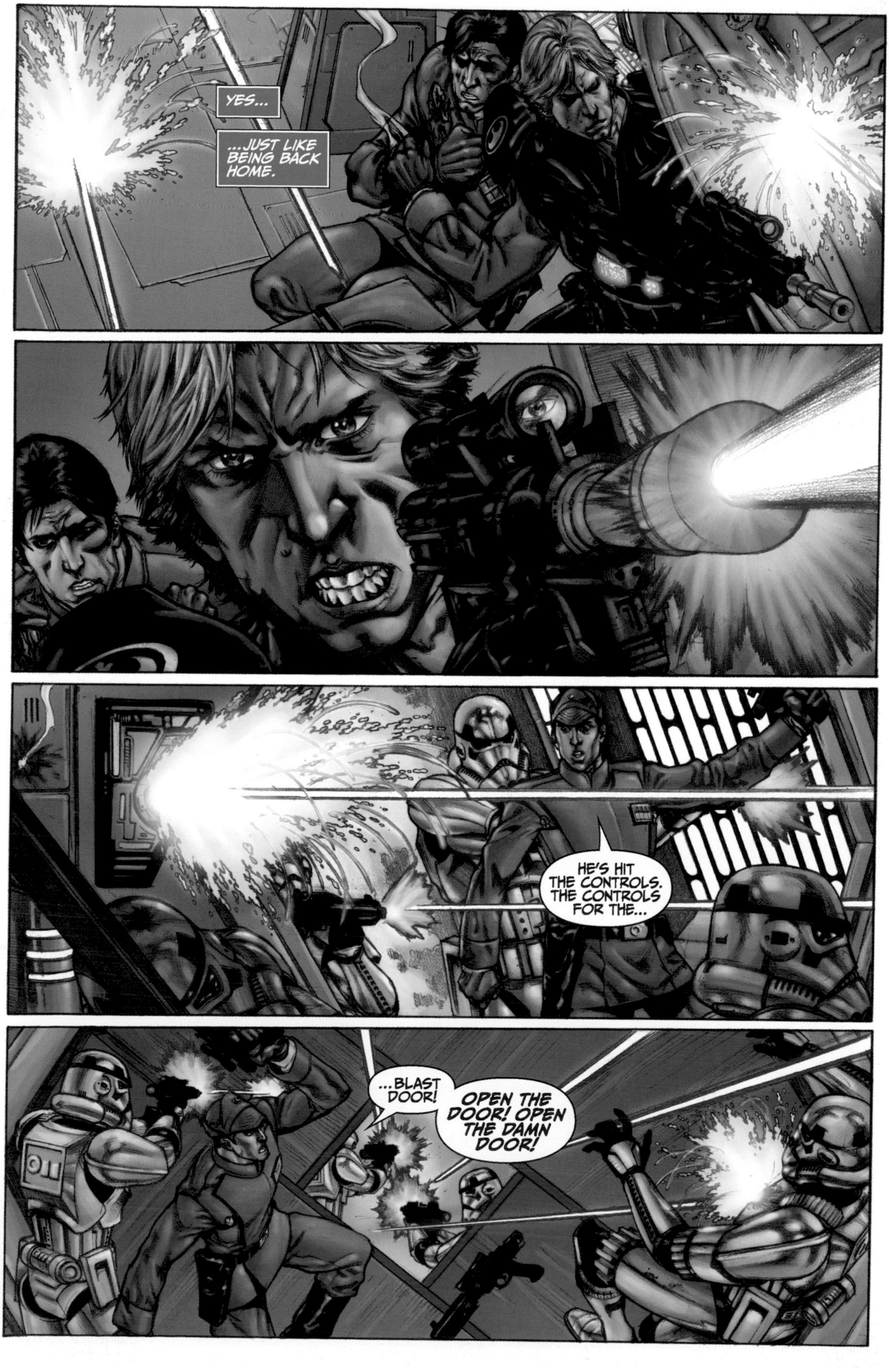
YES...
...JUST LIKE BEING BACK HOME.
HE'S HIT THE CONTROLS. THE CONTROLS FOR THE...
...BLAST DOOR!
OPEN THE DOOR! OPEN THE DAMN DOOR!

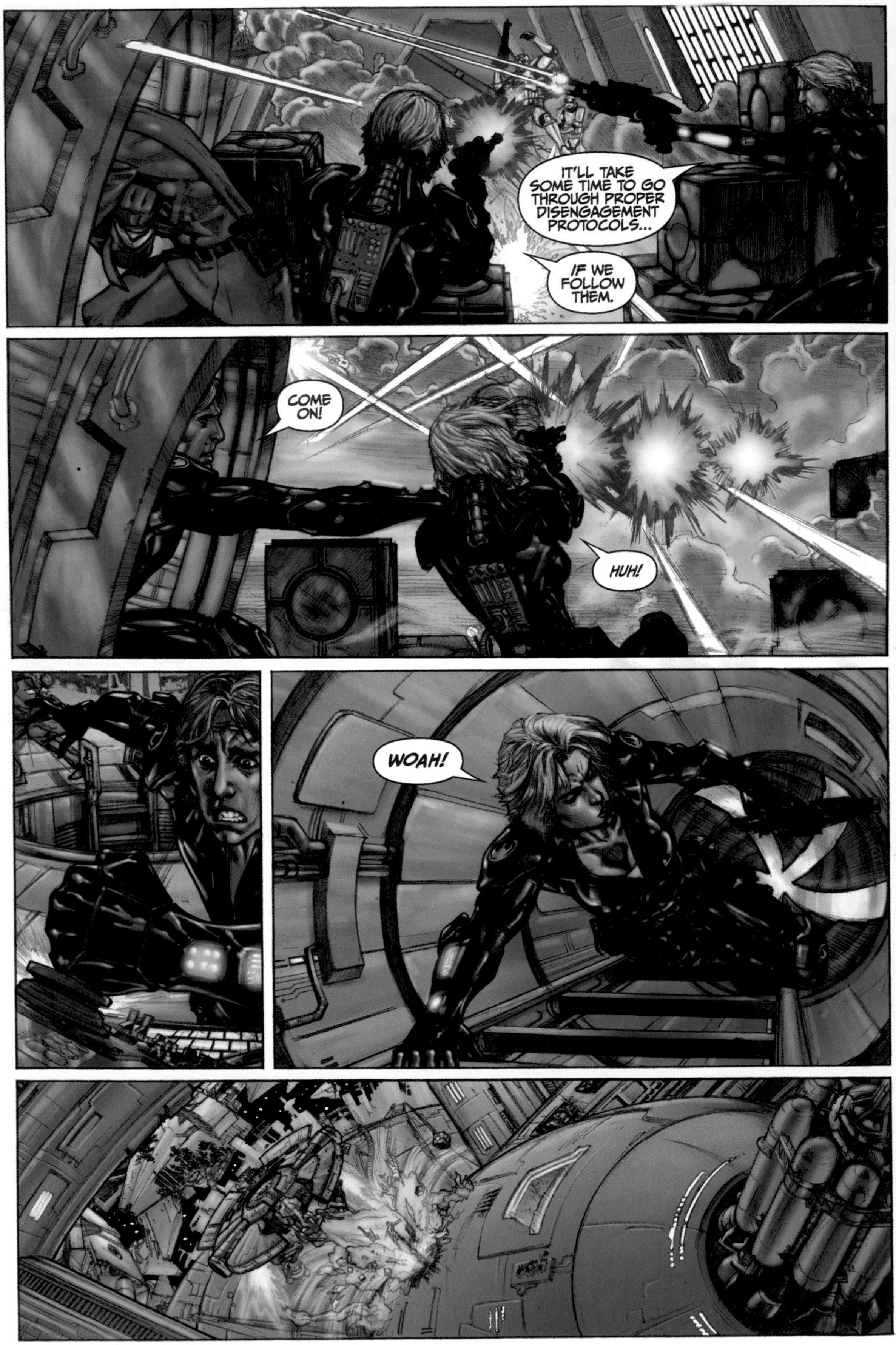

IT'LL TAKE SOME TIME TO GO THROUGH PROPER DISENGAGEMENT PROTOCOLS...
IF WE FOLLOW THEM.
COME ON!
HUH!
WOAH!

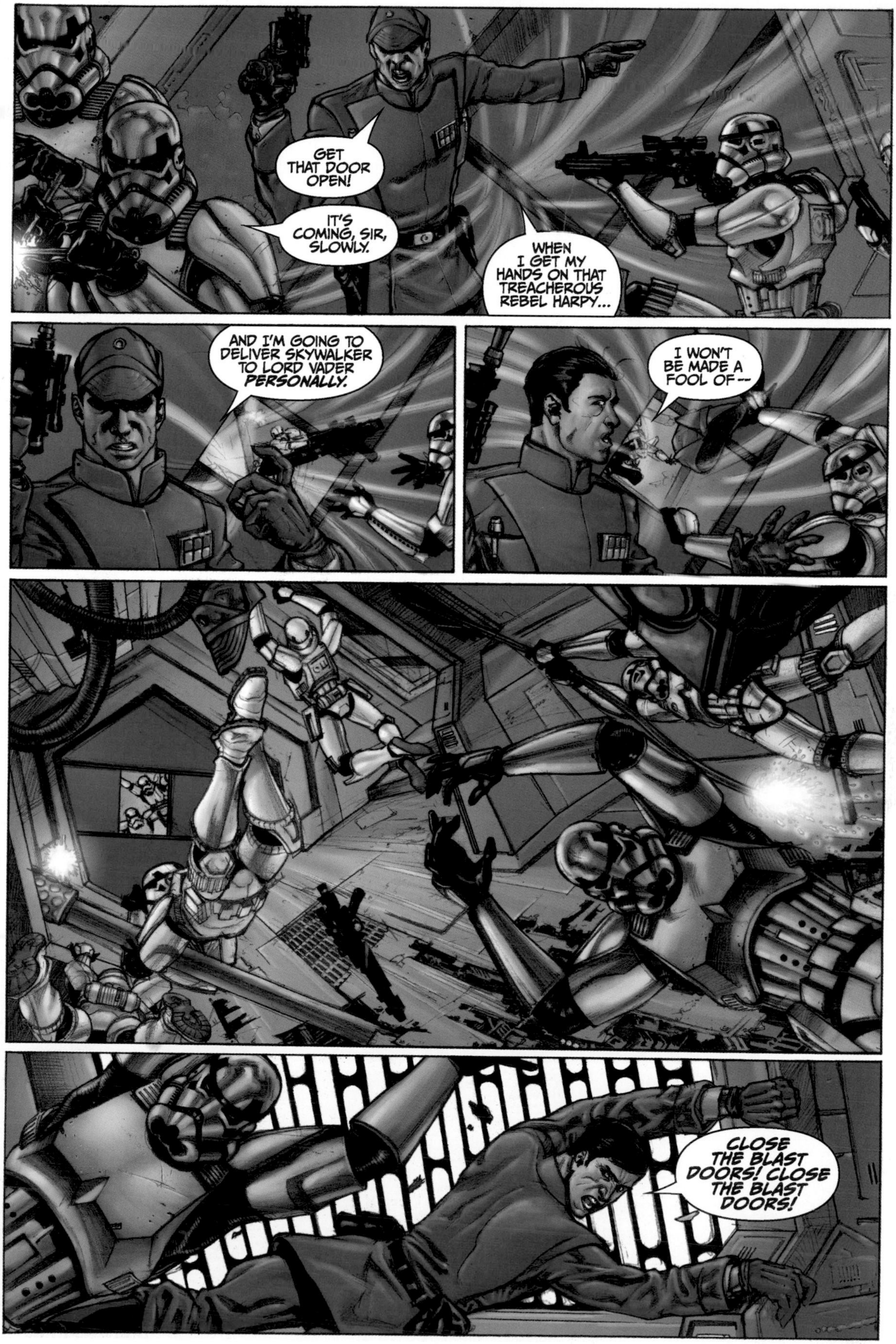
GET THAT DOOR OPEN!
IT'S COMING, SIR, SLOWLY.
WHEN I GET MY HANDS ON THAT TREACHEROUS REBEL HARPY...
AND I'M GOING TO DELIVER SKYWALKER TO LORD VADER *PERSONALLY.*
I WON'T BE MADE A FOOL OF--
CLOSE THE BLAST DOORS! CLOSE THE BLAST DOORS!

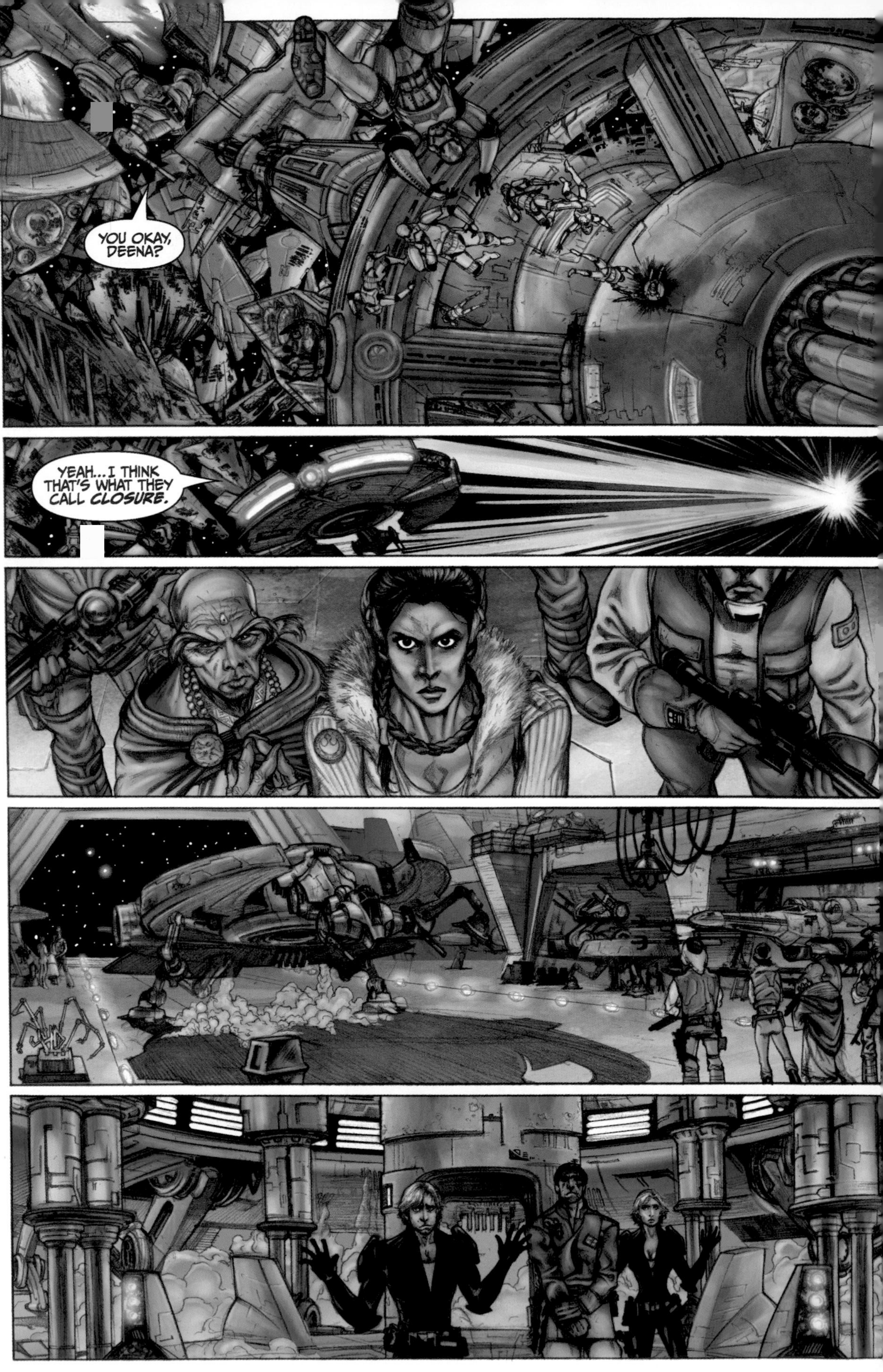
YOU OKAY, DEENA?
YEAH... I THINK THAT'S WHAT THEY CALL *CLOSURE*.

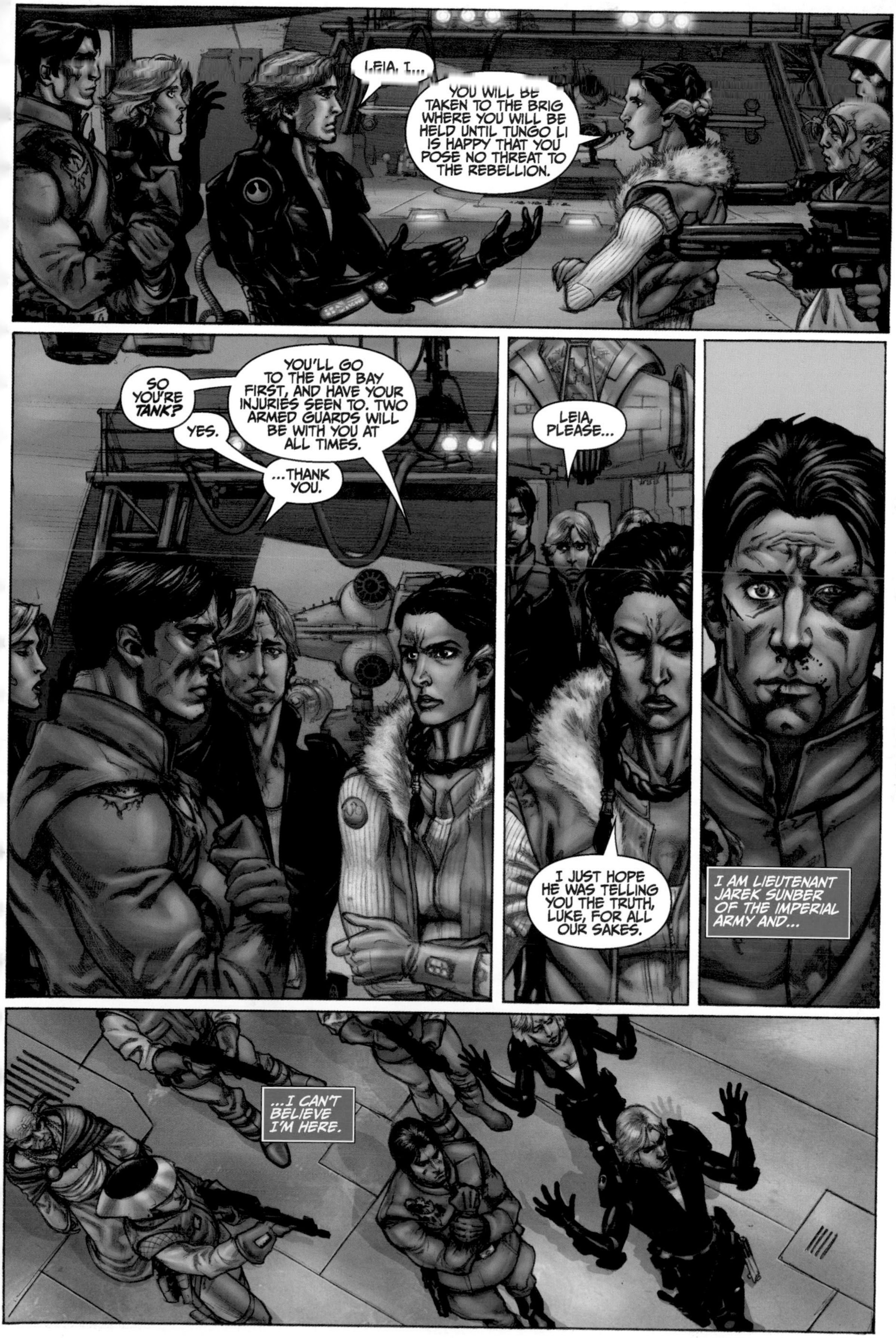
LEIA, I...
YOU WILL BE TAKEN TO THE BRIG WHERE YOU WILL BE HELD UNTIL TUNGO LI IS HAPPY THAT YOU POSE NO THREAT TO THE REBELLION.
SO YOU'RE TANK?
YES.
YOU'LL GO TO THE MED BAY FIRST, AND HAVE YOUR INJURIES SEEN TO. TWO ARMED GUARDS WILL BE WITH YOU AT ALL TIMES.
...THANK YOU.
LEIA, PLEASE...
I JUST HOPE HE WAS TELLING YOU THE TRUTH, LUKE, FOR ALL OUR SAKES.
I AM LIEUTENANT JAREK SUNBER OF THE IMPERIAL ARMY AND...
...I CAN'T BELIEVE I'M HERE.

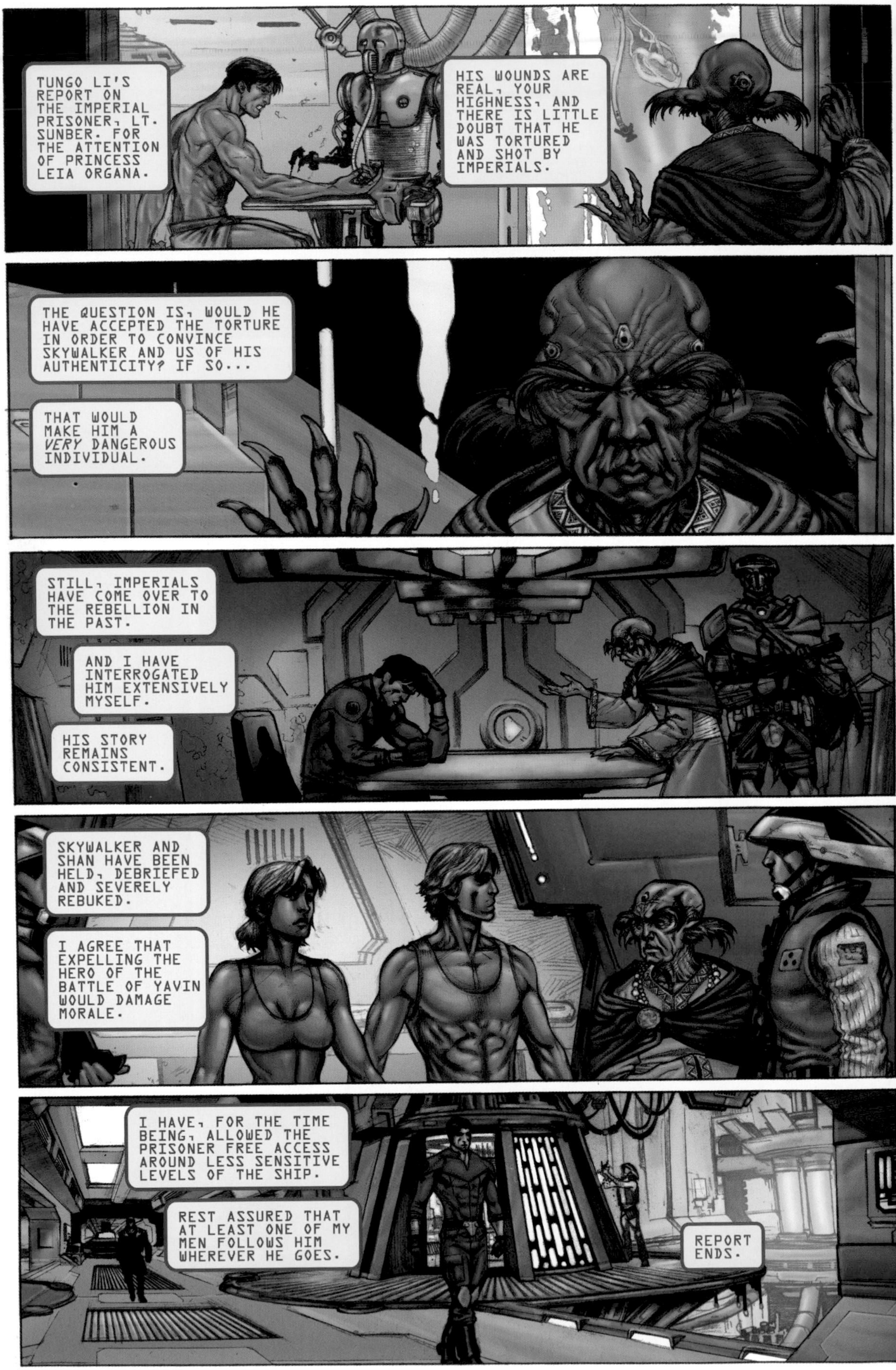
TUNGO LI'S REPORT ON THE IMPERIAL PRISONER, LT. SUNBER. FOR THE ATTENTION OF PRINCESS LEIA ORGANA.
HIS WOUNDS ARE REAL, YOUR HIGHNESS, AND THERE IS LITTLE DOUBT THAT HE WAS TORTURED AND SHOT BY IMPERIALS.
THE QUESTION IS, WOULD HE HAVE ACCEPTED THE TORTURE IN ORDER TO CONVINCE SKYWALKER AND US OF HIS AUTHENTICITY? IF SO...
THAT WOULD MAKE HIM A *VERY* DANGEROUS INDIVIDUAL.
STILL, IMPERIALS HAVE COME OVER TO THE REBELLION IN THE PAST.
AND I HAVE INTERROGATED HIM EXTENSIVELY MYSELF.
HIS STORY REMAINS CONSISTENT.
SKYWALKER AND SHAN HAVE BEEN HELD, DEBRIEFED AND SEVERELY REBUKED.
I AGREE THAT EXPELLING THE HERO OF THE BATTLE OF YAVIN WOULD DAMAGE MORALE.
I HAVE, FOR THE TIME BEING, ALLOWED THE PRISONER FREE ACCESS AROUND LESS SENSITIVE LEVELS OF THE SHIP.
REST ASSURED THAT AT LEAST ONE OF MY MEN FOLLOWS HIM WHEREVER HE GOES.
REPORT ENDS.

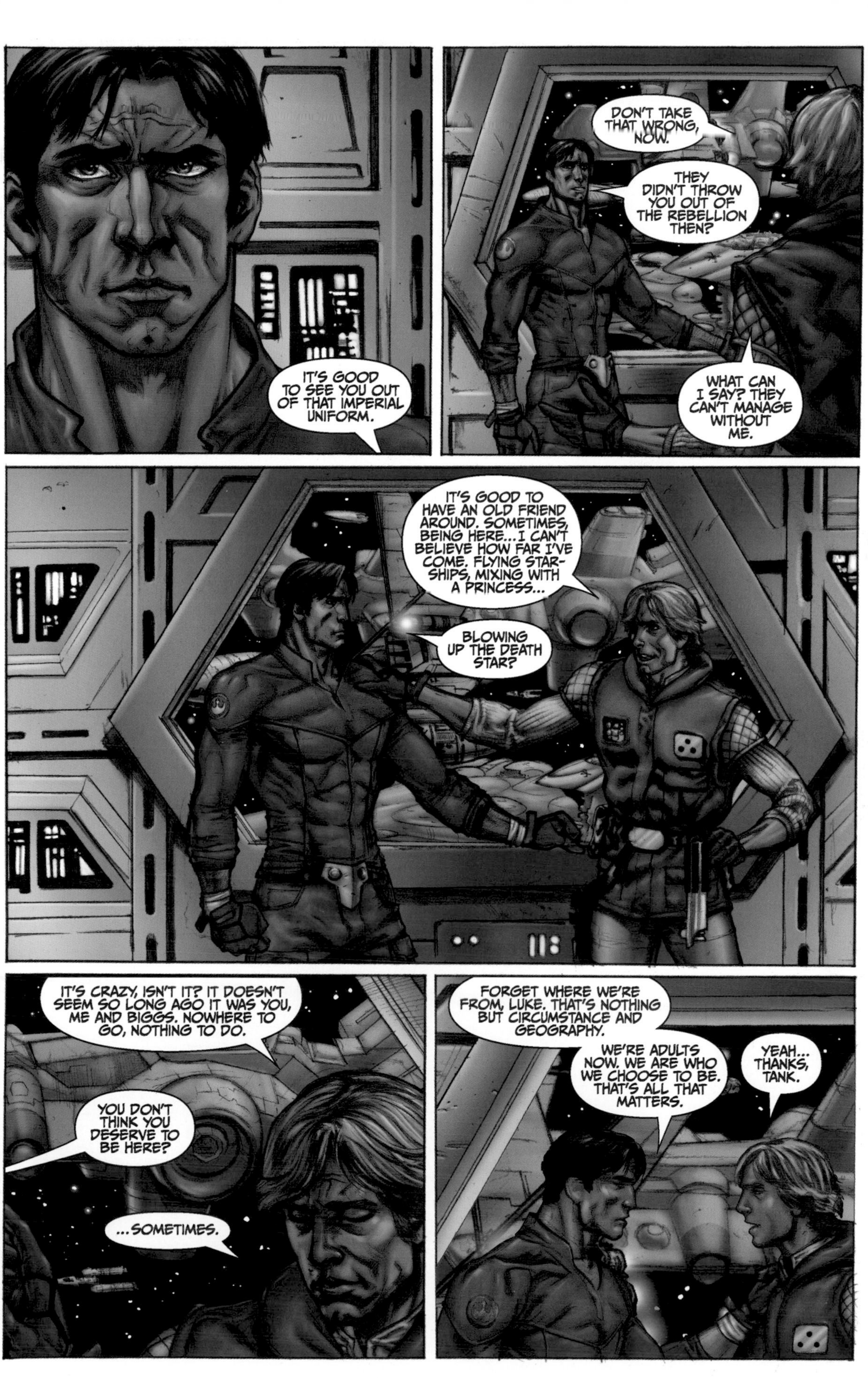
IT'S GOOD TO SEE YOU OUT OF THAT IMPERIAL UNIFORM.
DON'T TAKE THAT WRONG, NOW.
THEY DIDN'T THROW YOU OUT OF THE REBELLION THEN?
WHAT CAN I SAY? THEY CAN'T MANAGE WITHOUT ME.
IT'S GOOD TO HAVE AN OLD FRIEND AROUND. SOMETIMES, BEING HERE... I CAN'T BELIEVE HOW FAR I'VE COME. FLYING STAR-SHIPS, MIXING WITH A PRINCESS...
BLOWING UP THE DEATH STAR?
IT'S CRAZY, ISN'T IT? IT DOESN'T SEEM SO LONG AGO IT WAS YOU, ME AND BIGGS. NOWHERE TO GO, NOTHING TO DO.
YOU DON'T THINK YOU DESERVE TO BE HERE?
...SOMETIMES.
FORGET WHERE WE'RE FROM, LUKE. THAT'S NOTHING BUT CIRCUMSTANCE AND GEOGRAPHY.
WE'RE ADULTS NOW. WE ARE WHO WE CHOOSE TO BE. THAT'S ALL THAT MATTERS.
YEAH... THANKS, TANK.

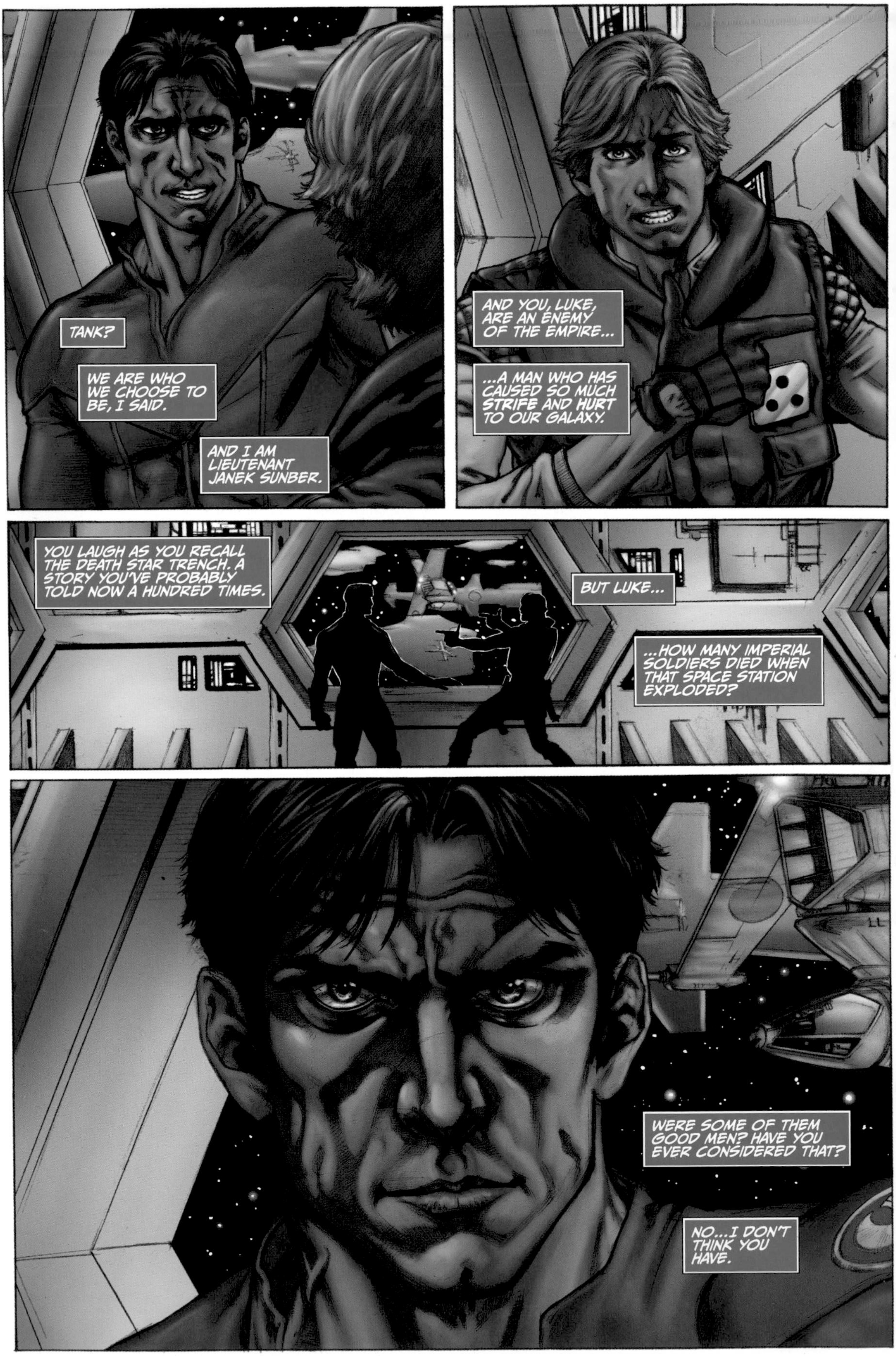
TANK?
WE ARE WHO WE CHOOSE TO BE, I SAID.
AND I AM LIEUTENANT JANEK SUNBER.
AND YOU, LUKE, ARE AN ENEMY OF THE EMPIRE...
...A MAN WHO HAS CAUSED SO MUCH STRIFE AND HURT TO OUR GALAXY.
YOU LAUGH AS YOU RECALL THE DEATH STAR TRENCH. A STORY YOU'VE PROBABLY TOLD NOW A HUNDRED TIMES.
BUT LUKE...
...HOW MANY IMPERIAL SOLDIERS DIED WHEN THAT SPACE STATION EXPLODED?
WERE SOME OF THEM GOOD MEN? HAVE YOU EVER CONSIDERED THAT?
NO...I DON'T THINK YOU HAVE.

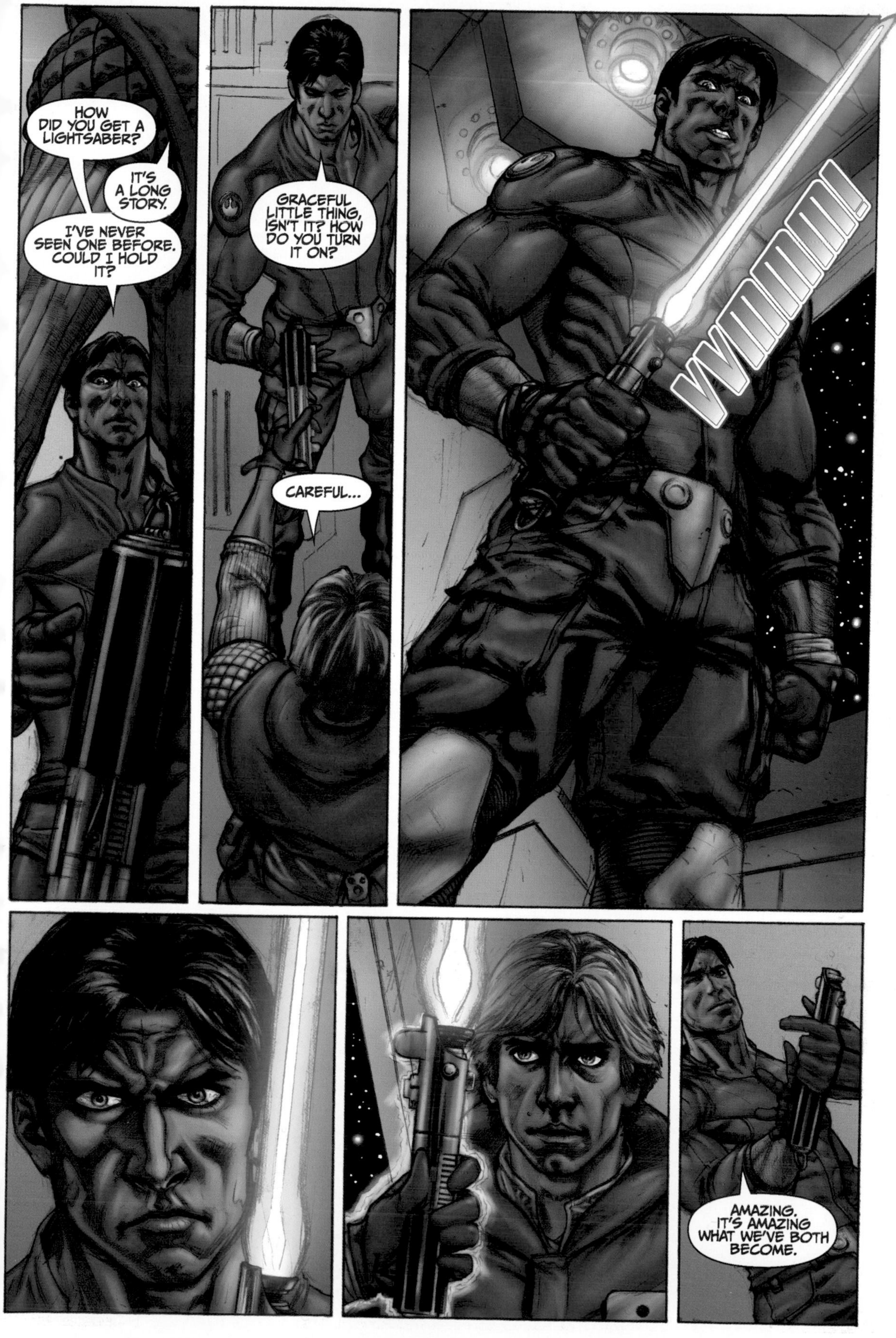
HOW DID YOU GET A LIGHTSABER?
IT'S A LONG STORY.
I'VE NEVER SEEN ONE BEFORE. COULD I HOLD IT?
GRACEFUL LITTLE THING, ISN'T IT? HOW DO YOU TURN IT ON?
CAREFUL...
VVMMMM!
AMAZING. IT'S AMAZING WHAT WE'VE BOTH BECOME.

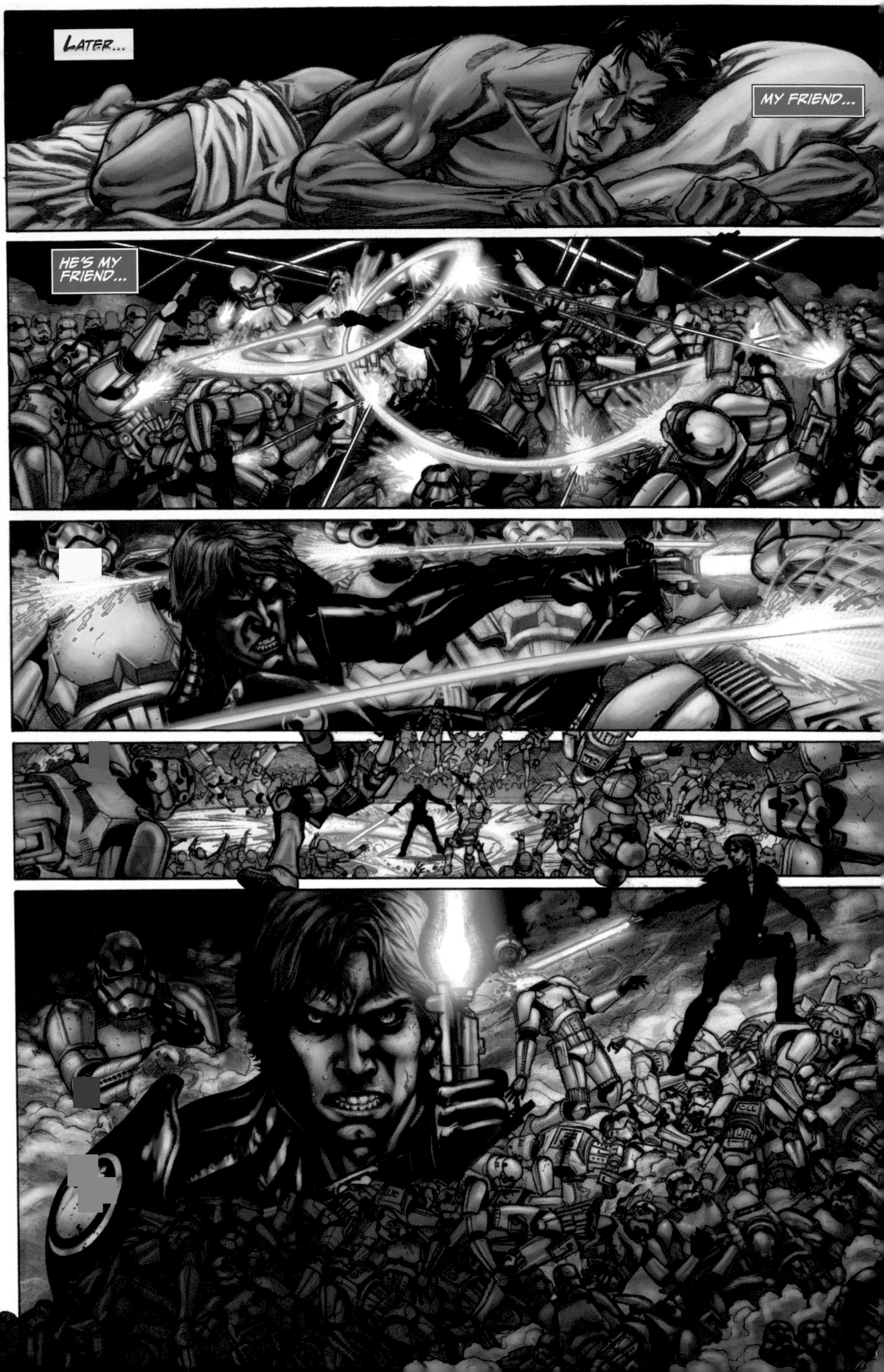
LATER...
MY FRIEND...
HE'S MY FRIEND...

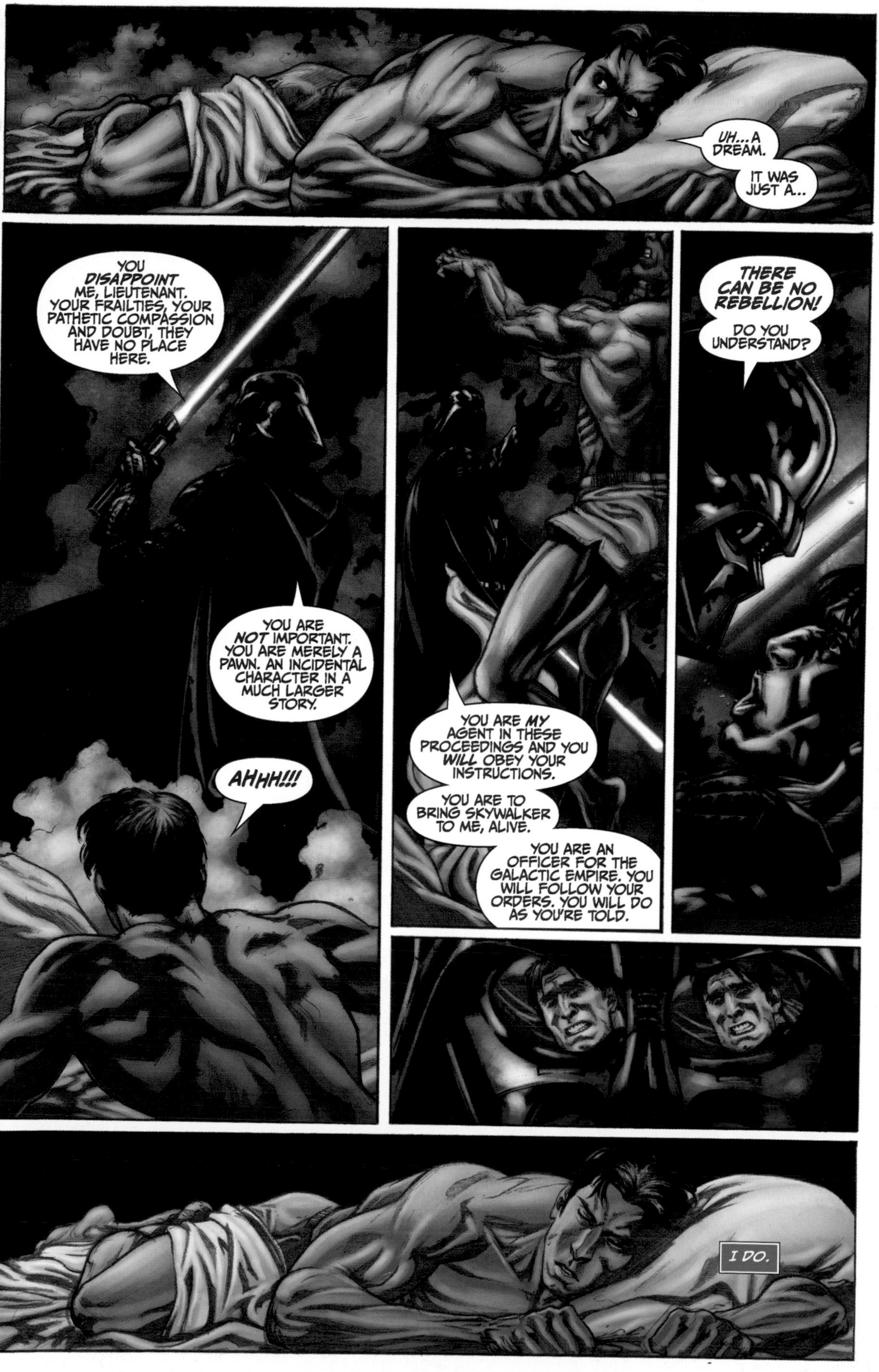
UH...A DREAM.
IT WAS JUST A...
YOU DISAPPOINT ME, LIEUTENANT. YOUR FRAILTIES, YOUR PATHETIC COMPASSION AND DOUBT, THEY HAVE NO PLACE HERE.
YOU ARE NOT IMPORTANT. YOU ARE MERELY A PAWN. AN INCIDENTAL CHARACTER IN A MUCH LARGER STORY.
AHHH!!!
YOU ARE MY AGENT IN THESE PROCEEDINGS AND YOU WILL OBEY YOUR INSTRUCTIONS.
YOU ARE TO BRING SKYWALKER TO ME, ALIVE.
YOU ARE AN OFFICER FOR THE GALACTIC EMPIRE. YOU WILL FOLLOW YOUR ORDERS. YOU WILL DO AS YOU'RE TOLD.
THERE CAN BE NO REBELLION!
DO YOU UNDERSTAND?
I DO.

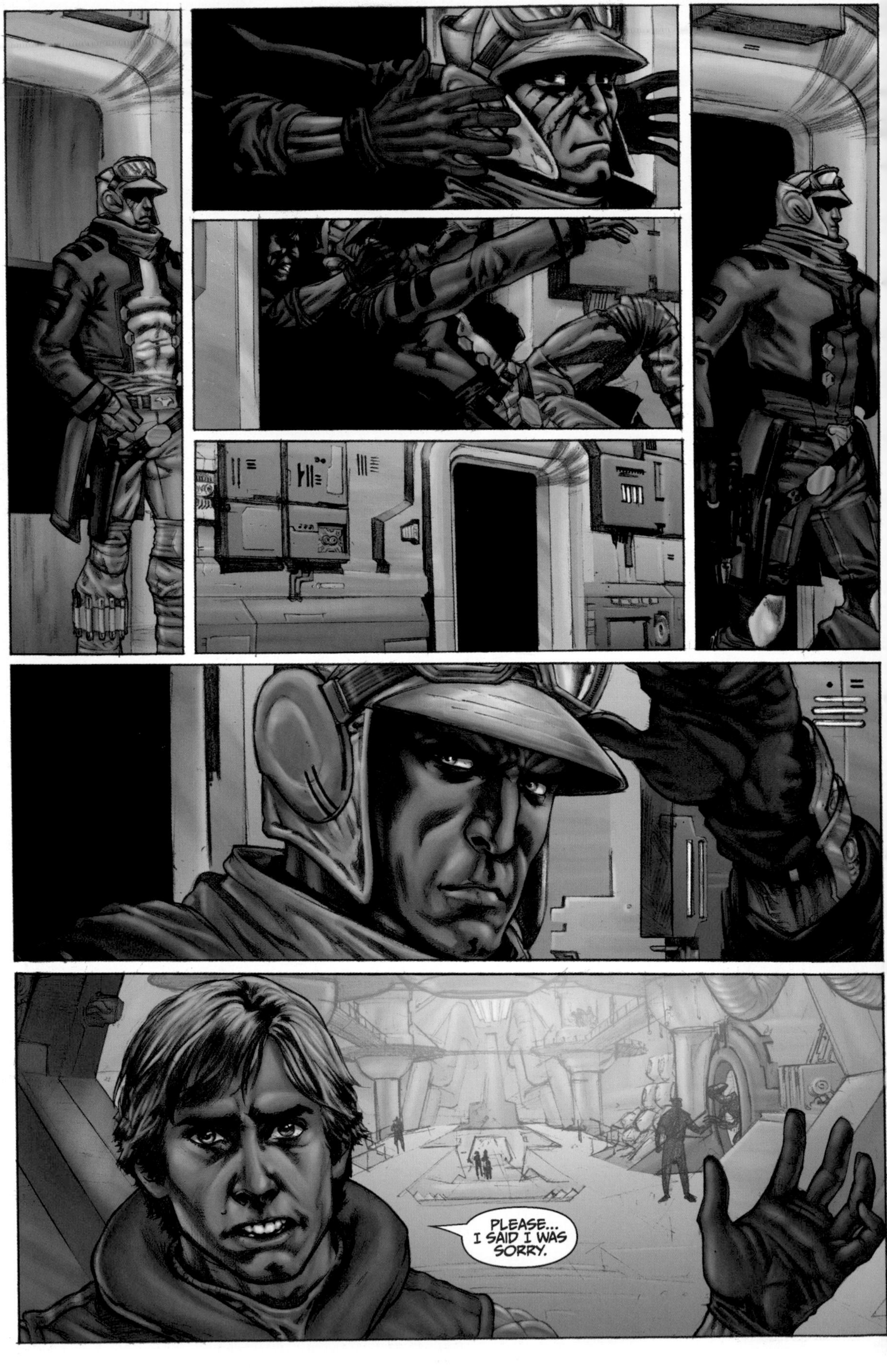
PLEASE... I SAID I WAS SORRY.

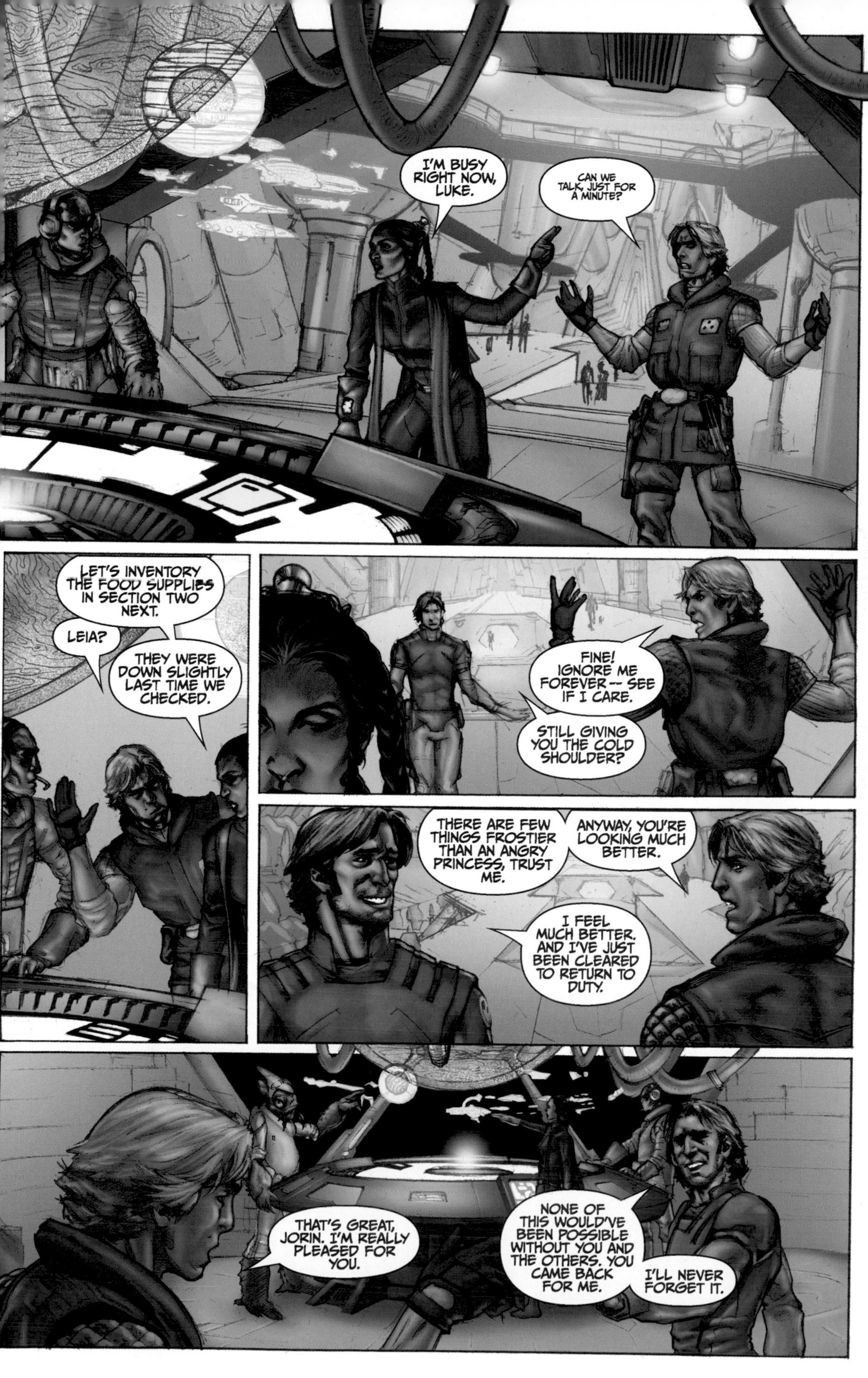
I'M BUSY RIGHT NOW, LUKE.
CAN WE TALK, JUST FOR A MINUTE?
LET'S INVENTORY THE FOOD SUPPLIES IN SECTION TWO NEXT.
LEIA?
THEY WERE DOWN SLIGHTLY LAST TIME WE CHECKED.
FINE! IGNORE ME FOREVER -- SEE IF I CARE.
STILL GIVING YOU THE COLD SHOULDER?
THERE ARE FEW THINGS FROSTIER THAN AN ANGRY PRINCESS, TRUST ME.
ANYWAY, YOU'RE LOOKING MUCH BETTER.
I FEEL MUCH BETTER. AND I'VE JUST BEEN CLEARED TO RETURN TO DUTY.
THAT'S GREAT, JORIN. I'M REALLY PLEASED FOR YOU.
NONE OF THIS WOULD'VE BEEN POSSIBLE WITHOUT YOU AND THE OTHERS. YOU CAME BACK FOR ME.
I'LL NEVER FORGET IT.

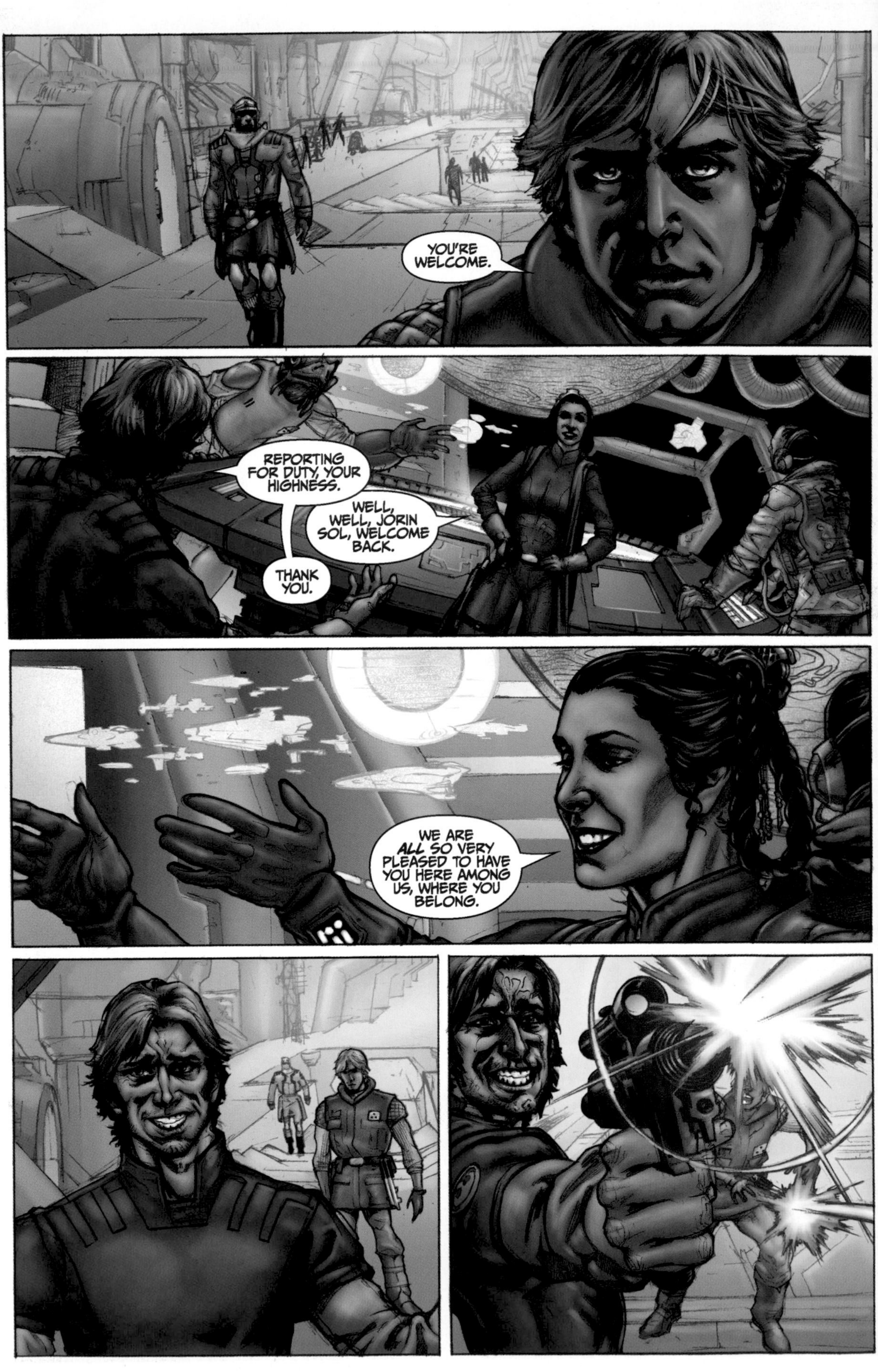
YOU'RE WELCOME.
REPORTING FOR DUTY, YOUR HIGHNESS.
WELL, WELL, JORIN SOL, WELCOME BACK.
THANK YOU.
WE ARE ALL SO VERY PLEASED TO HAVE YOU HERE AMONG US, WHERE YOU BELONG.

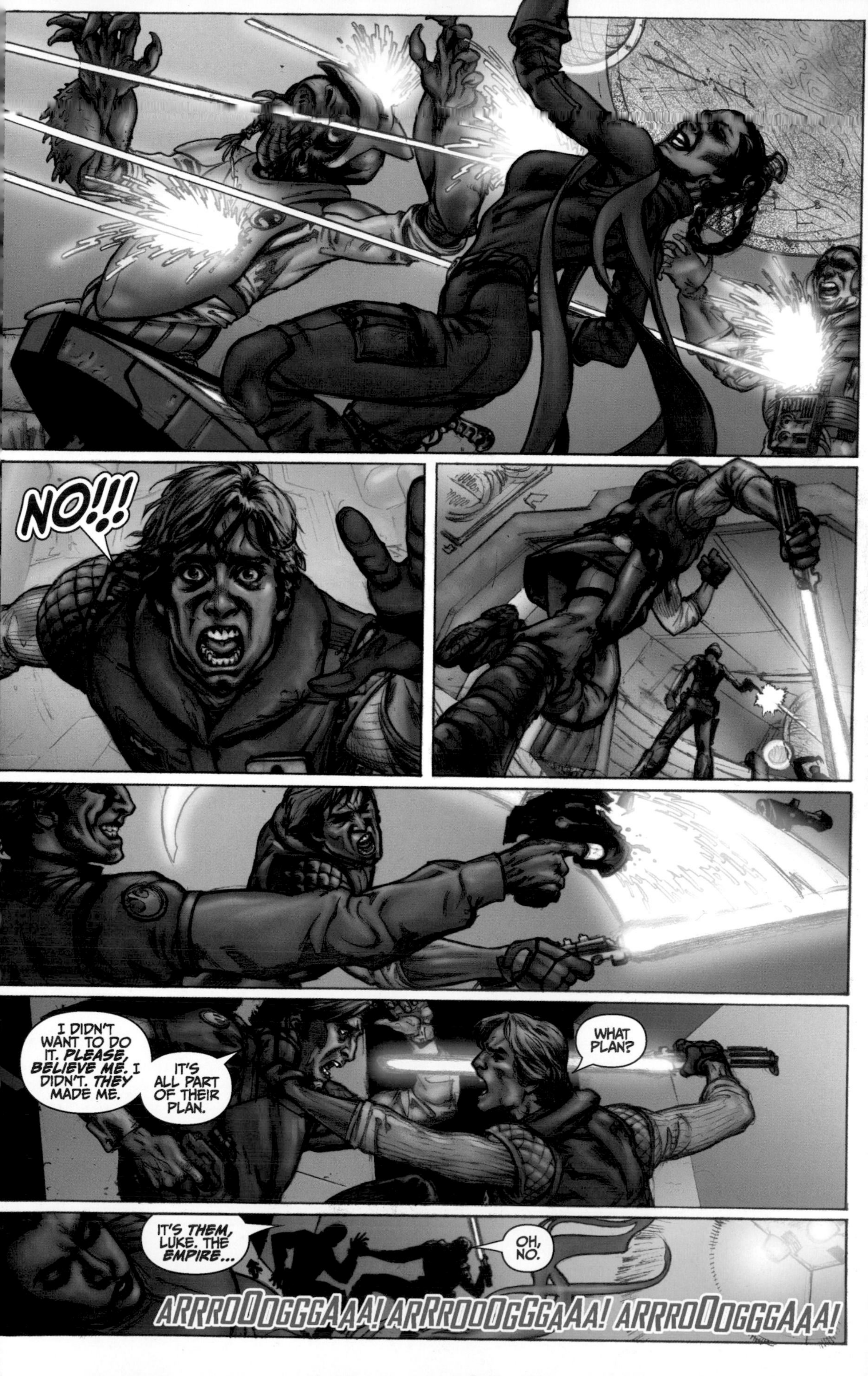
NO!!!
I DIDN'T WANT TO DO IT. *PLEASE, BELIEVE ME.* I DIDN'T. *THEY* MADE ME.
IT'S ALL PART OF THEIR PLAN.
WHAT PLAN?
IT'S *THEM,* LUKE. THE *EMPIRE...*
OH, NO.
ARRROOOGGGAAA! ARRROOOGGGAAA! ARRROOOGGGAAA!

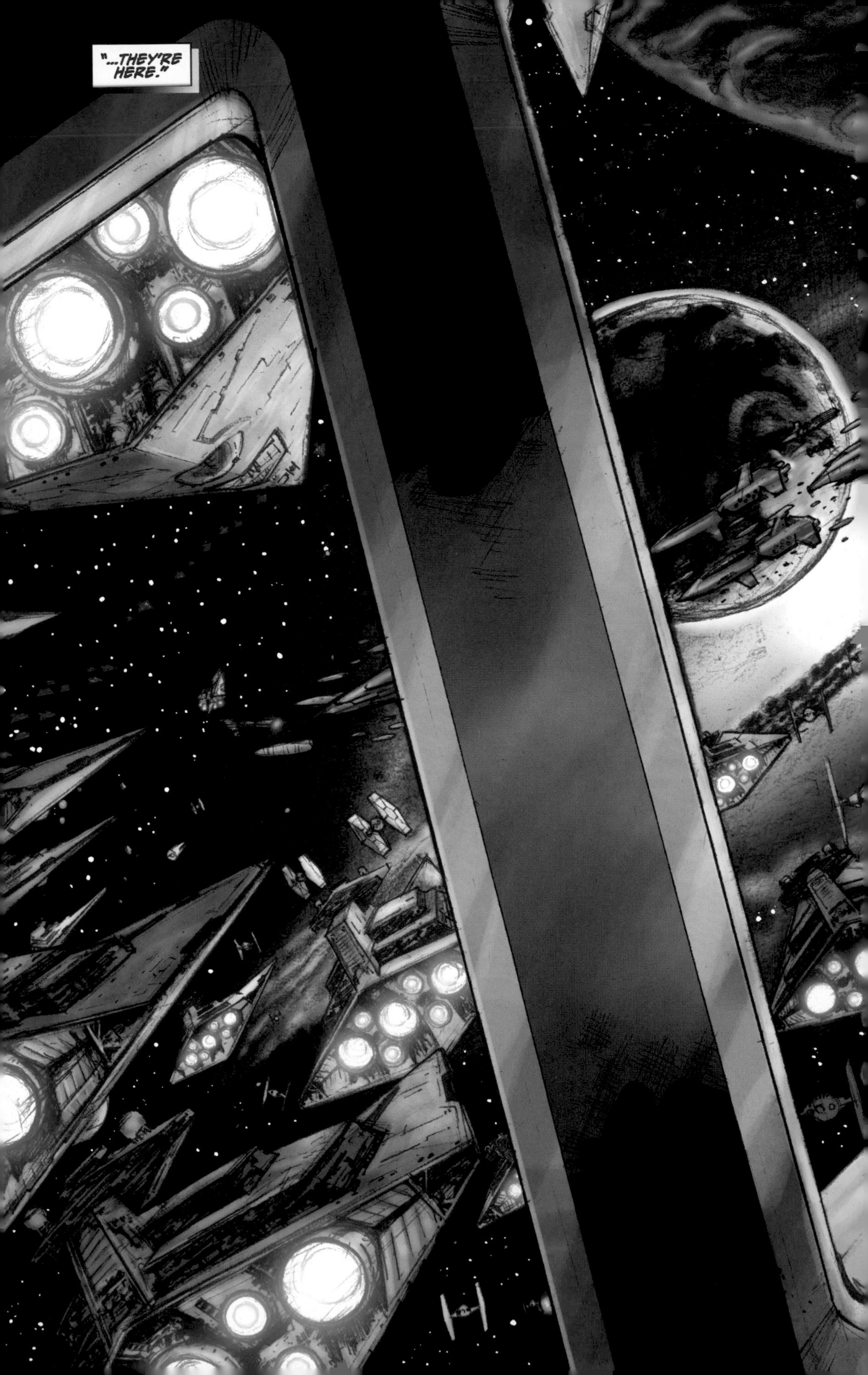
"...THEY'RE HERE."

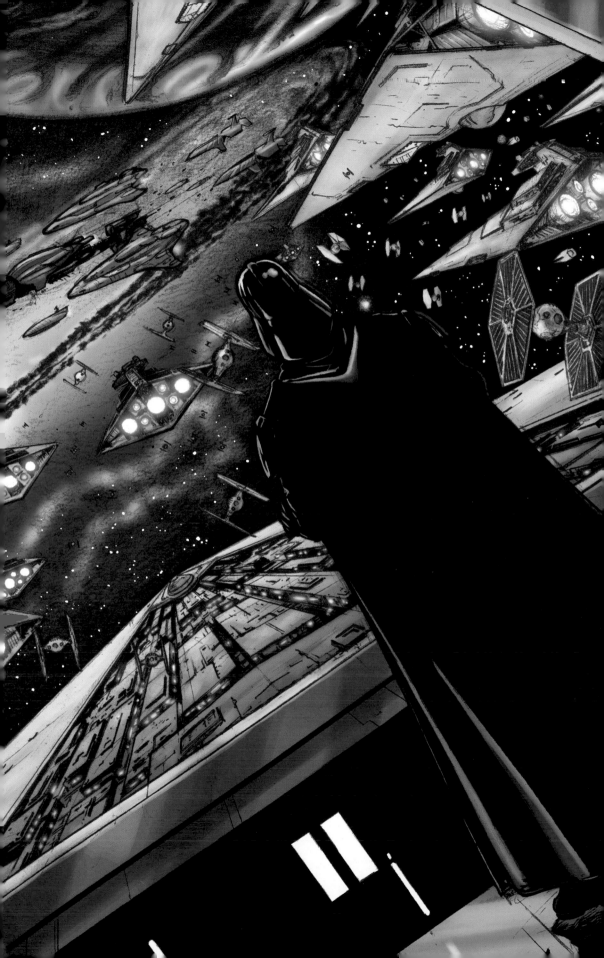

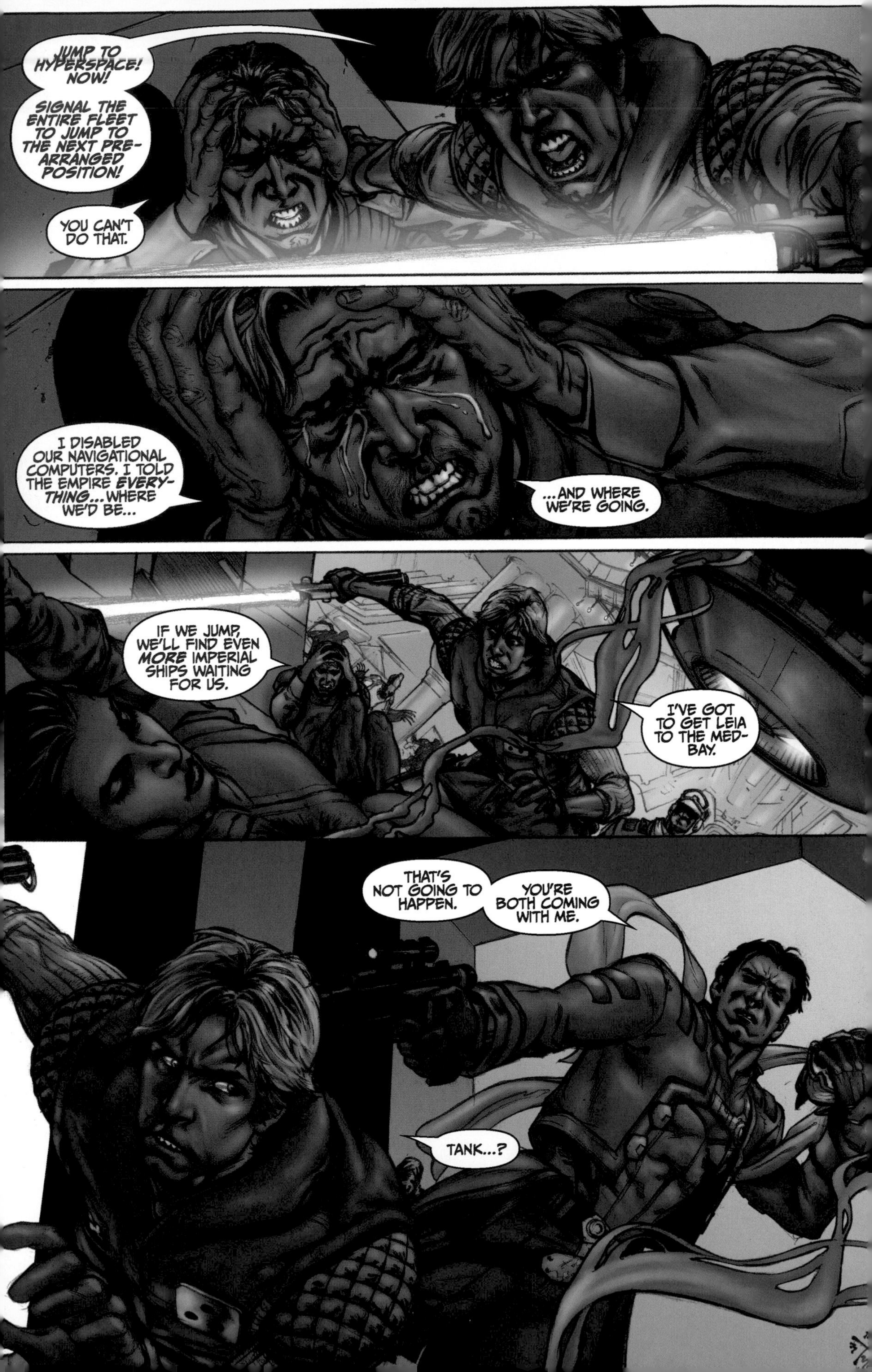
JUMP TO HYPERSPACE! NOW!
SIGNAL THE ENTIRE FLEET TO JUMP TO THE NEXT PRE-ARRANGED POSITION!
YOU CAN'T DO THAT.
I DISABLED OUR NAVIGATIONAL COMPUTERS. I TOLD THE EMPIRE *EVERYTHING*... WHERE WE'D BE...
...AND WHERE WE'RE GOING.
IF WE JUMP, WE'LL FIND EVEN *MORE* IMPERIAL SHIPS WAITING FOR US.
I'VE GOT TO GET LEIA TO THE MED-BAY.
THAT'S NOT GOING TO HAPPEN.
YOU'RE BOTH COMING WITH ME.
TANK...?

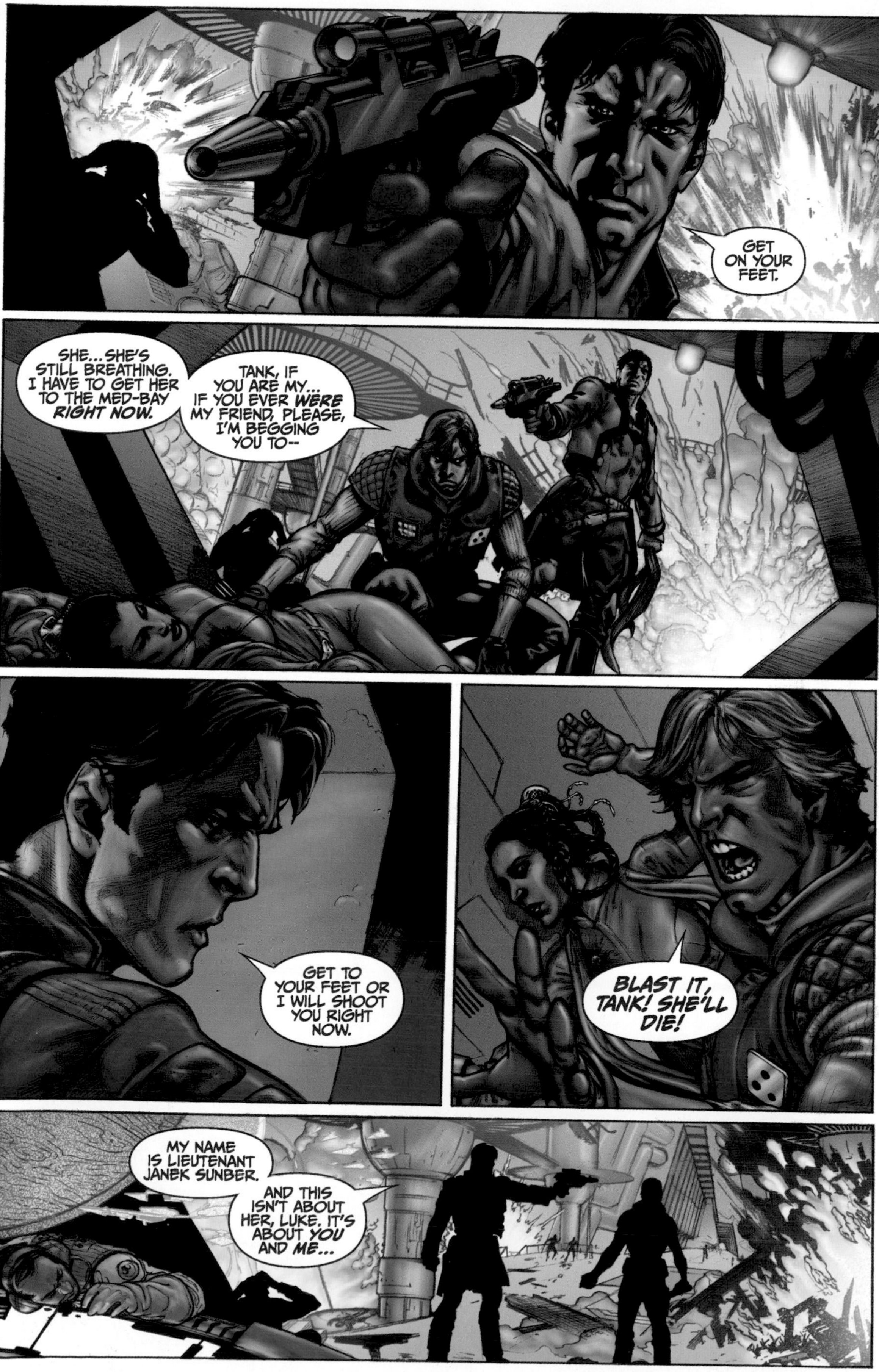
GET ON YOUR FEET.
SHE...SHE'S STILL BREATHING. I HAVE TO GET HER TO THE MED-BAY RIGHT NOW.
TANK, IF YOU ARE MY... IF YOU EVER WERE MY FRIEND, PLEASE, I'M BEGGING YOU TO--
GET TO YOUR FEET OR I WILL SHOOT YOU RIGHT NOW.
BLAST IT, TANK! SHE'LL DIE!
MY NAME IS LIEUTENANT JANEK SUNBER.
AND THIS ISN'T ABOUT HER, LUKE. IT'S ABOUT YOU AND ME...

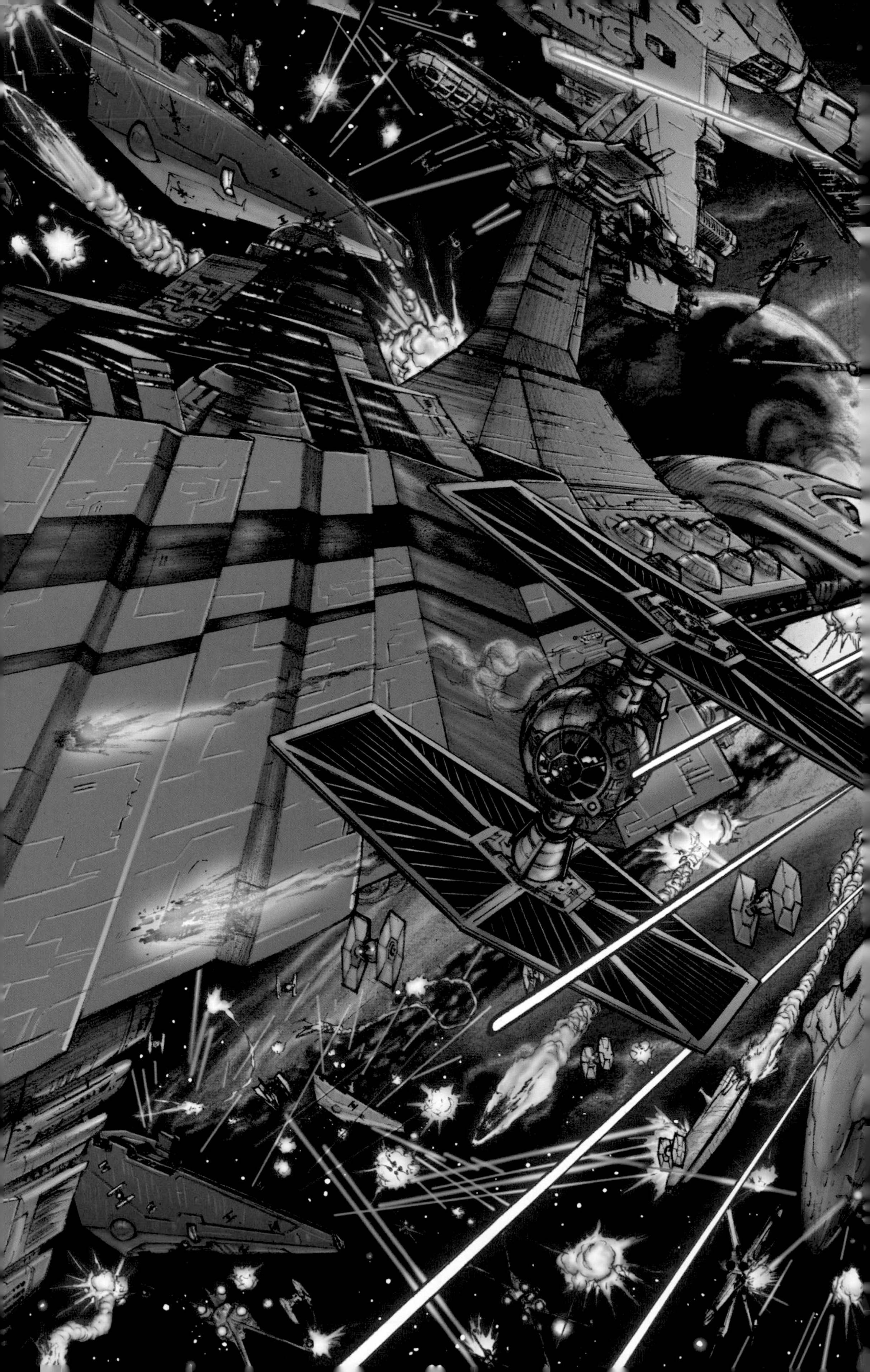

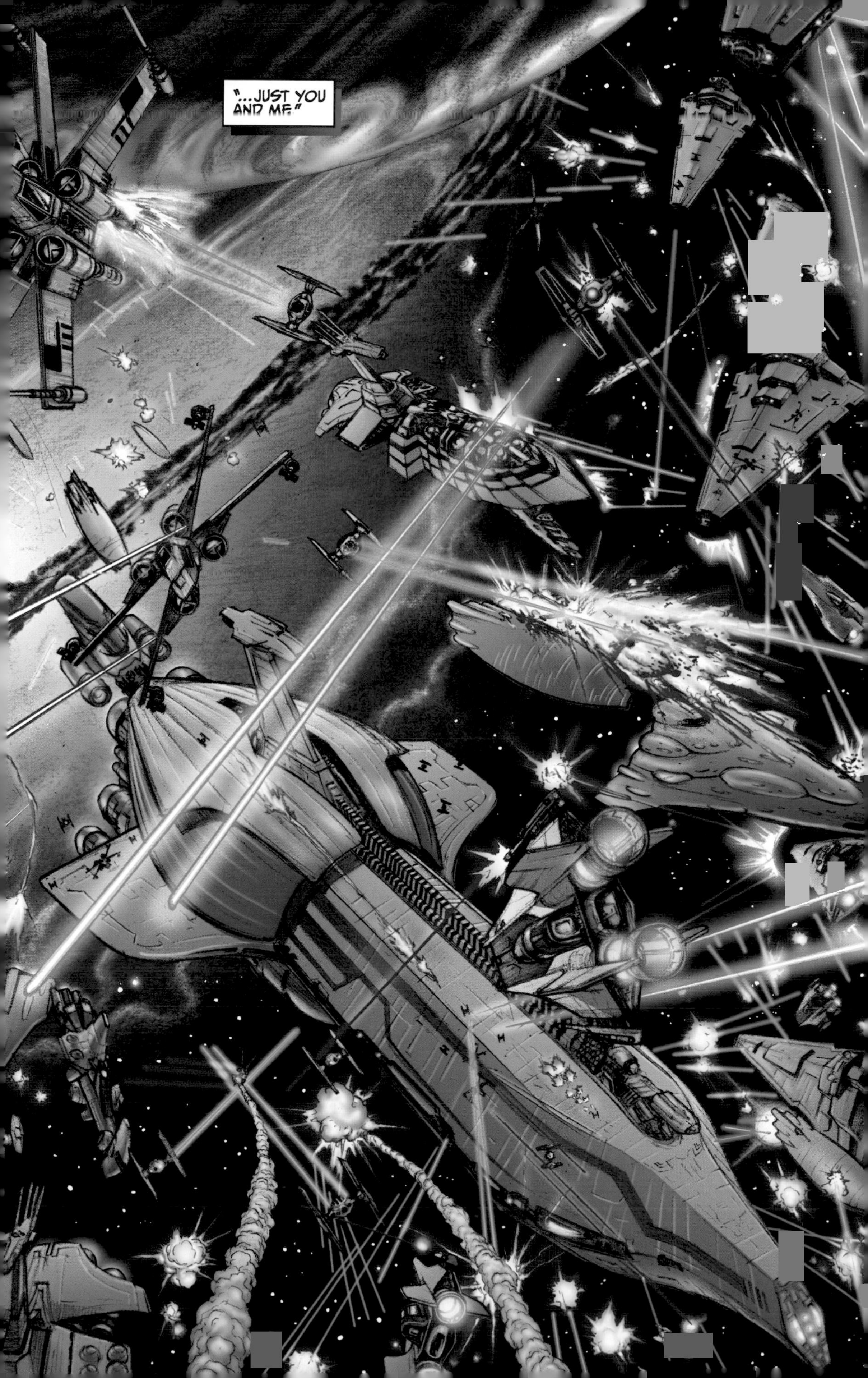
"...JUST YOU AND ME."

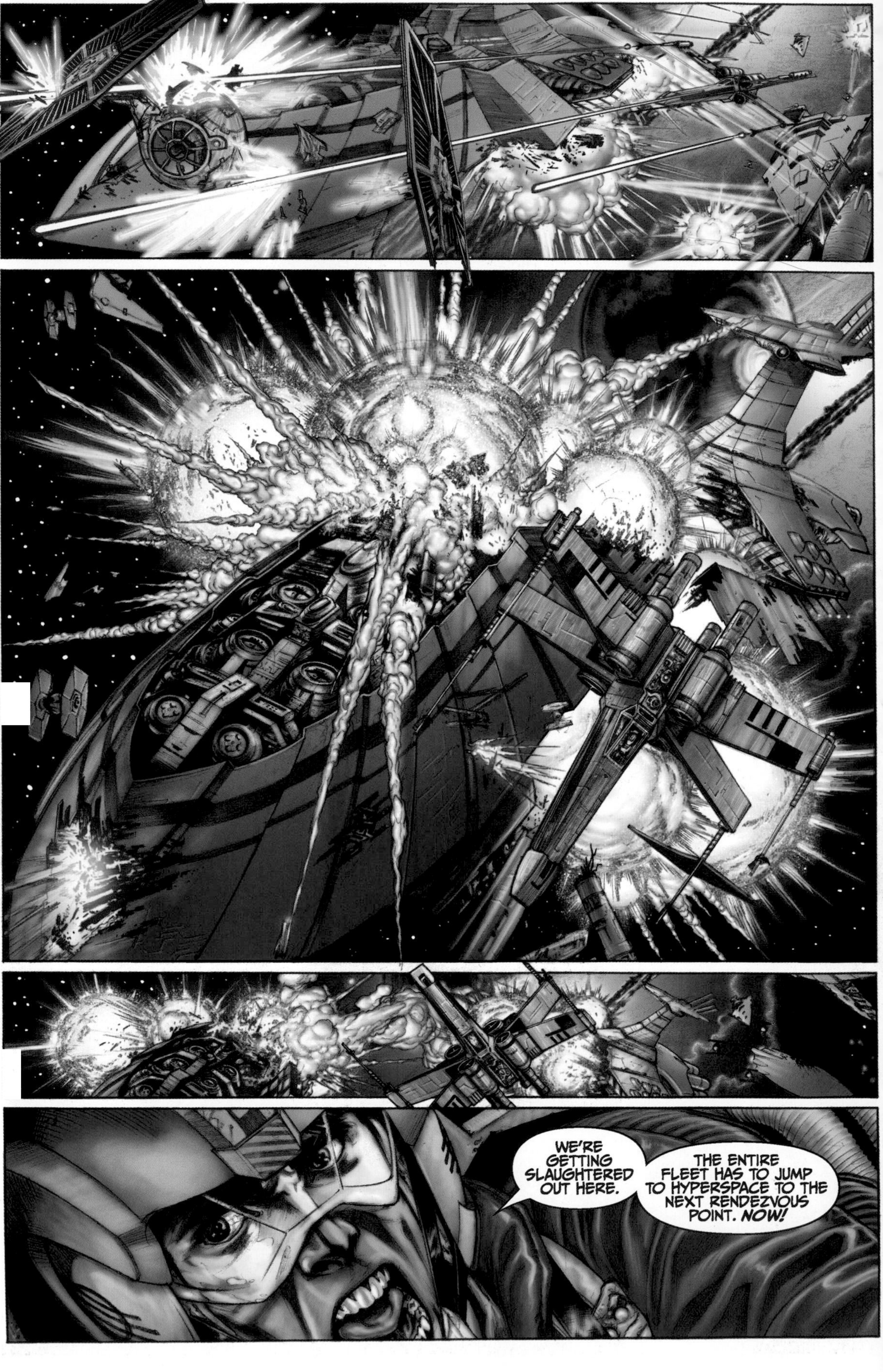
WE'RE GETTING SLAUGHTERED OUT HERE.
THE ENTIRE FLEET HAS TO JUMP TO HYPERSPACE TO THE NEXT RENDEZVOUS POINT. *NOW!*

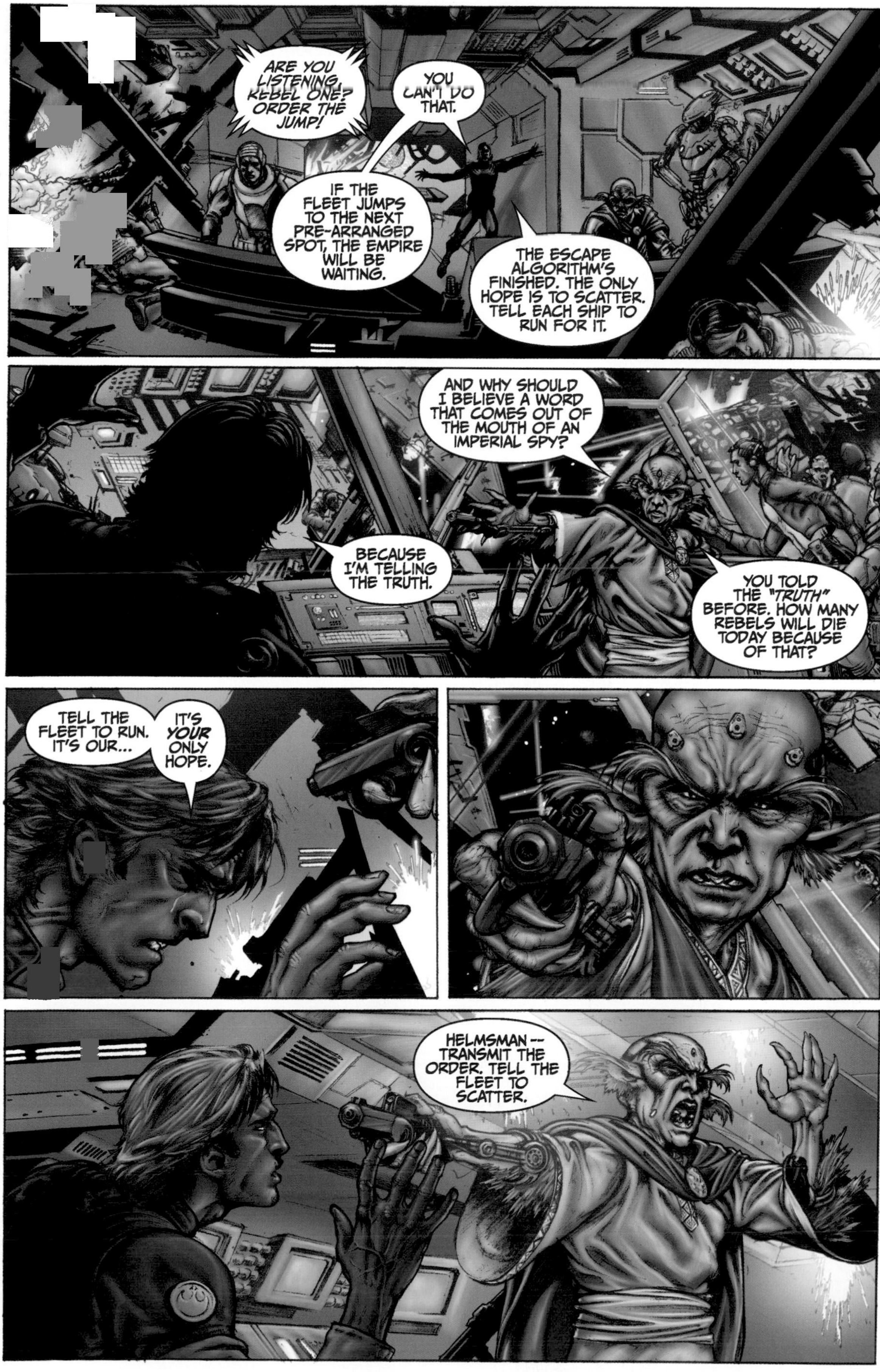
ARE YOU LISTENING, REBEL ONE? ORDER THE JUMP!
YOU CAN'T DO THAT.
IF THE FLEET JUMPS TO THE NEXT PRE-ARRANGED SPOT, THE EMPIRE WILL BE WAITING.
THE ESCAPE ALGORITHM'S FINISHED. THE ONLY HOPE IS TO SCATTER. TELL EACH SHIP TO RUN FOR IT.
AND WHY SHOULD I BELIEVE A WORD THAT COMES OUT OF THE MOUTH OF AN IMPERIAL SPY?
BECAUSE I'M TELLING THE TRUTH.
YOU TOLD THE "TRUTH" BEFORE. HOW MANY REBELS WILL DIE TODAY BECAUSE OF THAT?
TELL THE FLEET TO RUN. IT'S OUR...
IT'S YOUR ONLY HOPE.
HELMSMAN-- TRANSMIT THE ORDER. TELL THE FLEET TO SCATTER.

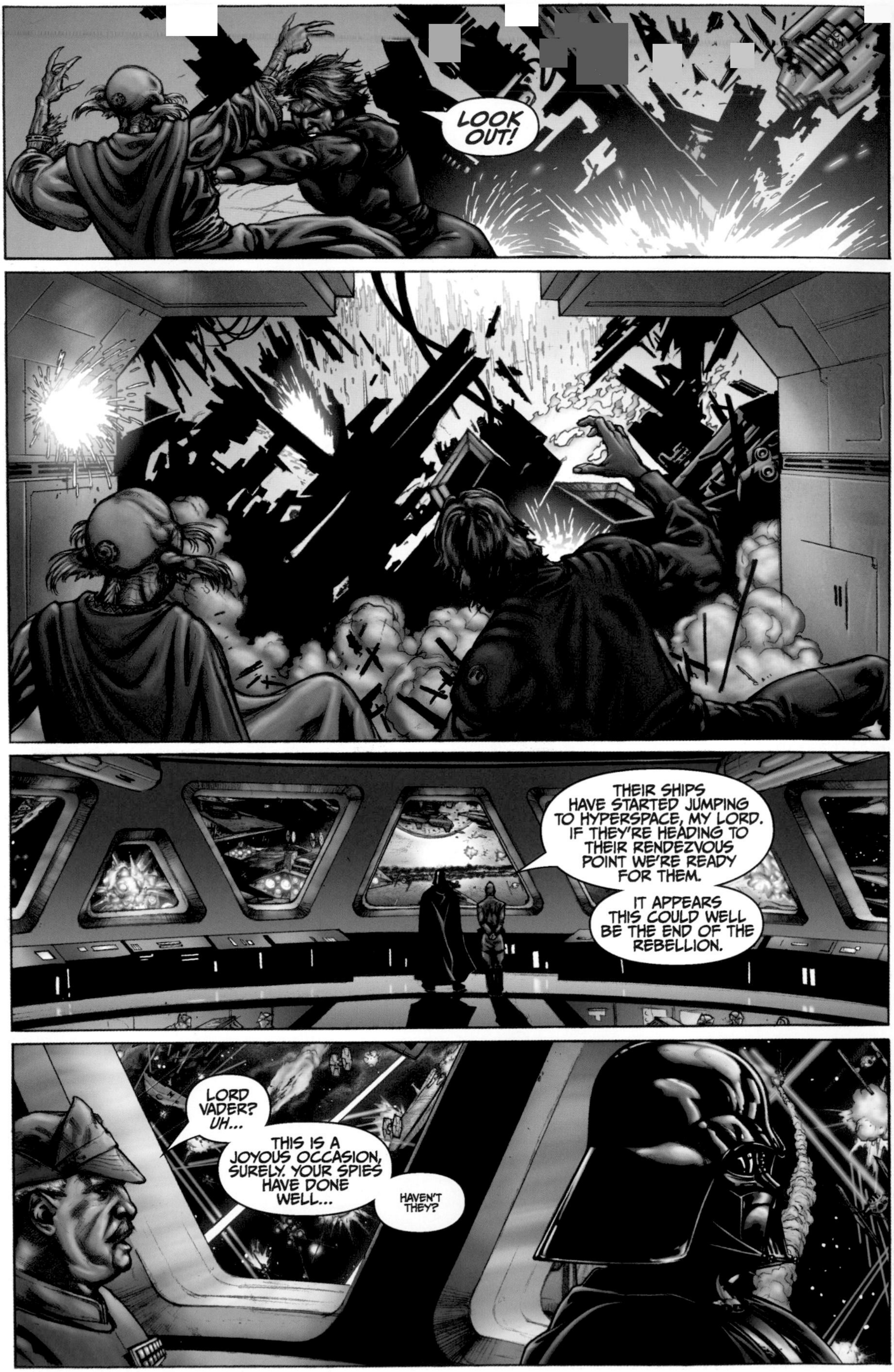
LOOK OUT!
THEIR SHIPS HAVE STARTED JUMPING TO HYPERSPACE, MY LORD. IF THEY'RE HEADING TO THEIR RENDEZVOUS POINT WE'RE READY FOR THEM.
IT APPEARS THIS COULD WELL BE THE END OF THE REBELLION.
LORD VADER? UH...
THIS IS A JOYOUS OCCASION, SURELY. YOUR SPIES HAVE DONE WELL...
HAVEN'T THEY?

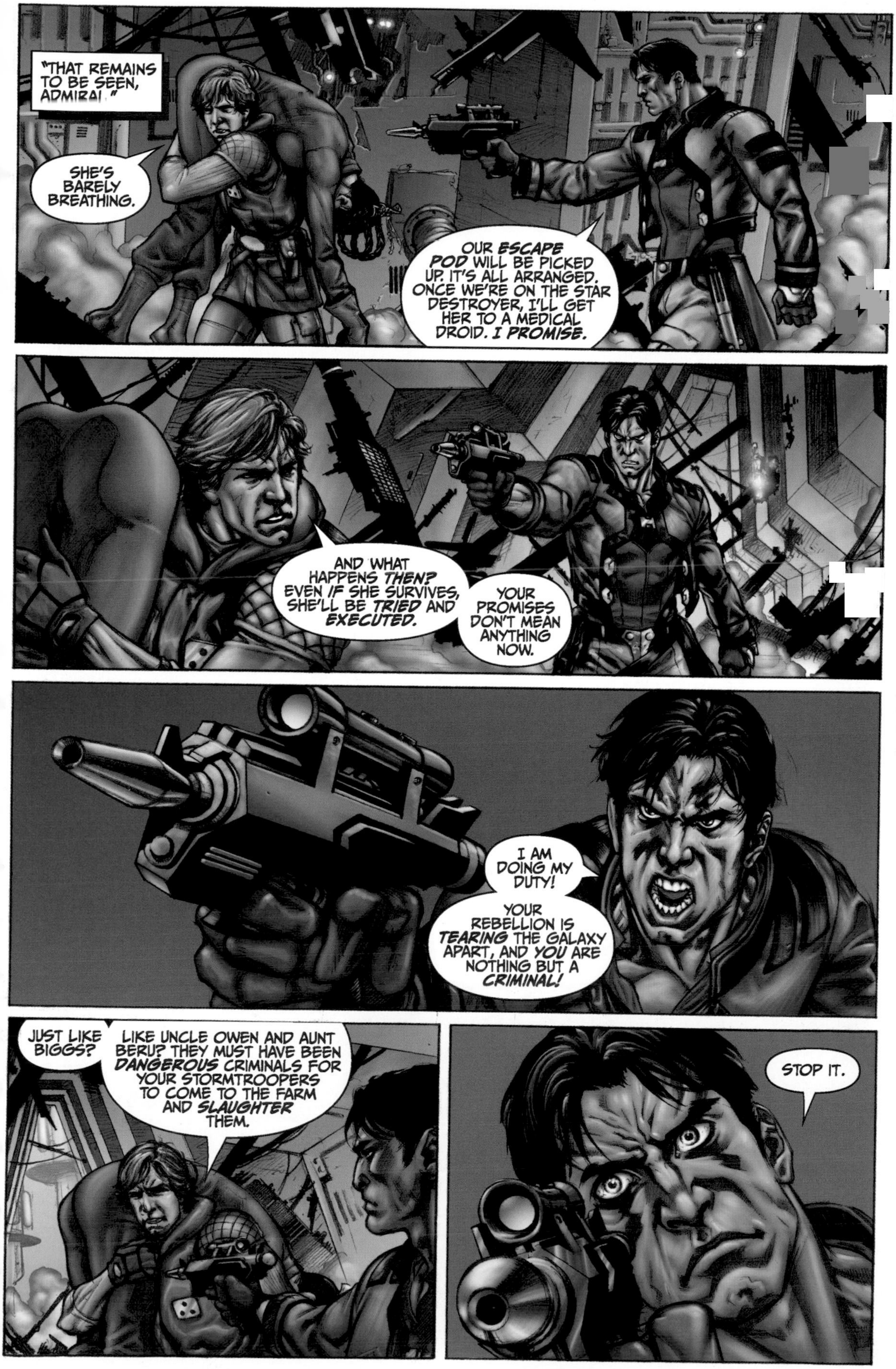
"THAT REMAINS TO BE SEEN, ADMIRAL."
SHE'S BARELY BREATHING.
OUR ESCAPE POD WILL BE PICKED UP. IT'S ALL ARRANGED. ONCE WE'RE ON THE STAR DESTROYER, I'LL GET HER TO A MEDICAL DROID. I PROMISE.
AND WHAT HAPPENS THEN? EVEN IF SHE SURVIVES, SHE'LL BE TRIED AND EXECUTED.
YOUR PROMISES DON'T MEAN ANYTHING NOW.
I AM DOING MY DUTY!
YOUR REBELLION IS TEARING THE GALAXY APART, AND YOU ARE NOTHING BUT A CRIMINAL!
JUST LIKE BIGGS?
LIKE UNCLE OWEN AND AUNT BERU? THEY MUST HAVE BEEN DANGEROUS CRIMINALS FOR YOUR STORMTROOPERS TO COME TO THE FARM AND SLAUGHTER THEM.
STOP IT.

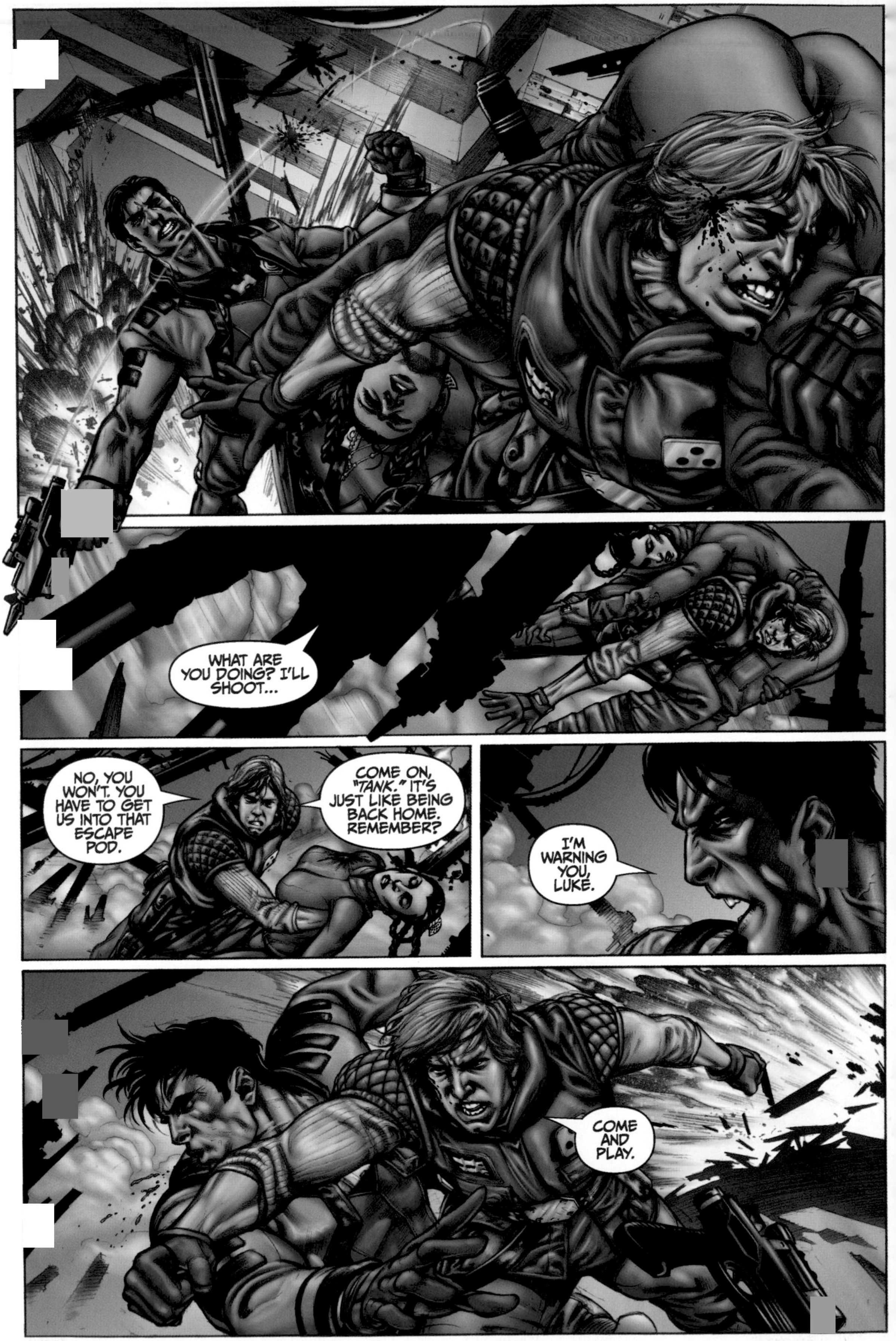
WHAT ARE YOU DOING? I'LL SHOOT...
NO, YOU WON'T. YOU HAVE TO GET US INTO THAT ESCAPE POD.
COME ON, "TANK." IT'S JUST LIKE BEING BACK HOME. REMEMBER?
I'M WARNING YOU, LUKE.
COME AND PLAY.

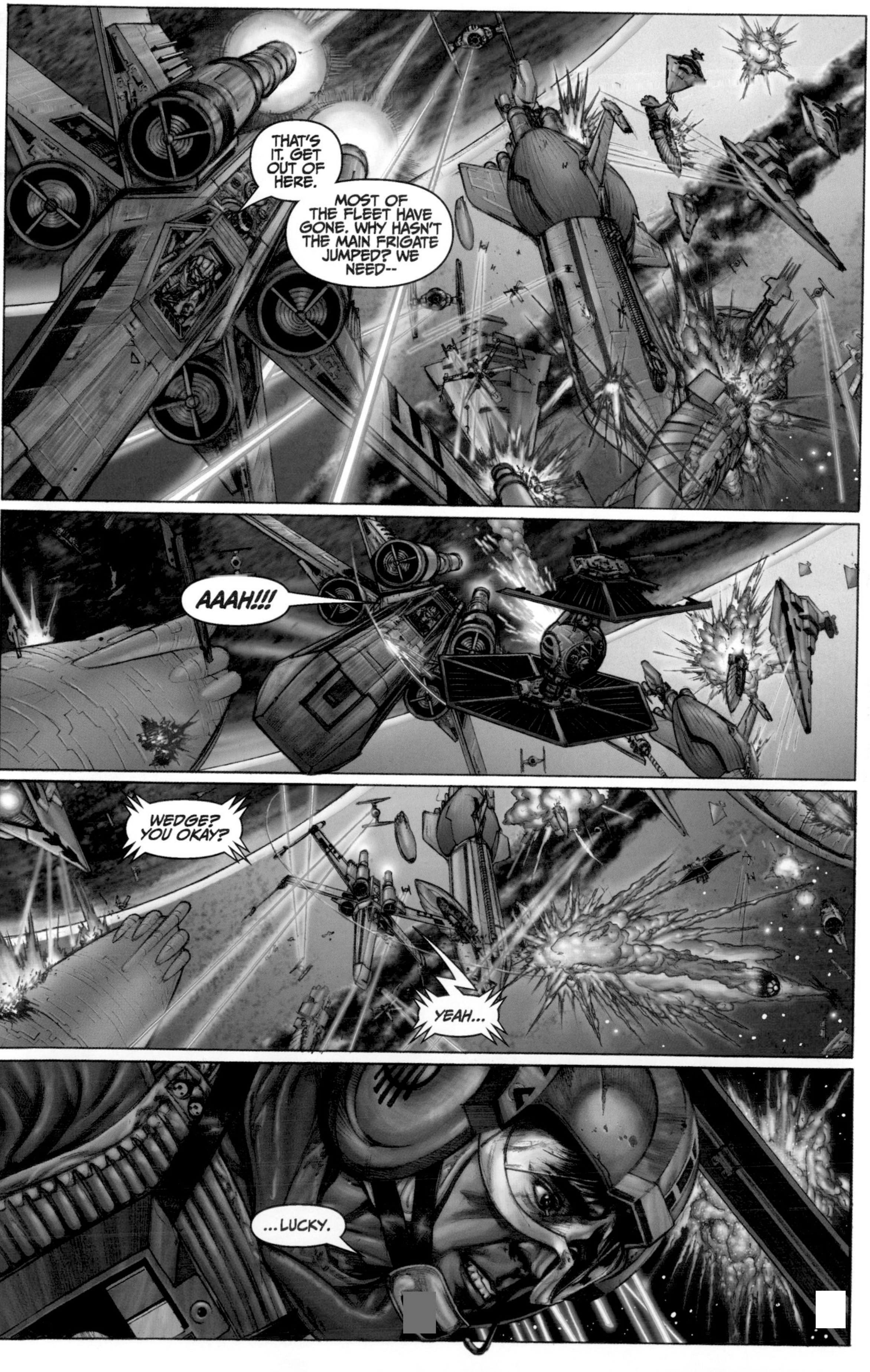
THAT'S IT. GET OUT OF HERE.
MOST OF THE FLEET HAVE GONE. WHY HASN'T THE MAIN FRIGATE JUMPED? WE NEED--
AAAH!!!
WEDGE? YOU OKAY?
YEAH...
...LUCKY.

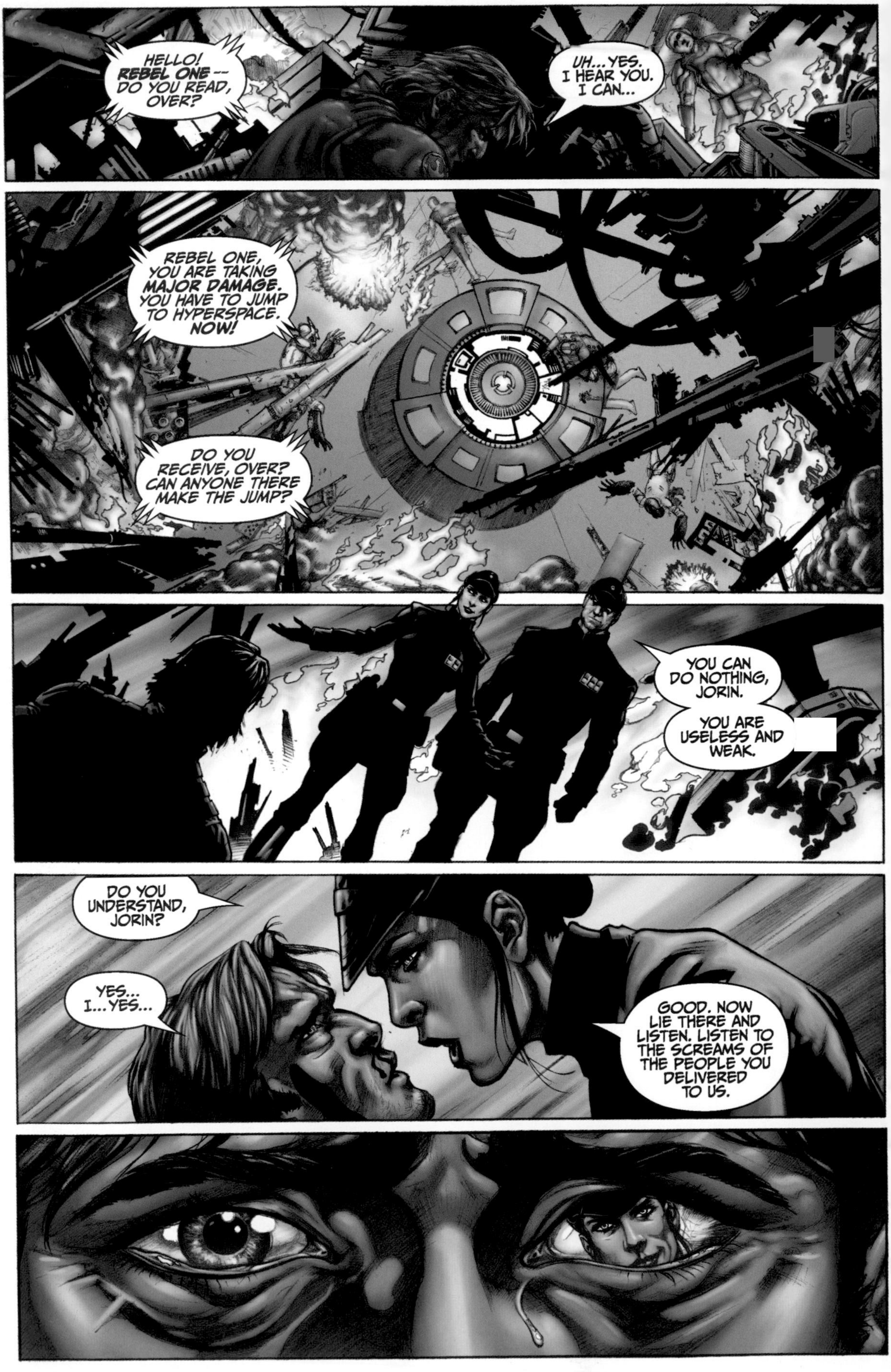
HELLO! REBEL ONE -- DO YOU READ, OVER?
UH... YES. I HEAR YOU. I CAN...
REBEL ONE, YOU ARE TAKING MAJOR DAMAGE. YOU HAVE TO JUMP TO HYPERSPACE. NOW!
DO YOU RECEIVE, OVER? CAN ANYONE THERE MAKE THE JUMP?
YOU CAN DO NOTHING, JORIN.
YOU ARE USELESS AND WEAK.
DO YOU UNDERSTAND, JORIN?
YES... I... YES...
GOOD. NOW LIE THERE AND LISTEN. LISTEN TO THE SCREAMS OF THE PEOPLE YOU DELIVERED TO US.

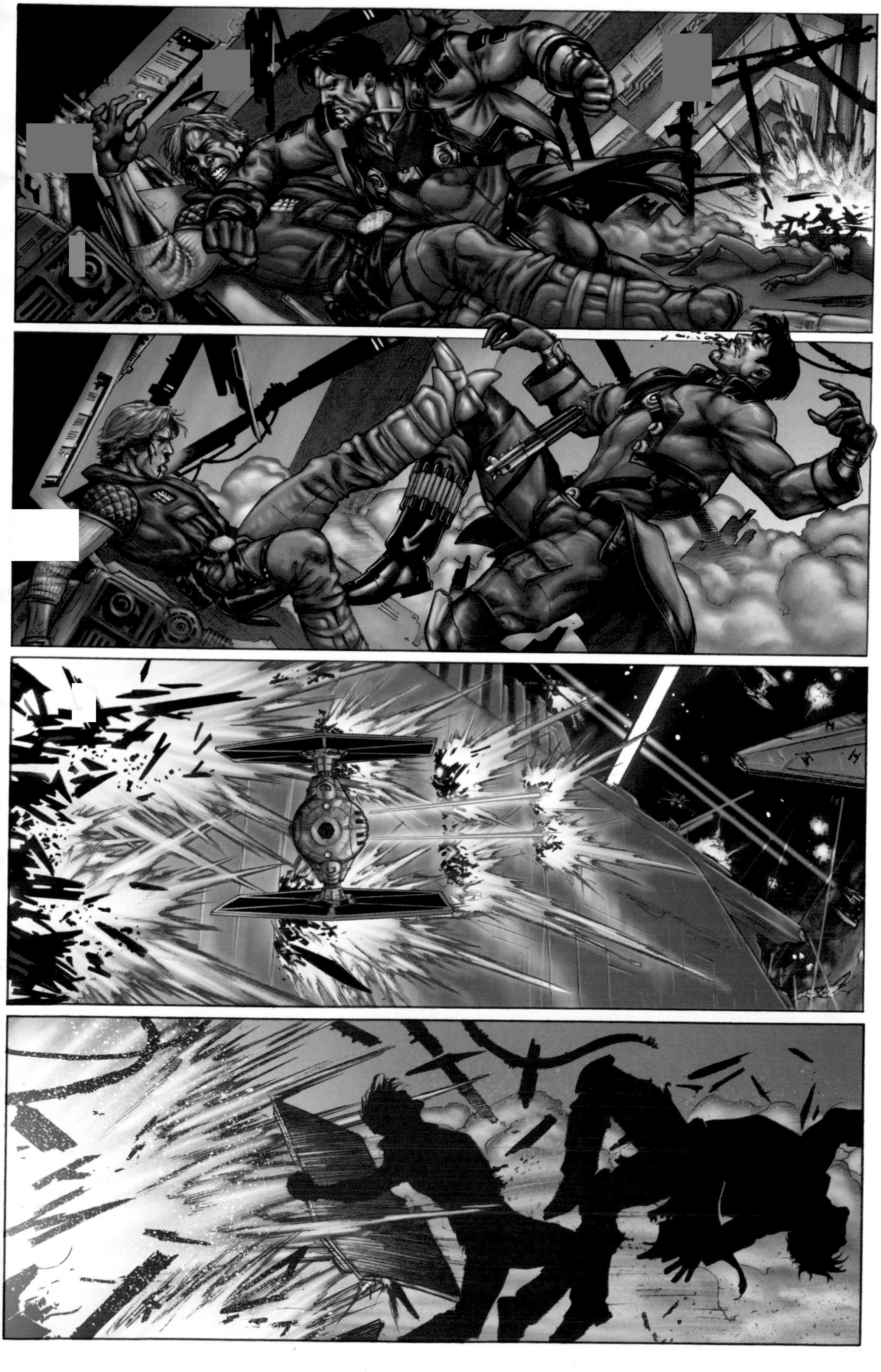

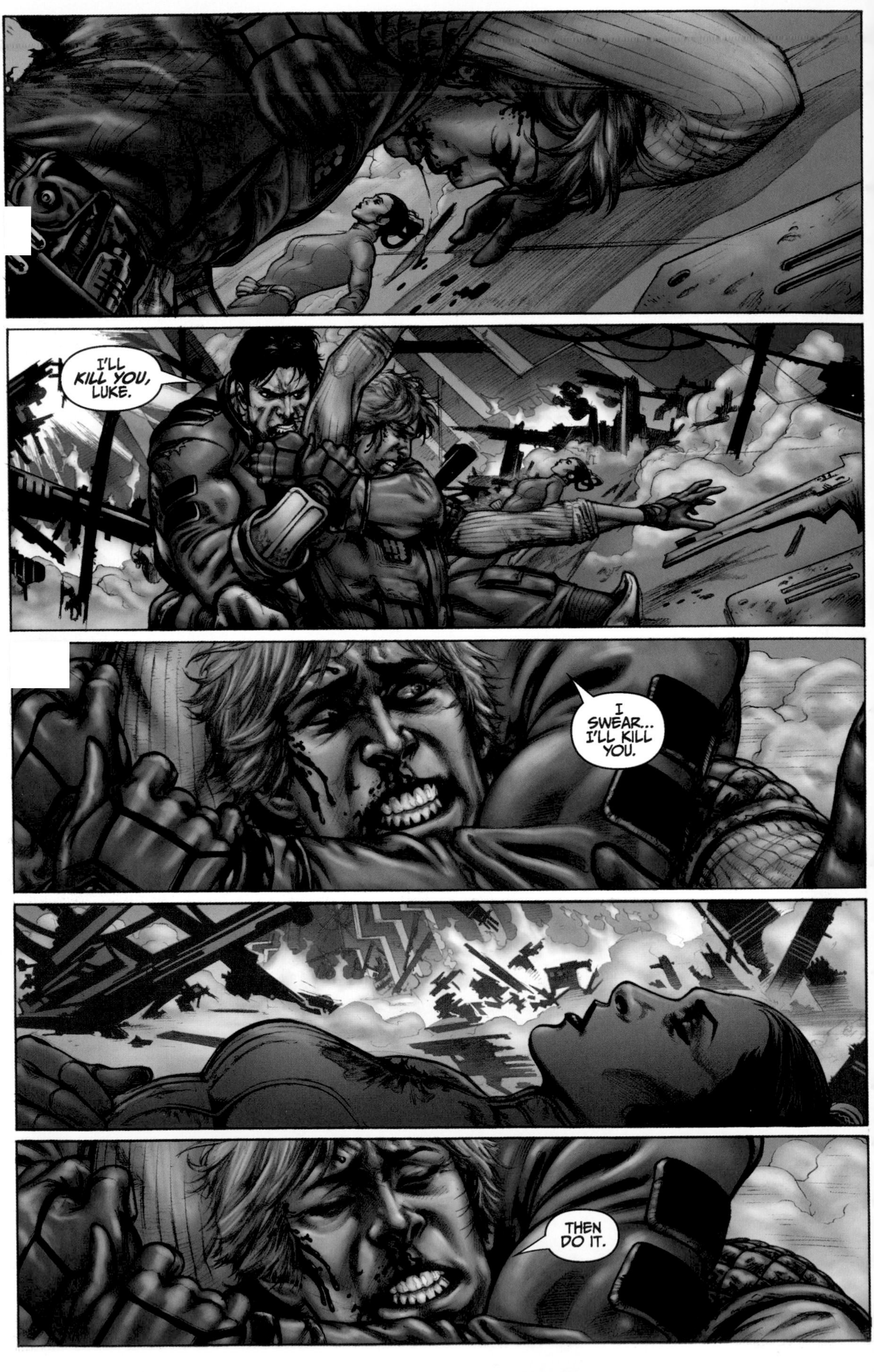
I'LL KILL YOU, LUKE.
I SWEAR... I'LL KILL YOU.
THEN DO IT.

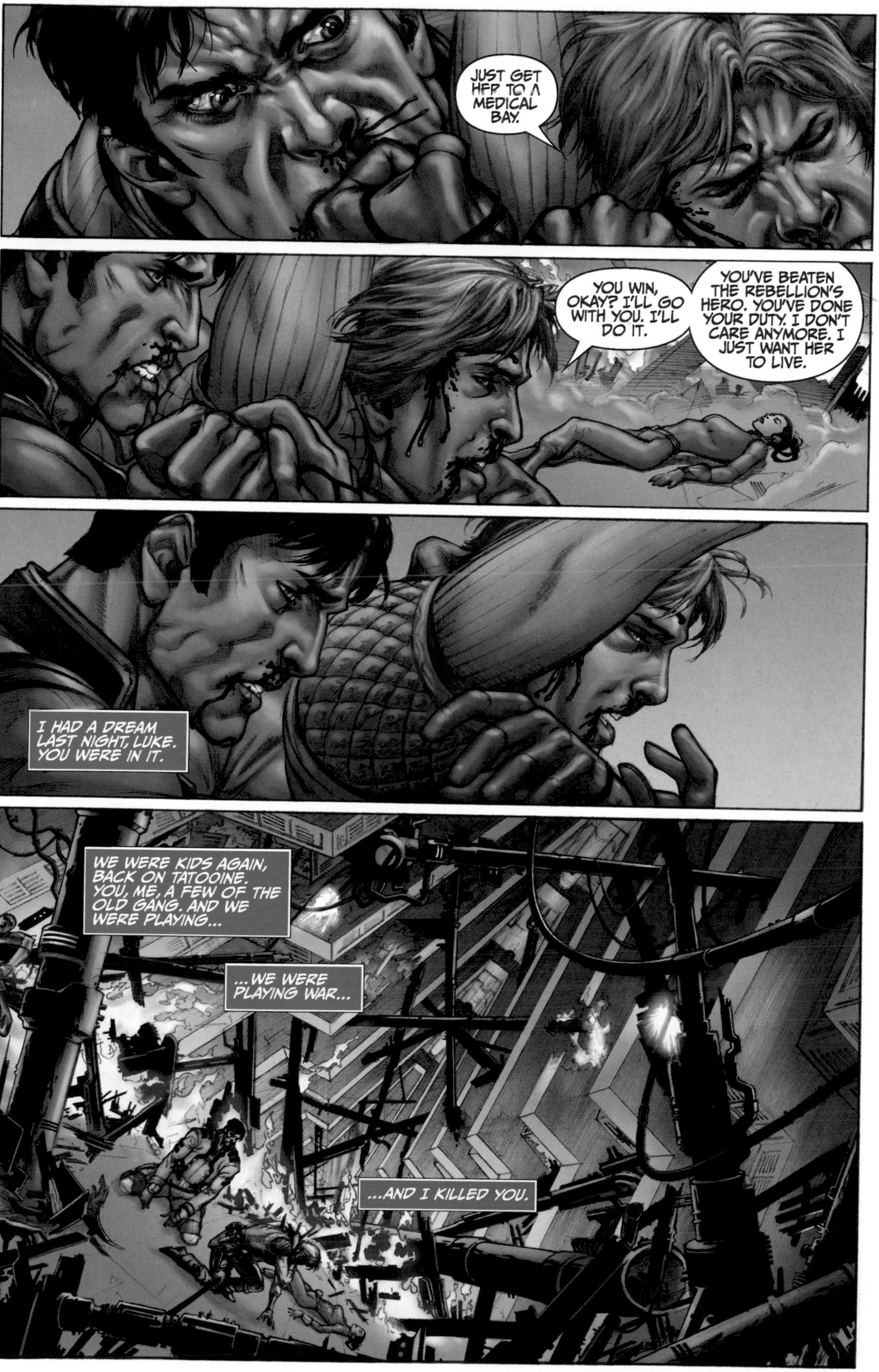
JUST GET HER TO A MEDICAL BAY.
YOU WIN, OKAY? I'LL GO WITH YOU. I'LL DO IT.
YOU'VE BEATEN THE REBELLION'S HERO. YOU'VE DONE YOUR DUTY. I DON'T CARE ANYMORE. I JUST WANT HER TO LIVE.
I HAD A DREAM LAST NIGHT, LUKE. YOU WERE IN IT.
WE WERE KIDS AGAIN, BACK ON TATOOINE. YOU, ME, A FEW OF THE OLD GANG. AND WE WERE PLAYING...
...WE WERE PLAYING WAR...
...AND I KILLED YOU.

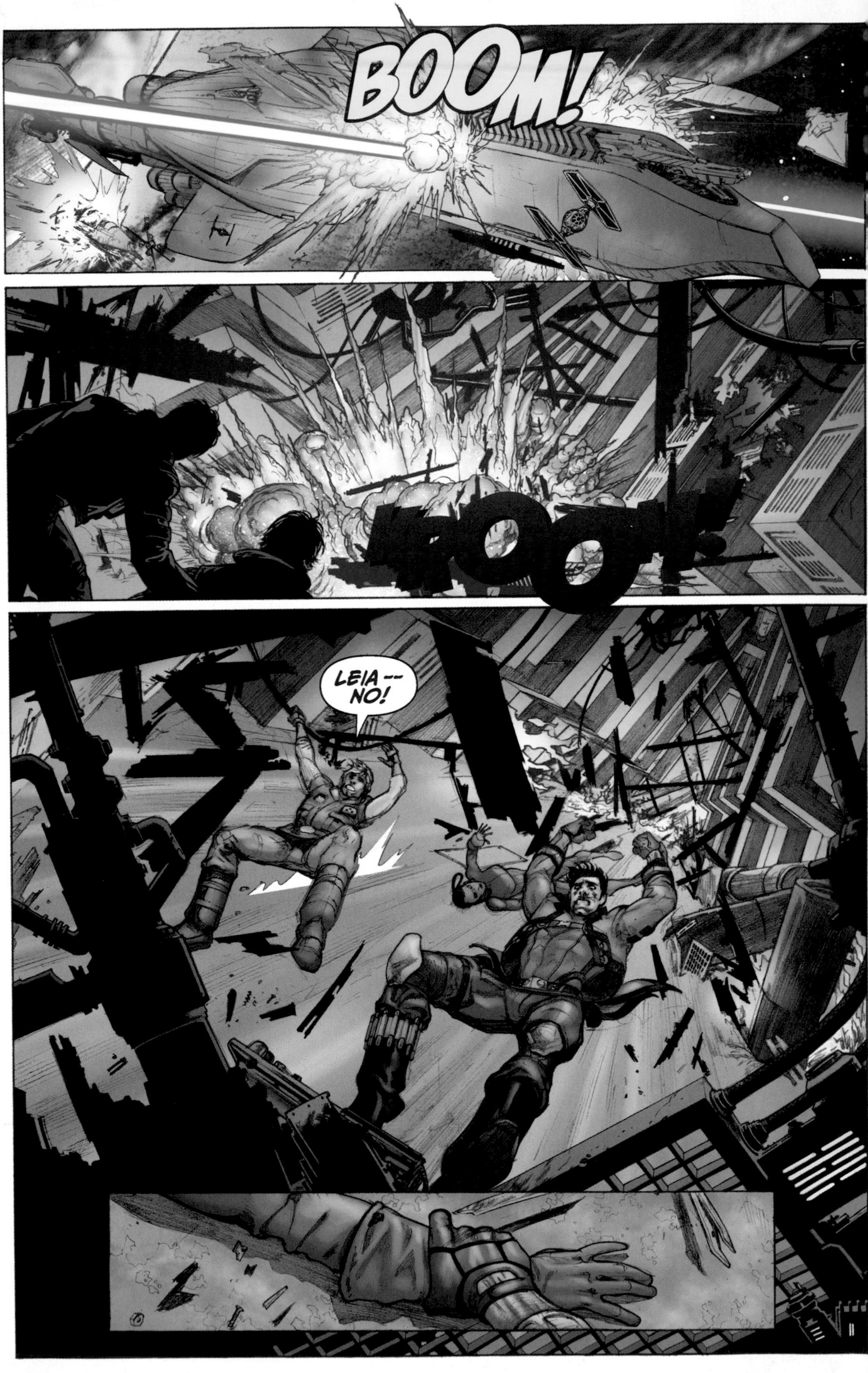
BOOM!
KROOM!
LEIA -- NO!

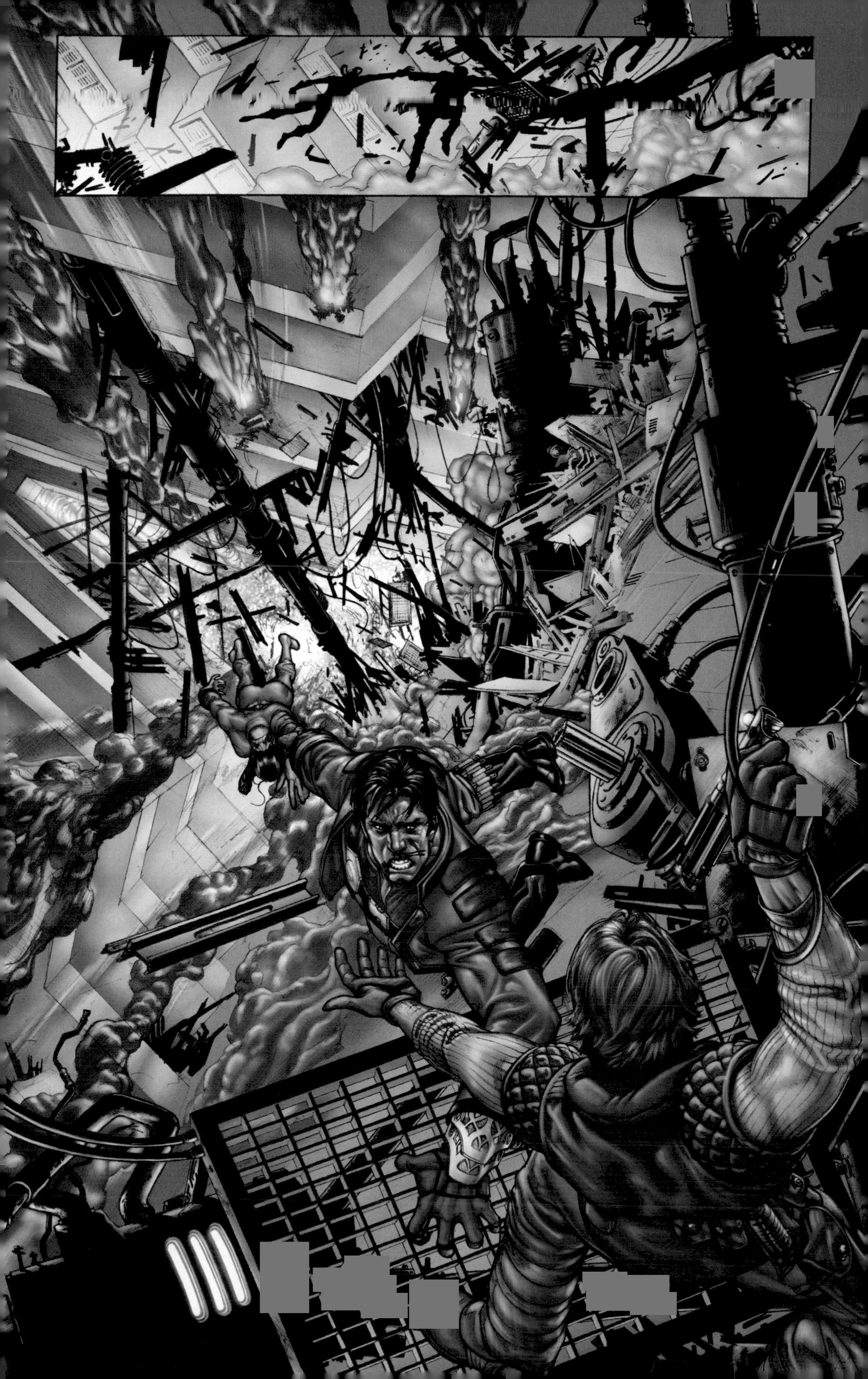

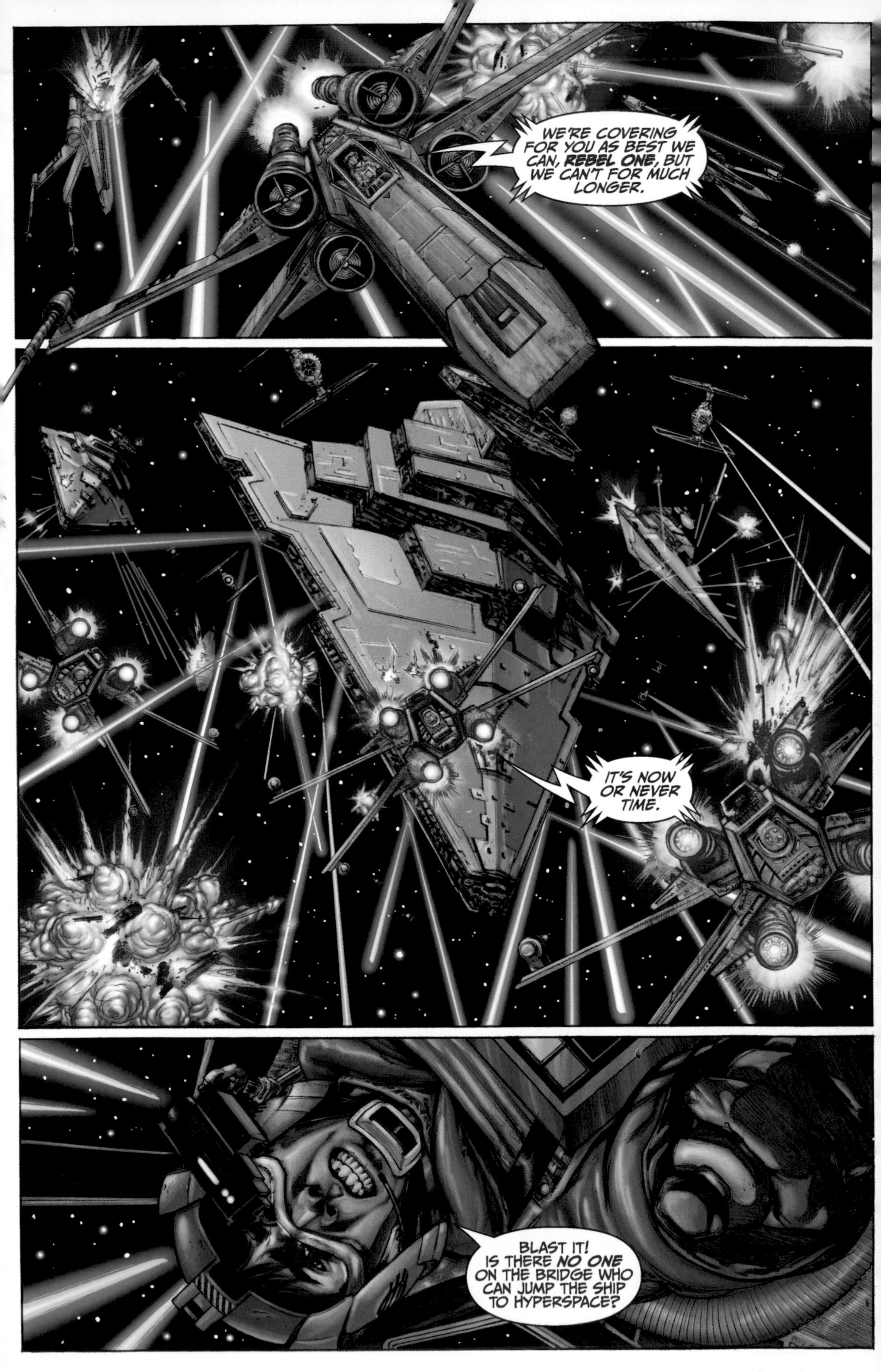
WE'RE COVERING FOR YOU AS BEST WE CAN, **REBEL ONE**, BUT WE CAN'T FOR MUCH LONGER.
IT'S NOW OR NEVER TIME.
BLAST IT! IS THERE *NO ONE* ON THE BRIDGE WHO CAN JUMP THE SHIP TO HYPERSPACE?

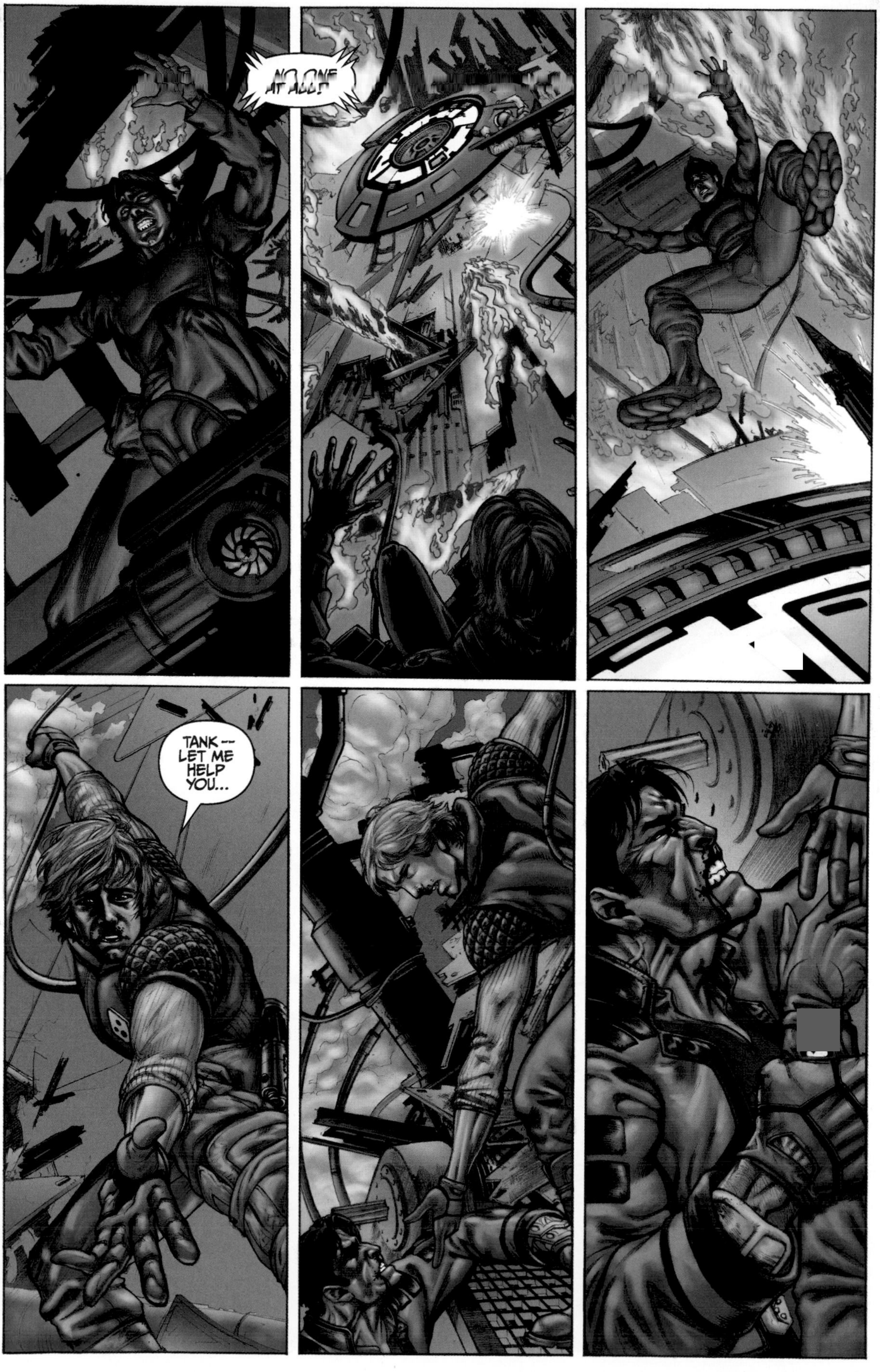
NO ONE AT ALL!?
TANK -- LET ME HELP YOU...

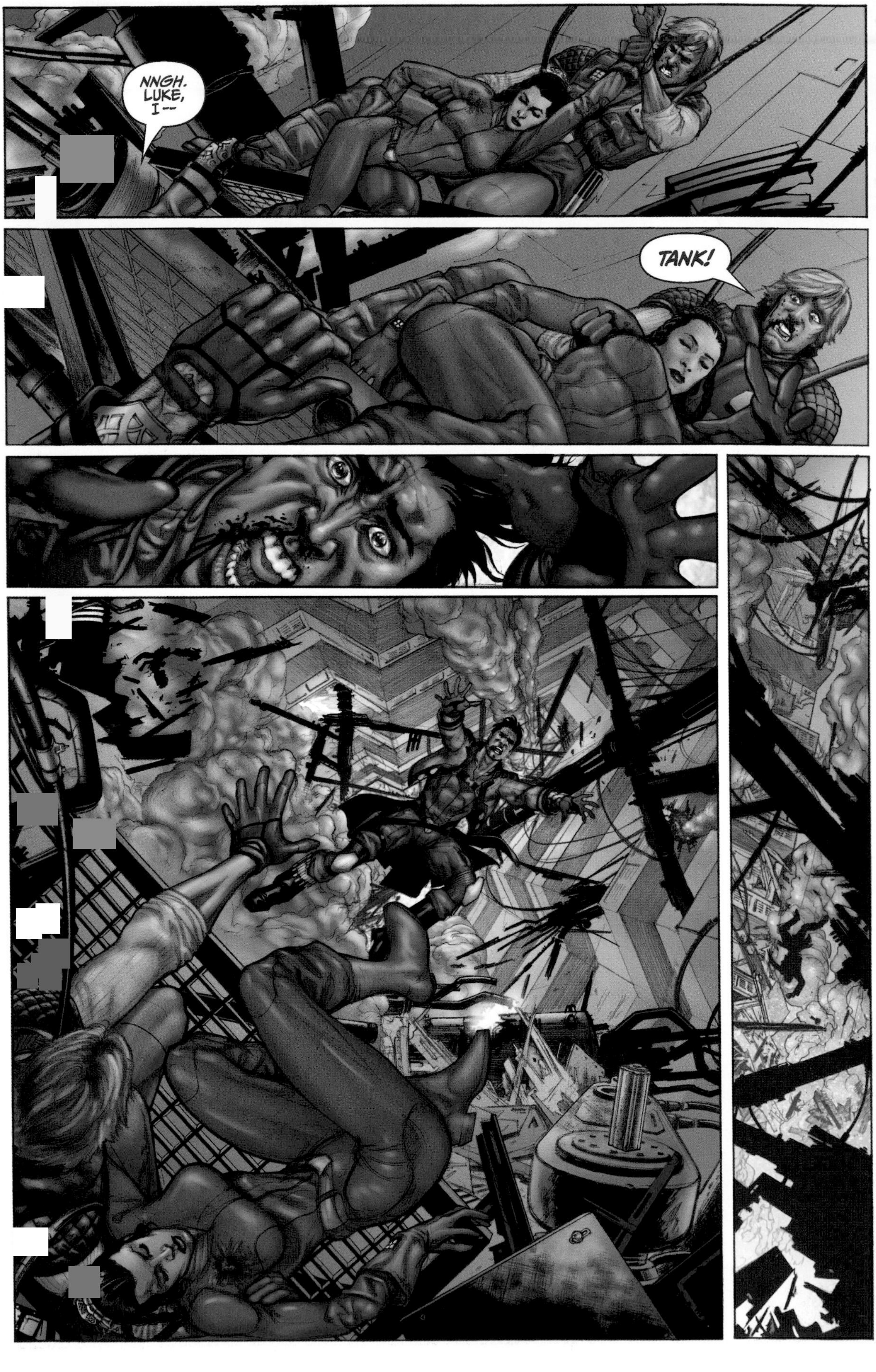
NNGH. LUKE, I--
TANK!

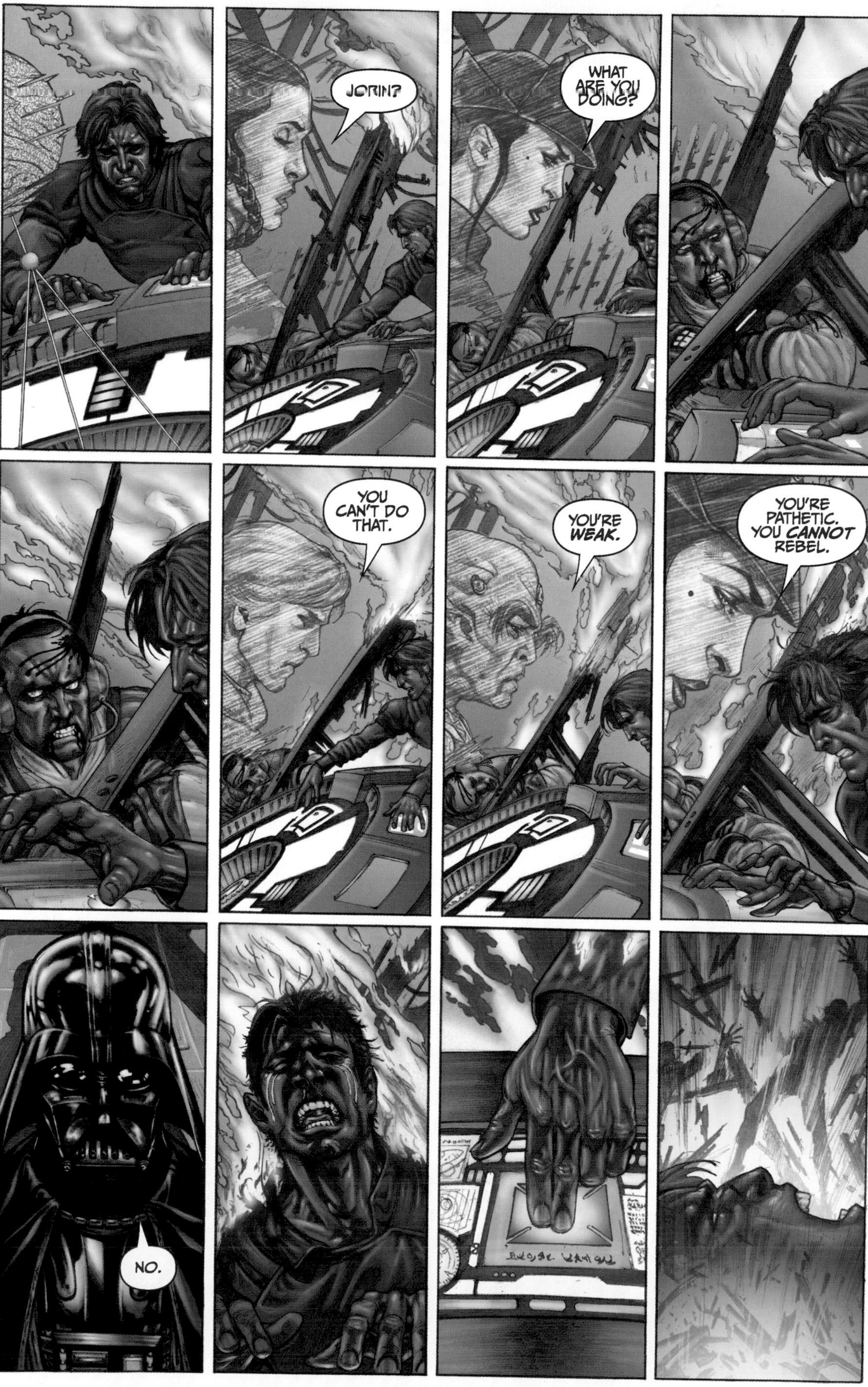
JORIN?
WHAT ARE YOU DOING?
YOU CAN'T DO THAT.
YOU'RE *WEAK.*
YOU'RE PATHETIC. YOU *CANNOT* REBEL.
NO.

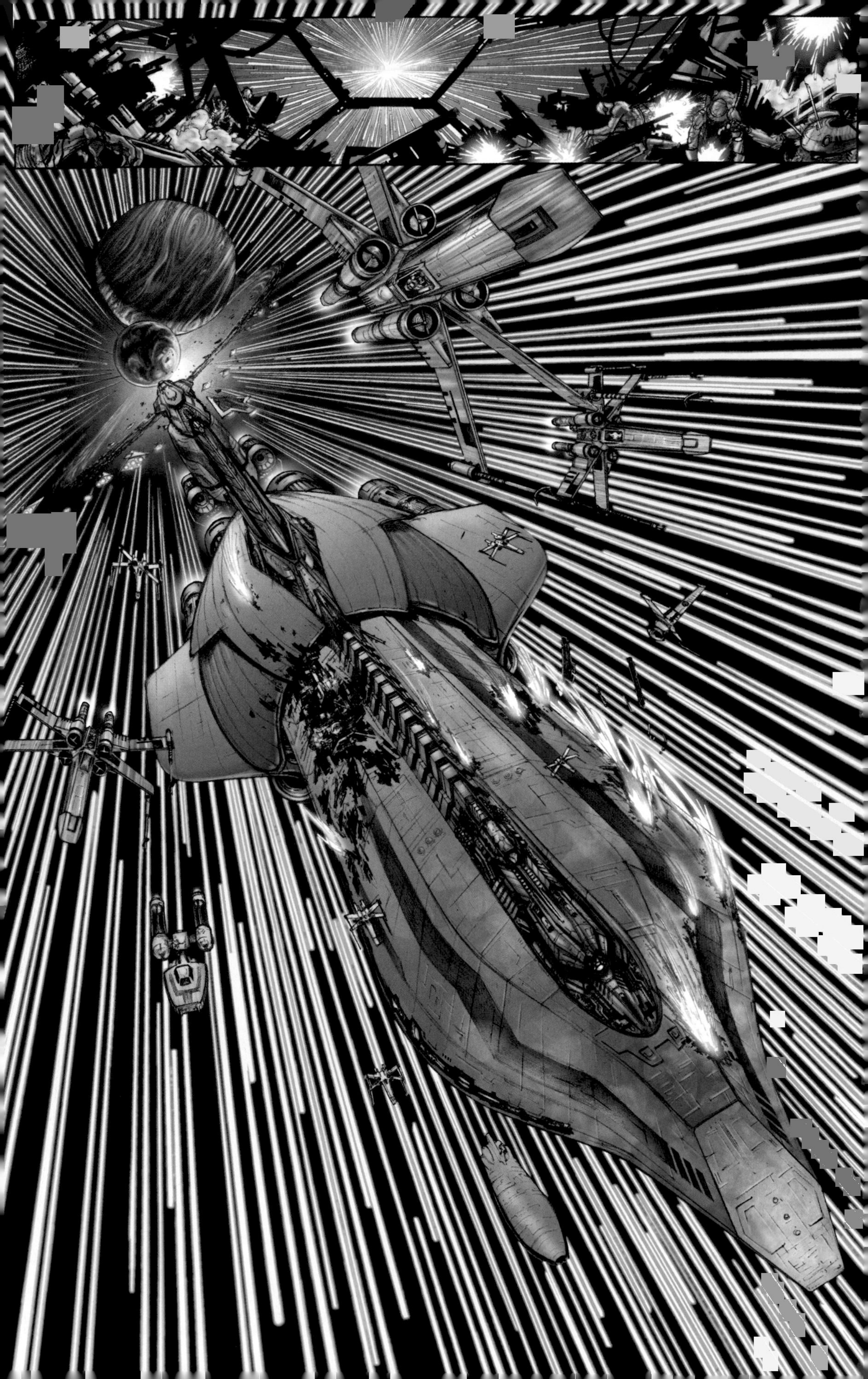

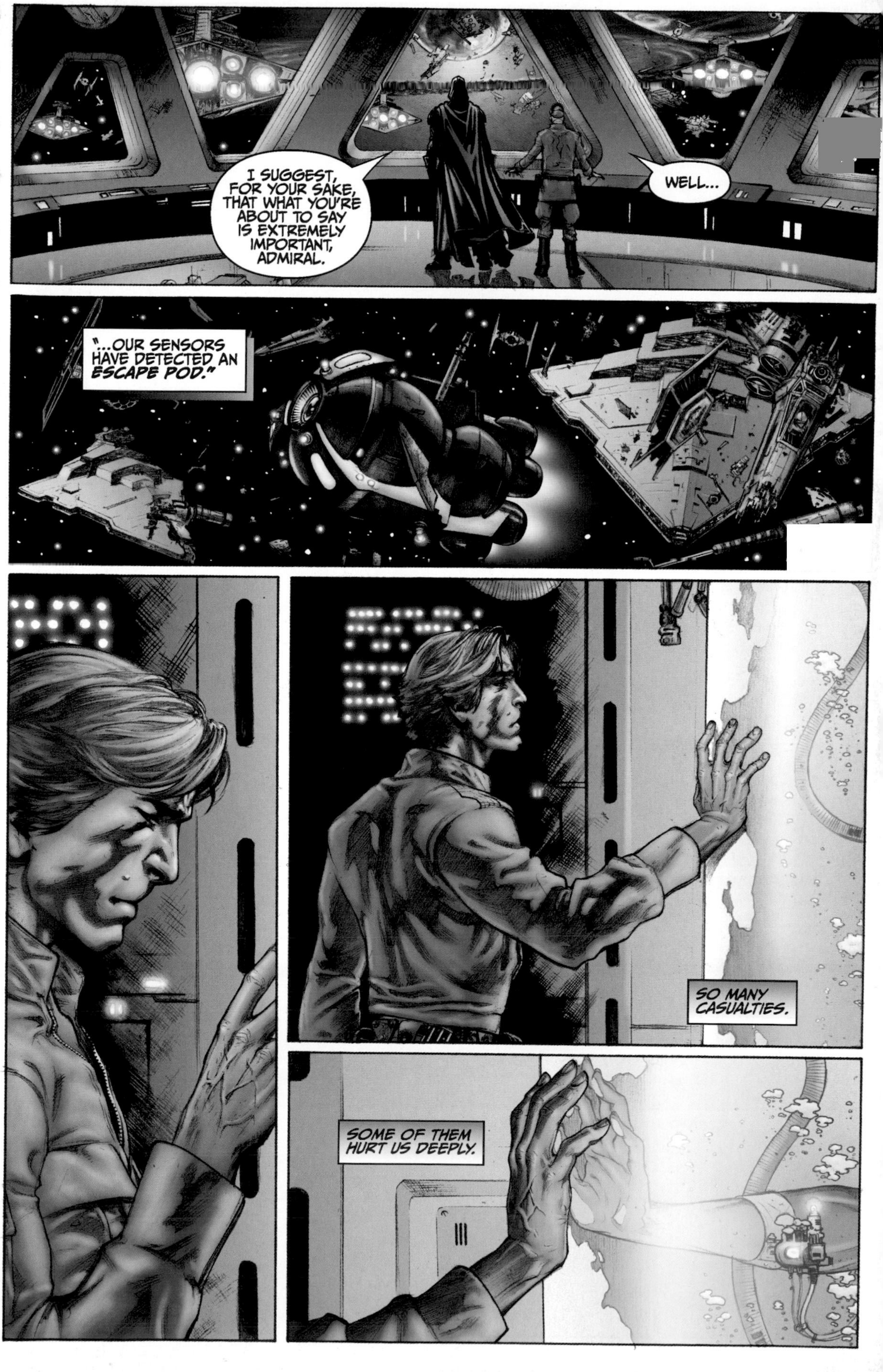
I SUGGEST, FOR YOUR SAKE, THAT WHAT YOU'RE ABOUT TO SAY IS EXTREMELY IMPORTANT, ADMIRAL.
WELL...
"...OUR SENSORS HAVE DETECTED AN ESCAPE POD."
SO MANY CASUALTIES.
SOME OF THEM HURT US DEEPLY.

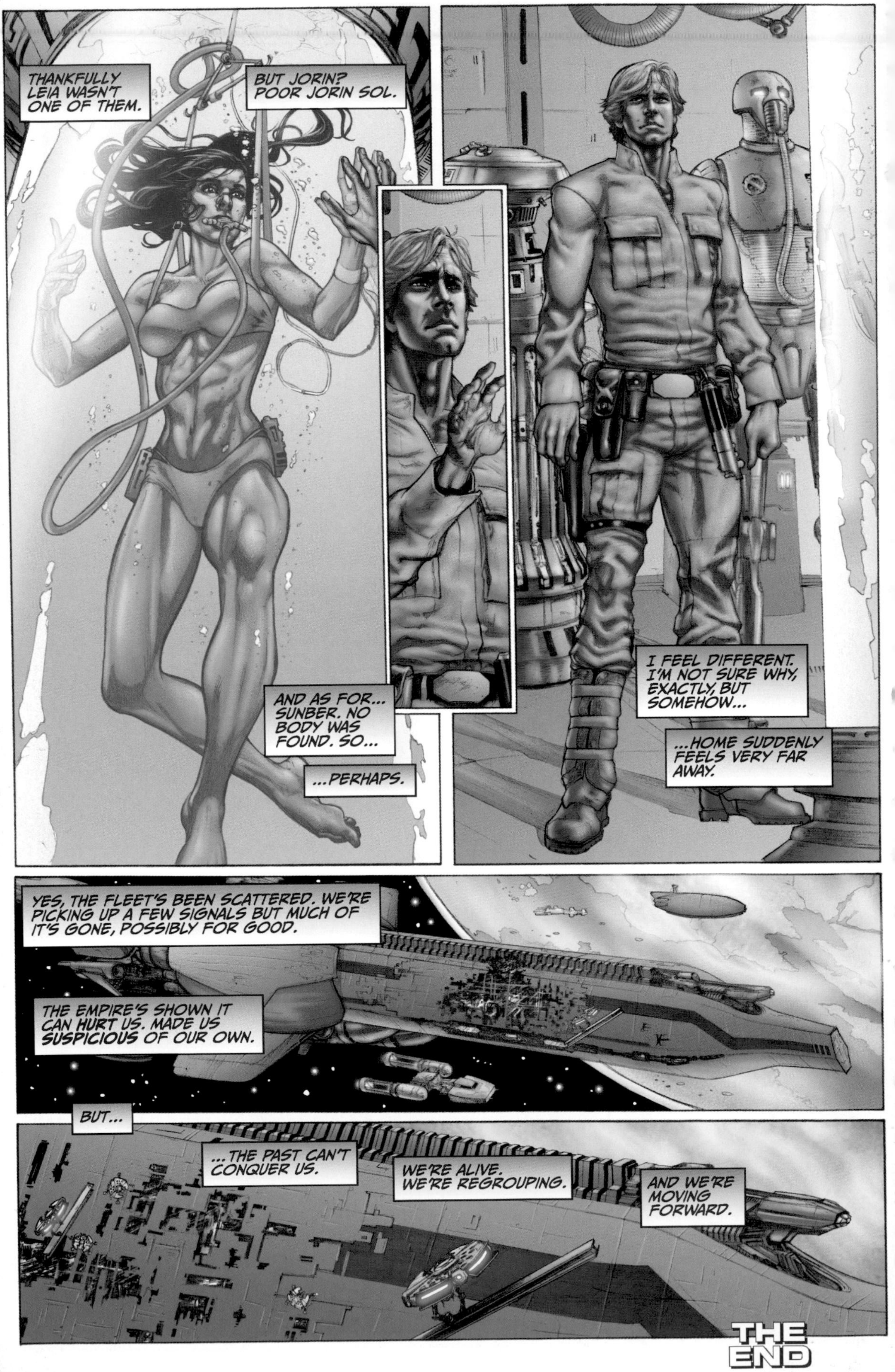
THANKFULLY LEIA WASN'T ONE OF THEM.
BUT JORIN? POOR JORIN SOL.
AND AS FOR... SUNBER. NO BODY WAS FOUND. SO...
...PERHAPS.
I FEEL DIFFERENT. I'M NOT SURE WHY, EXACTLY, BUT SOMEHOW...
...HOME SUDDENLY FEELS VERY FAR AWAY.
YES, THE FLEET'S BEEN SCATTERED. WE'RE PICKING UP A FEW SIGNALS BUT MUCH OF IT'S GONE, POSSIBLY FOR GOOD.
THE EMPIRE'S SHOWN IT CAN HURT US. MADE US SUSPICIOUS OF OUR OWN.
BUT...
...THE PAST CAN'T CONQUER US.
WE'RE ALIVE. WE'RE REGROUPING.
AND WE'RE MOVING FORWARD.
THE END

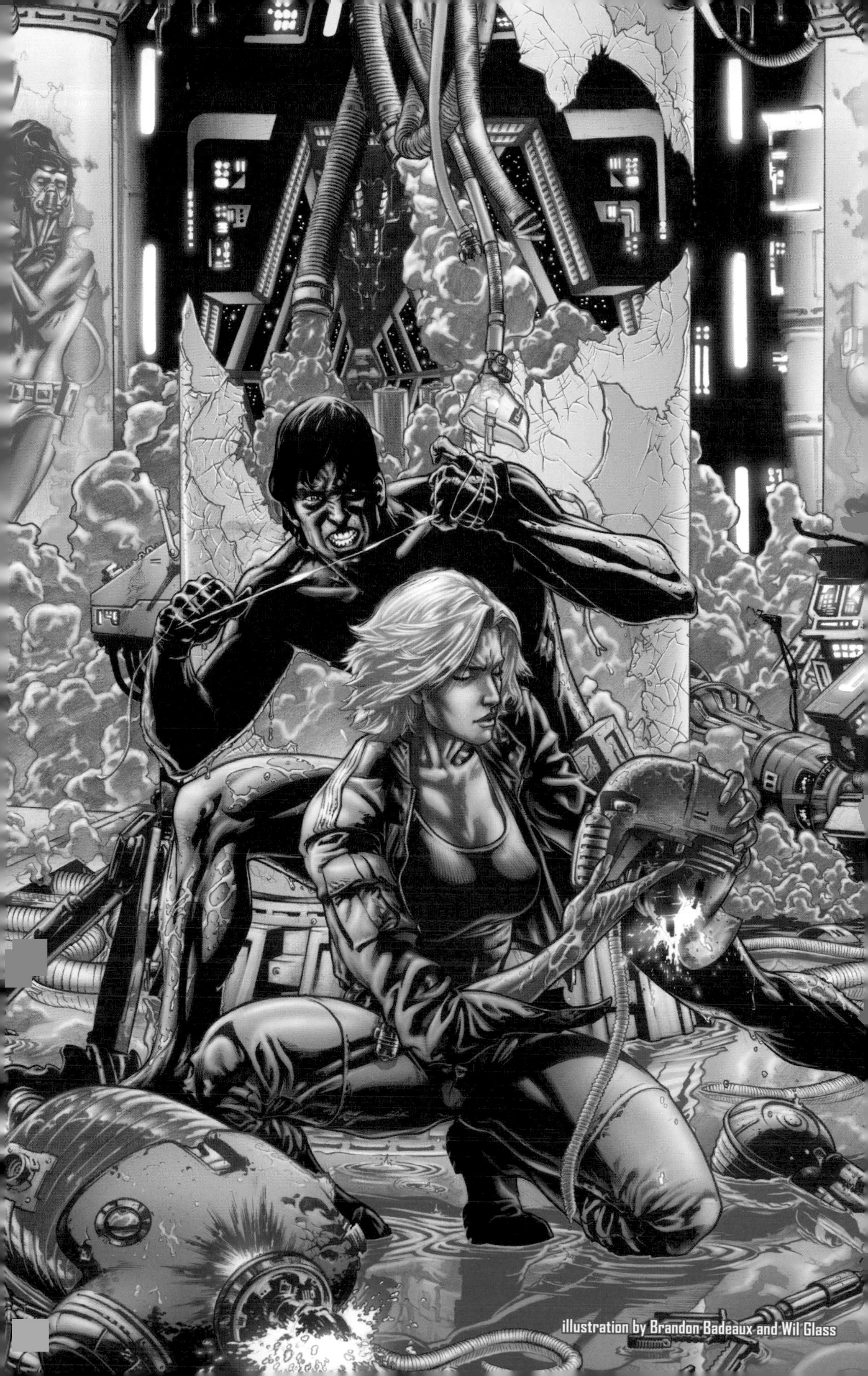

illustration by Brandon Badeaux and Wil Glass

illustration by Brandon Badeaux and Dan Jackson

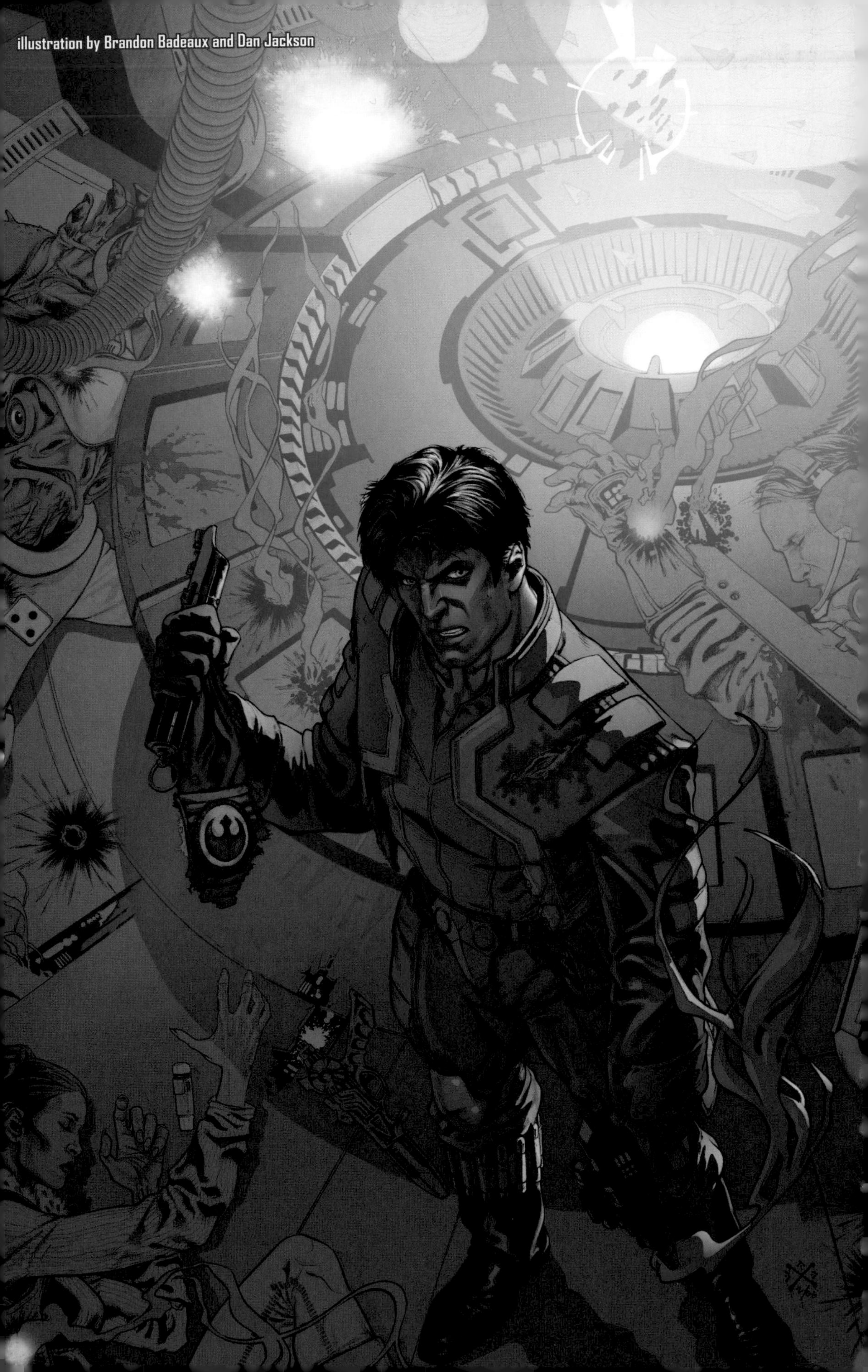

illustration by Brandon Badeaux and Michael Atiyeh

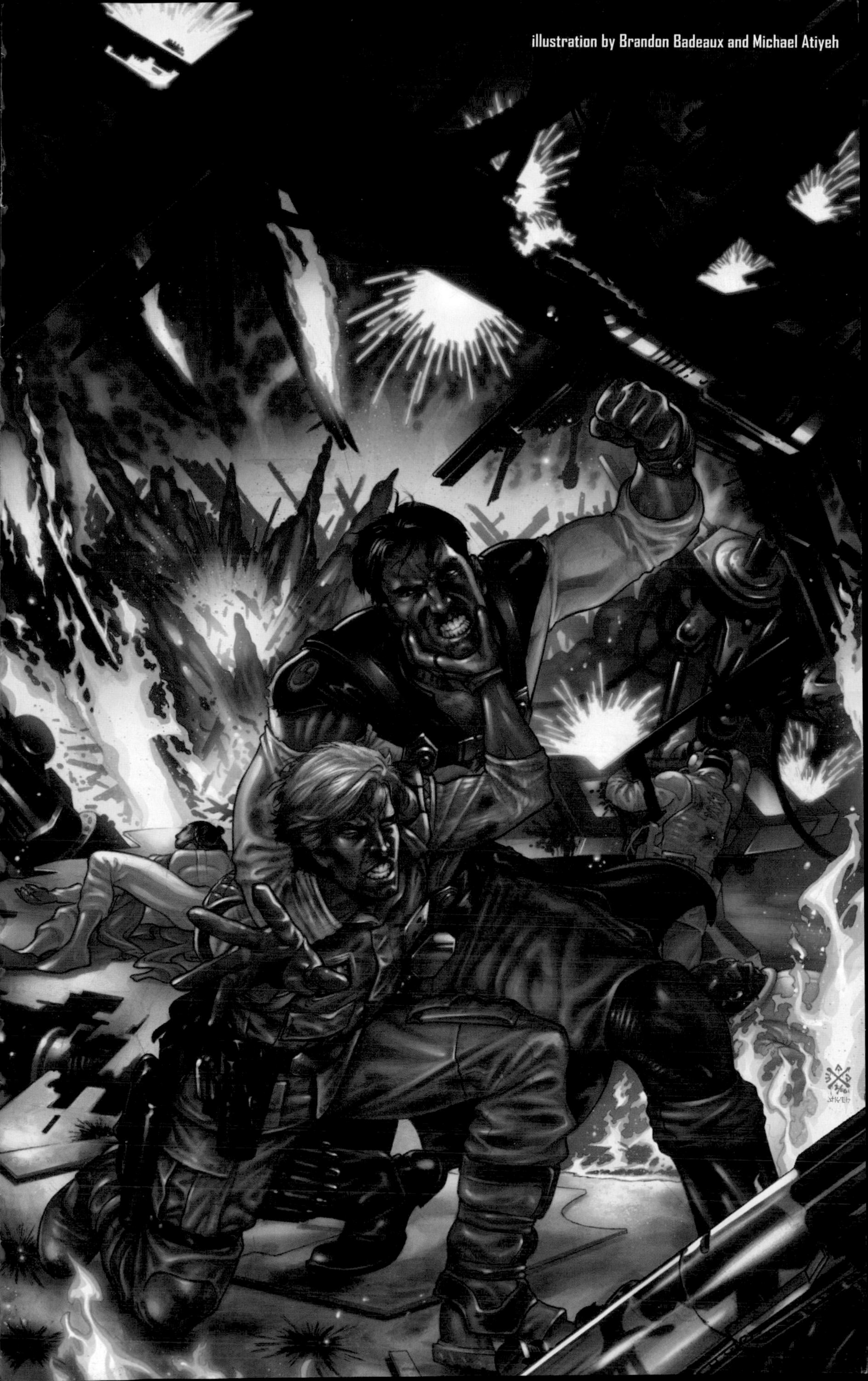

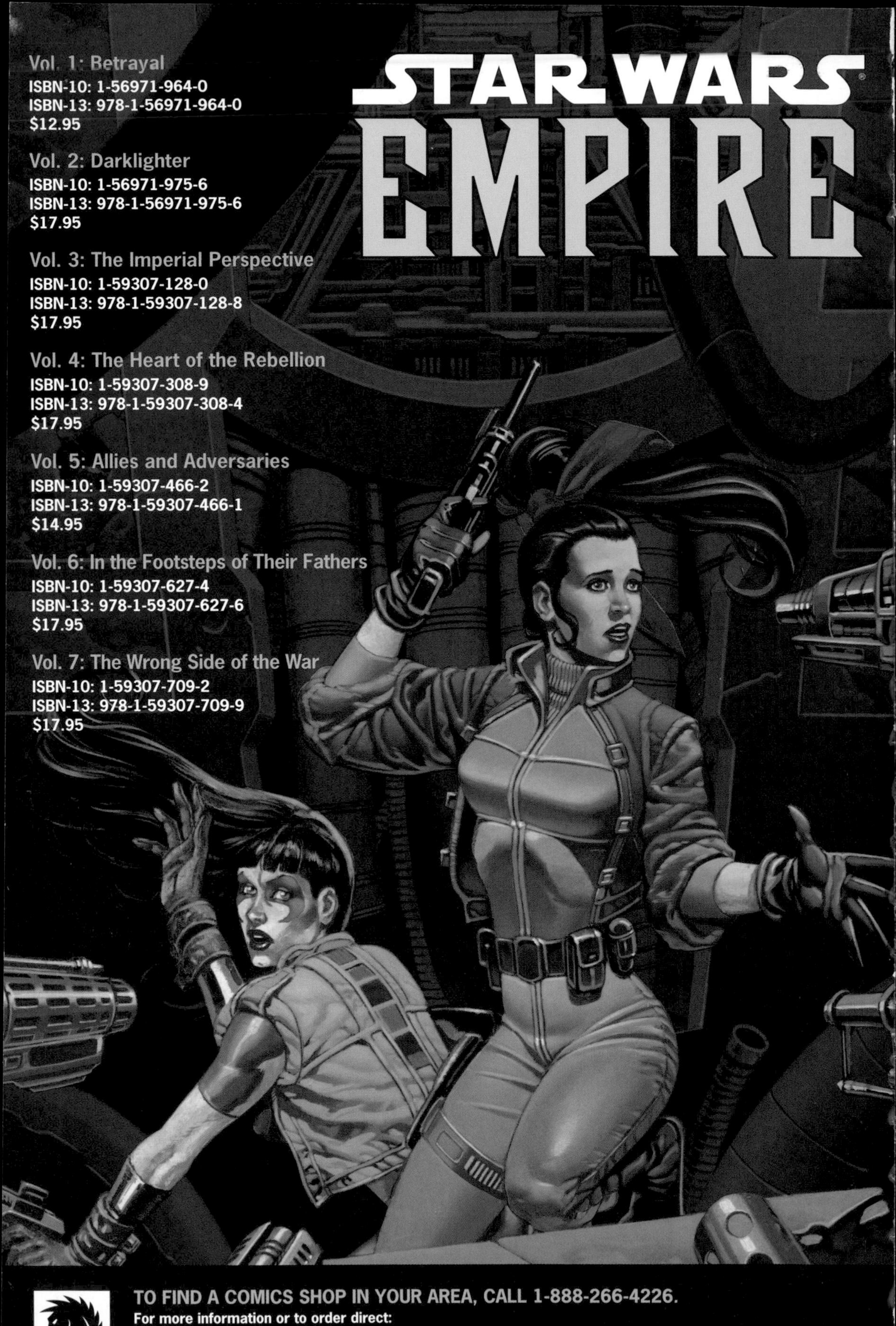
STAR WARS
EMPIRE
Vol. 1: Betrayal
ISBN-10: 1-56971-964-0
ISBN-13: 978-1-56971-964-0
$12.95
Vol. 2: Darklighter
ISBN-10: 1-56971-975-6
ISBN-13: 978-1-56971-975-6
$17.95
Vol. 3: The Imperial Perspective
ISBN-10: 1-59307-128-0
ISBN-13: 978-1-59307-128-8
$17.95
Vol. 4: The Heart of the Rebellion
ISBN-10: 1-59307-308-9
ISBN-13: 978-1-59307-308-4
$17.95
Vol. 5: Allies and Adversaries
ISBN-10: 1-59307-466-2
ISBN-13: 978-1-59307-466-1
$14.95
Vol. 6: In the Footsteps of Their Fathers
ISBN-10: 1-59307-627-4
ISBN-13: 978-1-59307-627-6
$17.95
Vol. 7: The Wrong Side of the War
ISBN-10: 1-59307-709-2
ISBN-13: 978-1-59307-709-9
$17.95